Adoniram Judson

Adoniram Judson:

Devoted for Life

VANCE CHRISTIE

All Scripture quotations are taken from the *King James Version*.

Vance Christie is a pastor and author specializing in missionary biographies. He lives in Aurora, Nebraska, and has previously written for the 'Heroes of the Faith' series. He has also written *John and Betty Stam* (ISBN 978-1-84550-376-5) and *David Brainerd* (ISBN 978-1-84550-478-6) in the Historymakers series. His website, www.vancechristie.com, has a complete list of his books in the field of historic Christian biography.

Copyright © Vance Christie 2013
paperback ISBN 978-1-78191-147-1
epub ISBN 978-1-78191-217-1
Mobi ISBN 978-1-78191-220-1

10 9 8 7 6 5 4 3 2 1

Published in 2013
by
Christian Focus Publications Ltd,
Geanies House, Fearn, Ross-shire,
IV20 1TW, Great Britain.

www.christianfocus.com

Cover design by Daniel Van Straaten

Printed and bound by
Nørhaven A/S, Denmark

CONTENTS

INTRODUCTION

Adoniram Judson holds the twin distinction of being chief among the very first missionaries ever sent out from the United States and of becoming America's first great foreign missionary hero. He and his family carried out nearly four decades of colorful but costly missionary service in Burma (modern Myanmar). Accounts of their trials, triumphs and tragedies captured the hearts of Americans and British alike and became the most widely read American missionary lore of the nineteenth and early twentieth centuries. To this day their story remains one of the most inspiring and compelling sagas of the modern missionary movement.

When Judson and three of his fellow seminary students first declared publicly their desire to go as missionaries to a foreign land, the formal document they presented stated with emphasis of them, *"they consider themselves as devoted to this work for life*, whenever God, in his providence, shall open the way."[1] More than twenty years later, at the midpoint of his missionary career, Judson stated, "The motto of every missionary, whether preacher, printer, or schoolmaster, ought to be, *'Devoted for life'.*"[2] Whenever he had occasion to correspond with prospective missionaries, he invariably listed as an indispensable qualification for missionary service the intention to devote one's entire life to it.

---

1   Francis Wayland, *Memoir of the Life and Labors of the Rev. Adoniram Judson, D.D.* (Boston: Phillips, Sampson and Co., 1853), vol. 1, p. 55.

2   ibid., vol. 2, p. 62.

Judson earned the right to his firmly-held conviction. He witnessed and experienced first-hand the numerous marked sacrifices and hardships missionaries had to embrace in order to fulfill their vocational calling. The trials he himself endured included: permanent separation from family and friends in the homeland; isolation and loneliness; spartan living conditions; challenging ministry circumstances in a pagan religious culture that resisted and opposed Christianity; recurring illness from foreign disease; the deaths of several family members and missionary colleagues; a brutal and protracted period of imprisonment.

Judson persevered through such staggering difficulties with unremitting labor, unshakable trust in God's all-wise, ever-loving providential will, and undimmed faith in the power and ultimate conquest of God's Word and the Christian Gospel. As he did so, he was used by the Lord to spread the Gospel throughout Burma, to translate the entire Bible into the Burmese language and to see healthy, growing Christian congregations established in various parts of the country. Judson's example became an inspiration to untold thousands of Christians in his own day and still has the power to instruct and motivate believers today.

Judson was married three times, having been twice widowed. His wives – Ann, Sarah and Emily – shared fully and willingly in his missionary endeavors and hardships. Though quite different from one another, each wife proved to be a committed, capable heroine in her own right. While the main focus of the current biography is on Judson himself, effort has been made to include some of the highlights of his wives' faithful ministry with him in an attempt to give them a portion of their well-deserved honor.

Quite a number of words – names of people and places, common nouns and verbs, English and foreign terms – have variant spellings in previous Judson biographies. In order to promote clarity and reduce confusion, liberty has been taken in the present work to spell those words uniformly, even when that involved emending their spelling within quoted citations from earlier sources. Other than such spelling changes for uniformity's sake, quoted citations are recorded as they originally appeared.

1

"OLD VIRGIL DUG UP"
(1788-1804)

Rev. Adoniram Judson, father of the eventual celebrated pioneer missionary to Burma, experienced a rather inauspicious beginning to his own career as a Congregational minister.[1] In 1776, after graduating at age twenty-six from Yale in New Haven, Connecticut, Judson continued to study for the ministry under Joseph Bellamy, a prominent pastor in Bethlehem, Connecticut.[2] During the decade that followed, three congregations in Massachusetts invited Judson to become their minister. But he declined each of those invitations because they did not measure up to his inflexible, idealized conviction that he should not accept a pastoral call unless it was unanimous.

In the summer of 1786, however, he accepted the invitation to pastor the First Church of Malden, Massachusetts, though that call was far from unanimous. (At that time Malden was a town of 1,000 inhabitants, located five miles north of Boston, then a thriving city of some 20,000.) A year before Judson's arrival at Malden, the congregation suffered a split when members from the southern portion of the parish withdrew and set up their own

1 Adoniram Judson senior was born in Woodbury, Connecticut, in June, 1752, the seventh and final child of Elnathan and Mary Judson. Wayland, *Memoir*, vol. 1, pp. 11-12, provides genealogical information dating back to William Judson, progenitor of the Judson clan in America, who came to Massachusetts from Yorkshire, England, in 1634.

2 Bellamy had played an active role in promoting the Great Awakening when it swept through New England in the early 1740s. At that earlier time he helped encourage another young ministerial candidate, David Brainerd, who afterward became the eminent missionary to Colonial American Indians.

church. A substantial minority of those who remained at First Church opposed the Calvinistic theology of their new minister, Judson.

Perhaps ministerial acquaintances or his repeated lost opportunities to minister had finally persuaded Judson to moderate his idealized standard for a pastoral call. Likely an even more significant factor that led to his change of heart just at that time was the fact that he had fallen in love and desired to marry. By accepting the Malden pastorate, which paid a decent salary and included the use of a large, two-story parsonage, he would be able to provide adequately for a wife and family. Judson married Abigail Brown on November 23, 1786, just months after beginning his ministry at Malden.[3]

Abigail Judson gave birth to their first child, a son, on Saturday, August 9, 1788. He was named Adoniram after his father. A little over two and a half years later, on March 21, 1791, Mrs. Judson bore a daughter who was named, like her mother and grandmother, Abigail Brown. Unfortunately, less than two weeks after Abigail's birth, due to ongoing conflict with some members of his congregation, Rev. Judson received his "Dismission" from Malden's First Church.

Often during the many months that followed, Judson was away from his home for days at a time, participating in ministerial activities and investigating pastoral possibilities. His wife had a special surprise prepared for him upon his return from one such journey. In his absence of the past week she had taught their son, still just three years of age, to read. Judson listened in amazement as young Adoniram read aloud an entire chapter from the Bible. That was one of the first indications the Judsons had of their son's exceptional mind.

While still in Malden, after turning four years of age, Adoniram used to gather other young children of the neighborhood to play church, fulfilling the role of officiating minister himself. Even then his favorite hymn, appropriately enough in light of his later career, began with the words, "Go preach my Gospel, saith the Lord."

---

3   She had been born at Tiverton, Rhode Island, on December 15, 1759, and was the eldest daughter of Abraham and Abigail Brown.

In January, 1793, Rev. Judson assumed the pastorate (with a unanimous call) of the Congregational Church in Wenham, about twenty miles northeast of Malden and five miles north of Salem. Wenham, with its 500 residents, was about half the size of Malden. Though the Wenham church building had begun to fall into disrepair, Rev. Judson happily traded that slight disadvantage for the far greater advantage of ministering in peace to a unified congregation for which he was doctrinally well suited.

Two more children were born to the Judsons while they lived in Wenham. Mrs. Judson bore her second son on May 28, 1794, and he was named Elnathan after his paternal grandfather. A second daughter, Mary Ellice, was born on February 18, 1796, but died less than seven months later on September 12.

At the time of his sibling's death, Adoniram Judson, Jr, was eight years old. He was high-spirited, even "exceedingly enthusiastic". Though very active and energetic, he was more interested in reading than in play. He had a sharp, inquisitive mind and found riddles and brainteasers irresistible. He stored many of these in his memory and used them to confound his schoolmates. Adoniram manifested strong self-confidence and, like many firstborn children, was a natural leader.

When eight or nine years old, Adoniram spotted an "enigma" printed in a newspaper along with a challenge for the readers to solve it. He did not rest until he had worked out a satisfactory solution to the puzzle. Carefully writing out his answer in his best handwriting, he placed it in an envelope addressed to the editor and secretly delivered the missive to the post office. But the postmaster took the letter for some mischievous prank of the local minister's eldest son and returned it to his father. The boy was in awe of his father. An acquaintance of Rev. Judson described him:

> He was ... a man of decidedly imposing appearance. His stature was rather above the average height. His ... erect position, grave utterance, and somewhat taciturn manner, together with the position which he naturally took in society, left you somewhat at a loss whether to class him with a patriarch of the Hebrews, or a censor of the Romans.

He was, through life, esteemed a man of inflexible integrity, and uniform consistency of Christian character.[4]

Young Adoniram was stunned and immediately ill at ease when he spotted the returned letter on the family dining room table after tea. "Is that yours, Adoniram?" his father asked soberly.

"Yes, sir," he responded quietly.

"How came you to write it?" When the boy did not answer, another question followed, "What is it about?"

"Please read it, Father," he managed falteringly.

"I do not read other people's letters. Break the seal and read it yourself."

Adoniram complied, then placed the letter in his father's hands. Mr. Judson asked to see the newspaper that contained the riddle. After reading and rereading both the puzzle and the proffered solution, he laid them on the table, crossed his hands on his knees and gazed intently into the fire for a very long time, saying nothing. When at last he returned from his reverie, the topic of conversation was changed and the letter not mentioned again. Adoniram went to bed that night not knowing whether he was to be punished or commended.

The next morning the father, again in a grave tone, informed his son, "I have purchased a book of riddles for your use. It is a very common one but as soon as you have solved all that it contains you shall have more difficult books." Then with uncharacteristic affection he patted him on the head and added, "You are a very acute boy, Adoniram, and I expect you to become a great man."

The son eagerly accepted the "book of riddles" but was disappointed to discover it was merely the same mathematics textbook that the older boys were studying in Master Dodge's school where he too was a student. Still, he was thrilled that his father had praised him. And he consoled himself with the thought that if there was anything puzzling in the math book he was sure he would like it.

4   Wayland, *Memoir*, vol. 1, p. 14.

Of Rev. Judson's anticipation of greatness for his son expressed on this and other occasions, it has been noted: "Though not ... ambitious of personal distinction, he appears to have coveted eminence for his children with more than a wise eagerness; and to have been in the habit of stimulating his son to exertion by the assurance that he would certainly become a great man."[5] Another observed:

> His father stimulated his ambition to the utmost. He seems early to have formed the hope that his boy was to become a great man, and he took no pains to hide this expectation; so that even in childhood Adoniram's heart came to be full of worldly ambition, which in subsequent years had to be nailed to the cross.[6]

Rather early on Adoniram began to gain a reputation for his outstanding scholarship, especially in arithmetic and ancient languages. Not long after the newspaper "enigma" incident, a gentleman in the neighboring town of Beverly sent him a mathematical problem and offered him a dollar for the solution. Adoniram immediately shut himself in his bedroom where he worked hour after hour to solve the problem. While the reward was tempting, he was even more concerned to uphold his reputation.

The next morning he was summoned from his seclusion to amuse Elnathan who was ill. Adoniram began to build a house made of corncobs for the younger brother, laying a strong foundation then proceeding with the superstructure with unaccountable deliberation, seeming somewhat distracted. "That's it!" he suddenly exclaimed, "I've got it!" He jumped up, scattering the materials for the half-built house, dashed back to his bedroom and recorded the correct solution to the problem.

By age ten his proficiency in Greek and Latin had become clear at Master Dodge's school. His classmates nicknamed him Virgil or even "old Virgil dug up", likely after the renowned Roman poet of

5   ibid., p. 13.
6   Edward Judson, *The Life of Adoniram Judson* (Philadelphia: Judson Press, 1938), p. 2.

the first century B.C. Adoniram was a voracious reader and quite random in the types of books he enjoyed. He devoured everything from the theological tomes in his father's library to popular novels and plays that he borrowed from others. Rev. Judson, who granted his son a significant amount of unsupervised free time, probably was not aware of (and probably would not have approved) Adoniram's reading such secular, fictional fare.

The book of Scripture that most intrigued the boy was Revelation. Before he turned twelve he overheard visitors in his parents' home discussing a newly published exposition of the Apocalypse that was proving to be "a work of rare interest". A rather intimidating gentleman in the neighborhood owned a copy of the book and, after considerable wrestling with his own reserve, young Judson paid him a visit and asked to borrow it. When he was coldly and sternly refused, he was unable to conceal his disappointment from his father.

"Not lend it to you!" the indignant parent responded with unanticipated sympathy, "I wish *he* could understand it half as well. You shall have books, Adoniram, just as many as you can read, and I'll go to Boston myself for them." The father fulfilled his promise but, to the son's perplexity and further disappointment (which he dared not verbalize), the desired work on the Apocalypse was not obtained.

Due to a combination of declining health and inadequate compensation, Rev. Judson resigned from his Wenham pastorate in the summer of 1799. May of the following year found the Judsons living in Braintree, a few miles south of Boston. That summer Rev. Judson was employed by the Massachusetts Home Missionary Society as a missionary to the "interior parts of Vermont". After that, for the better part of two years, it is not known what ministry and work opportunities he had with which to provide for his family. In May of 1802, Judson was called as pastor of the newly-formed, conservative Third Congregational Church of Plymouth, Massachusetts. Plymouth was then a good-sized town of some 3,500 residents. Both the Third Church's new edifice and the spacious house Judson had built for his family not far from the church enjoyed a pleasant view of the harbor.

A few months after settling in Plymouth, Adoniram, then aged fourteen, became seriously ill. For a long time he was extremely weak and his recovery was doubtful. More than a year passed before he was able to resume normal activities. While he was laid aside he spent many long days and nights contemplating what he would like to do with his life. He considered becoming an orator, a poet or a statesman, or pursuing some other career by which he could attain the highest eminence. But such pleasant prospects were blasted when he realized that even if he achieved the prominence he desired, he could not hold on to that honor forever. What would it profit him after a hundred years had passed that America had never seen his equal? When he became alarmed at the boundless swelling of his own abominable pride as revealed by such thoughts, he tried to comfort himself with the notion that it was caused by the fever in his brain.

One day he pondered the possibility of becoming a prominent divine in order to gain the eminence he desired. Gradually, however, he concluded that the humble Gospel minister who labored only to please God and benefit his fellow man was worthy of greater honor than was the renowned worldly divine who pursued the same perishable objects of fame and fortune that other men sought to gain through their occupations. Only the selfless, humble minister would have his fame sounded before him as he entered the eternal world. But no sooner had he begun considering the possibility of gaining that type of eternal fame than the words flashed through his mind, "Not unto us, not unto us, but to Thy name be the glory" (Ps. 115:1). In light of that scriptural perspective, even the pursuit of eternal glory for oneself seemed inappropriate, perhaps blasphemous.

These musings left him confounded, and stirred up within him a flood of feelings that had till then remained dormant. He now clearly saw the vanity of worldly pursuits and was, on the whole, ready to admit the superiority of religious ones. But his father had often said he would one day be a great man and that was still what he was determined to be. He felt like he had ventured onto dangerous ground.

He had always said and thought, so far as he had thought anything about it, that he wished to become truly religious; but now religion seemed so entirely opposed to all his ambitious plans, that he was afraid to look into his heart, lest he should discover what he did not like to confess, even to himself – that he did not want to become a Christian.[7]

Such uncomfortable introspections were likely suppressed, at least to a degree, as Judson returned to health and normal activities. Having lost a year of schooling, he threw himself into his studies more intensely than ever before. In the next twelve months he completed two full years of schooling. As a result, by the time his sixteenth birthday arrived in 1804, he was ready to enter college.

7   ibid., p. 9.

2

RESCUED FROM UNBELIEF
(1804-1809)

Judson entered Rhode Island College in Providence on Friday, August 17, 1804, barely one week after his sixteenth birthday. Because of his advanced knowledge of several of the core subjects taught at the college, he was admitted as a sophomore. One month after his arrival, the school changed its name to Brown University, in recognition of the institution's chief financial benefactor, shipping magnate Nicholas Brown.

Brown and Providence were located about fifty miles southwest of Plymouth. Though officially a Baptist institution, Brown's catholic spirit attracted students from various denominations, including many Congregationalists. By the time Judson arrived, three times as many Rhode Island College graduates had become Congregational ministers (sixty-six) than had become Baptist pastors (twenty-two).[1]

The school's all-male student body then numbered less than 150. Its modest faculty consisted of three professors and two tutors. The campus was little more than a rough, eight-acre field with a few shade trees scattered here and there. The school's primary building was the "college edifice", now known as University Hall. Modeled after Nassau Hall at Princeton, the impressive structure was 150 feet long and four stories high. It contained classrooms, a chapel, a library, administration offices, a dining commons (where all the students ate) and the students' dorm rooms.

---

1 Many of the details concerning Brown University during Judson's time there are gleaned from Stacy R. Warburton, *Eastward! The Story of Adoniram Judson* (New York: Round Table Press, 1937), pp. 5–10.

The main courses of study were Latin, Greek, mathematics, rhetoric, oratory, history, geography, logic, moral philosophy and astronomy. Latin and Greek were heavily emphasized, with the former being commonly spoken on campus. Classroom and study hours, totaling nine each day and evening, were strictly enforced, and no student was to be out of his room after 9 p.m. On April 30, 1805, toward the end of Judson's first year at Brown, the university's president, Asa Messer, wrote a glowing letter of commendation and congratulations to his father:

> Rev. Sir: Notwithstanding the greatness of my present hurry, I must drop you a word respecting your son; and this, I can assure you, is not by way of complaint. A uniform propriety of conduct, as well as an intense application to study, distinguishes his character. Your expectations of him, however sanguine, must certainly be gratified. I most heartily congratulate you, my dear sir, on that charming prospect which you have exhibited in this very amiable and promising son; and I most heartily pray that the Father of mercies may make him now, while a youth, a son in his spiritual family, and give him an earnest of the inheritance of the saints in light.[2]

Rev. Judson's pleasure and pride at such a report would have been significantly moderated, however, had he possessed a clear understanding of the true spiritual condition of his son at that time. While Judson's scholarship and outward conduct were highly commendable, he had not yet been spiritually regenerated (as Messer's letter implies) and was manifesting little interest in spiritual matters.

Furthermore, he had fallen under the influence of one Jacob Eames of Belfast, Maine, a member of the class above him. Eames was intelligent, talented, witty and amiable but a confirmed Deist. Owing to similar tastes and sympathies, the two soon became fast friends, and before long Judson joined Eames in his disbelief of Christianity. They often discussed what they would

2   Wayland, *Memoir*, vol. 1, pp. 15–16.

like to do with their careers. They pondered the possibility of entering the law profession as it provided a ready platform for the pursuit of broad political ambitions. They also considered becoming prominent actors and playwrights.

Judson was nominated and received as a member of Brown's prestigious Philermenian Society, which met every other week for debates, speeches and the reading of essays and poems. He excelled academically throughout his time at Brown. One classmate testified that he had no recollection of Judson ever failing or even hesitating in the public recitation of any of his lessons. Judson's chief academic rival was John Bailey who later became a member of the United States Congress. Their class produced two other congressmen as well as several ministers, teachers and lawyers.

Despite being away from campus for six weeks in the middle of his senior year to teach school in Plymouth, Judson succeeded, at age nineteen, in graduating as the valedictorian of his class. Upon learning that he had achieved that honor, he dashed off a cryptic message to his father, who doubtless understood its meaning: "Dear Father, I have got it. Your affectionate son, A. J." So great was Judson's enthusiasm as he wrote those words that he feared he might seem overly exultant to his fellow students and insensitive to his disappointed rival, John Bailey. Judson secretly took a roundabout way to the town post office. By the time he arrived back at campus he was composed enough to accept his classmate's congratulations with proper personal humility and appropriate sensitivity toward Bailey.

In September 1807, two weeks after graduating with the Bachelor of Arts degree, Judson opened a private school back in Plymouth. It is not known how many pupils attended the school or where it met. Judson threw himself into those responsibilities with his typical enthusiasm and drive. In addition to teaching, he wrote and had two textbooks published in less than a year – *Elements of English Grammar* in February 1808, and *The Young Lady's Arithmetic* the following July.

But he was not content being a school teacher in his home town. He wanted to see more of the world and to make much more of his life. He also felt shackled and like a hypocrite living in his parents' home and attending their church, never having revealed to them the change of religious beliefs he had come to have while in college. Consequently, on his twentieth birthday, he closed his school and announced to his parents his intention to travel for a time.

When his father pressed him for an explanation of that sudden change of course, Judson was forced (or provoked) into divulging his new-held beliefs. His father, stunned and bitterly disappointed, responded severely, accusing him of irresponsibility and ingratitude for all the sacrifices that had been made in his behalf. He warned his son against rushing to his own destruction. He also sought to convince him of the truth of Christianity and the error of infidelity. But Judson, well prepared through countless discussions about these matters with Jacob Eames, had ready responses to all his father's contentions and objections. His mother, deeply distressed, responded with tears, protests, warnings and unconcealed prayers for his restoration. Her tears and pleading followed him day after day everywhere he went.

Finally, on August 15, after enduring six days of domestic anguish, Judson mounted a horse and rode westward out of town. He traveled some 150 miles to Sheffield in the southwest corner of Massachusetts, where his uncle, Ephraim Judson, then aged seventy, served as pastor. Leaving his horse in the uncle's care, Judson continued on more than fifty miles to the north and west, to Albany, New York. From there he was thrilled to take passage on the *Clermont*, the first successful steamboat, down the picturesque Hudson River to New York City. Along the way his fellow passengers mistook his name and called him "Mr. Johnson". It occurred to him that a disguised identity might prove helpful as he attempted to see more deeply into the world, so he adopted the alias.

Shortly after arriving in New York, he joined a small traveling theatrical troupe. In truth, it was little more than a group of vagrant actors who were trying their prospects wherever they could in and around the city. He did this partly out of curiosity and a desire for adventure. His higher motive, he convinced himself, was to familiarize himself with the regulations of the world of theatre in case he should ever pursue his literary dreams as a playwright. Of that period, he later divulged:

> In my early days of wildness I joined a band of strolling players. We lived a reckless, vagabond life, finding lodgings where we could, and bilking the landlord where we found opportunity – in other words, running up a score, and then decamping without paying the reckoning.[3]

Another revealed of that same period:

> He knew that he was on the verge of such a life as he despised. For the world he would not see a young brother in his perilous position; but "I," he thought, "am in no danger. I am only seeing the world – the dark side of it, as well as the bright; and I have too much self-respect to do anything mean or vicious."[4]

Judson soon grew tired and disillusioned with such a lifestyle and left it without notice one night.

After returning to Sheffield for his horse, he again traveled westward. He stopped at a country inn where the proprietor, while showing him to his room, stated apologetically, "I have been obliged to place you next door to a young man who is exceedingly ill, probably in a dying state. I hope that will occasion you no uneasiness." Judson assured him it would not but it proved to be a very restless night. The groans of the sick man and the movements of those caring for him came from the adjacent room.

But what really disturbed Judson was the landlord's statement that the young stranger was in a dying state. A related question kept pressing upon Judson's mind: Was he prepared? In the darkness Judson felt himself blush with shame, for the question exposed the shallowness of the beliefs he had come to profess in recent years. He wondered what the clear-thinking, intellectual Jacob Eames would say about his immature perspective. Still he

3   Edward Judson, *The Life of Adoniram Judson*, p. 11.

4   Wayland, *Memoir*, vol. 1, p. 24.

wondered if the dying individual was a strong Christian, calmly anticipating glorious immortality, or an unbeliever shuddering on the brink of a dark, unknown eternity. The fact that the ailing person was a *young* man led Judson, entirely against his will, to imagine himself on that deathbed facing eternity.

When at last morning came and sunlight flooded his room, dispelling all his "superstitious illusions", he felt much better. As soon as he was dressed, he sought out the innkeeper and asked about his fellow lodger. "He is dead," came the reply.

"Dead!"

"Yes, he is gone, poor fellow. The doctor said he would probably not survive the night."

"Do you know who he was?"

"O, yes. It was a young man from Providence College, a very fine fellow. His name was Eames, Jacob Eames."

Judson was so thoroughly stunned that several hours passed before he attempted to resume his journey. But as he set out again, one thought filled his dazed mind: Dead! Lost! Lost! If his deceased friend were mistaken about his beliefs then those words applied irrevocably to him. In a state of despair, Judson decided to abandon his travel plans. He needed to find resolution to these matters that had been brought so forcefully to his attention. Turning his horse around, he started back toward home. He arrived in Plymouth on September 22, five and a half weeks after he had departed.

Mere days after his return, two notable clergymen visited the Judson home. Dr Moses Stuart pastored the prominent, historic First Church of New Haven, Connecticut, while Dr Edward Dorr Griffin ministered at the eminent First Presbyterian Church of Newark, New Jersey. Both were Yale graduates and had recently agreed to serve as professors at a new theological seminary being established in the small town of Andover, some twenty-five miles northwest of Boston. As Stuart and Griffin discussed the opening of the seminary with Rev. Judson, they met and were immediately impressed with his son. Learning of the young man's crisis of faith they suggested he consider enrolling in the seminary as a sound setting in which to pursue further study and sort out his personal beliefs. The younger Judson listened politely but was noncommittal.

A day or two later he received an offer to become an assistant teacher in one of Boston's private academies. He left for Boston immediately and had no sooner assumed his new responsibilities there when Thomas Boston's theological treatise, *Human Nature in its Fourfold State*, came into his hands. Boston (1676–1732) was an eminent Scottish divine. His immensely popular and influential *Fourfold State* explored man's condition in: his original state of righteousness and innocence; his state as a fallen creature; his state as a redeemed and regenerated being; his eternal state in either heaven or hell.

Having been confronted again with issues of eternal import, Judson knew he must settle them in his own mind and heart. Consequently, he promptly resigned his teaching position and, on October 12, entered the Theological Institution at Andover. Because he was not a ministerial candidate or even a professing Christian, he was admitted simply as a special student. Due to his outstanding scholastic background he was again admitted as a second year student.

The seminary was located on the grounds of Phillips Academy, which had been incorporated as Massachusetts' first boys' academy thirty years earlier. The seminary's main building, Phillips Hall, stood at the base of Andover Hill, a low ridge that the students affectionately dubbed "Pisgah" or "Zion". Erected shortly before Judson's arrival, the unadorned building was made of red brick and had a slate roof. It contained a chapel, a reading room and thirty dormitory rooms.

The school had only two faculty members during Judson's first year there – Eliphalet Pearson, Professor of Sacred Literature, and Leonard Woods, Professor of Christian Theology. A year later the two prominent pastors Judson had met at his father's home in Plymouth joined the seminary faculty – Moses Stuart as Pearson's successor and Edward Griffin as Professor of Sacred Rhetoric. These men helped Judson work through his spiritual perplexities.

God's Spirit was also at work in his heart. His doubts concerning the Christian faith soon evaporated. By November he "began to entertain a hope of having received the regenerating influences of the Holy Spirit." On December 2 he "made a solemn dedication of himself to God". Francis Wayland, who served as Judson's official biographer after his death, testified of his conversion and subsequent consecration of himself to the Lord's service:

> I have often heard Dr Judson speak of his introduction to Andover, and of the state of utter darkness, and almost despair, in which he was at the time. I have also heard him tell of the gradual change which came over him ... There was none of his characteristic impetuosity exhibited in his conversion; and he had none of those overpowering ... exercises, either before or after, that would be looked for in a person of his ardent temperament. He was prayerful, reflective, and studious of proofs; and gradually faith, trust in God, and finally a hope through the merits of Christ, took possession of his soul, he scarcely knew how; and from the moment that he fully believed, I think he never doubted. He said he felt as sure that he was an entirely new creature, actuated by new motives and governed by new principles, as he was sure of his own existence. His old habits of thought and feeling, to some extent, clung to him, but they were made subservient to higher purposes; and though he might still have his objects of ambition, they could never again be of the first moment. The change, though gradual, was too marked, too entire, to admit of a moment's doubt. He had no exercises on the subject of entering the ministry; it became a matter of course immediately on his indulging a hope.[5]

The following spring, on May 28, 1809, to the unspeakable joy of his family, Judson made a public profession of his Christian faith and joined the membership of Plymouth's Third Congregational Church.

5   ibid., pp. 36–7.

3

Following the Star in the East
(1809-1810)

Less than a month after joining his parents' church, Judson was offered a tutorship at Brown University. Earlier he may have jumped at the opportunity but now he declined it.

> His plans of life were, of course, entirely reversed. He banished forever those dreams of literary and political ambition in which he had formerly indulged, and simply asked himself, 'How shall I so order my future being as best to please God?' The portions of his correspondence which belong to this period indicate an earnest striving after personal holiness, and an enthusiastic consecration of every endowment to the service of Christ.[1]

In September 1809, at the outset of his senior year of seminary, Judson came across a printed sermon that was to have a profound influence on the direction of his future life. The pamphlet, entitled "The Star in the East", contained a message preached not long before by Dr Claudius Buchanan in the parish church he then pastored in Bristol, England. For several years Buchanan had served in India as a chaplain with the East India Company. The text for his sermon was Matthew 2:2: "for we have seen his star in the east, and are come to worship him." In the message he described the progress of the Christian Gospel in India and emphasized that the time was ripe for Christianity to be spread among Eastern peoples by even greater efforts than had been made

1   Wayland, *Memoir*, vol. 1, pp. 28–9.

to that point. Buchanan highlighted the endeavors of German Lutheran missionary Christian Frederick Schwartz (1726–1798), who had served for nearly fifty years in India.

In recent years American Christians of various denominations had become acquainted with and had contributed several thousand dollars to help support British Baptist missionary William Carey and his colleagues in their undertakings at Serampore, near Calcutta, India. Many American Christians were also aware of Robert Morrison, an English missionary who, early in 1807, went out under the London Missionary Society as the first ever Protestant missionary to China.[2] Morrison sailed to Canton, China, from Boston, Massachusetts, aboard an American vessel because the East India Company, with its monopoly over British shipping to the Orient, refused to transport him there.

A number of missionary societies, representing a variety of denominations, had come into existence in America during the previous twenty years. In addition, in the first decade of the nineteenth century, numerous "mite" and "cent" societies sprang up to help support missionary endeavor.[3] All those societies focused their efforts on sending evangelists and missionaries to North American Indians and to frontier settlements that lacked a Gospel witness. Other than sponsoring some missionaries to Canada, none of those societies were attempting to send out representatives to foreign countries.

The Lord used "The Star in the East" to direct Judson's attention beyond spiritual conditions and ministry prospects in his own country to the even greater spiritual needs and opportunities in another part of the world. Many years later Judson recalled the significant impact that reading Buchanan's treatise had on him:

> Though I do not now consider that sermon as peculiarly excellent, it produced a very powerful effect on my mind.

2   Until 1818 the London Missionary Society was known simply as The Missionary Society. The London Missionary Society designation will be used in the present volume to readily distinguish that society from other mission organizations.

3   Warburton, *Eastward!*, pp. 23–4, provides a detailed listing of several of those missionary and mite societies.

For some days I was unable to attend to the studies of my class, and spent my time in wondering at my past stupidity, depicting the most romantic scenes in missionary life, and roving about the college rooms declaiming on the subject of missions. My views were very incorrect, and my feelings extravagant; but yet I have always felt thankful to God for bringing me into that state of excitement, which was perhaps necessary, in the first instance, to enable me to break the strong attachment I felt to home and country, and to endure the thought of abandoning all my wonted pursuits and animating prospects. That excitement soon passed away; but it left a strong desire to prosecute my inquiries and ascertain the path of duty.[4]

After that Judson "devoured with great greediness every scrap of information concerning Eastern countries". He discovered and eagerly read a volume entitled *An Account of an Embassy to the Kingdom of Ava*. It was written by Michael Symes, a British army officer, who in 1795 had been sent by the Governor General of India to carry out military negotiations with the royal court of Burma. While Symes's mission proved largely fruitless, his book provided Judson with intriguing glimpses of the mysterious Burmese empire. Burma was a feudal kingdom thought to have an immense population. Its people were civilized, could read and write, and boasted an extensive literature. The vast majority of Burmans were Buddhists. Yet the king, an absolute monarch, purportedly granted toleration to all sects. An Italian Catholic missionary had a sizeable congregation made up of the descendants of former Portuguese colonists. Judson noted all this with keen interest. From then on the missionary prospects of not only India but also Burma were much on his mind.

Judson's sudden enthusiasm for foreign missions seemed peculiar and outlandish to his fellow students. Years later he divulged that initially his missionary perspectives were "condemned by all and not infrequently ridiculed and reproached".[5] He further revealed:

4   Wayland, *Memoir*, vol. 1, pp. 51–2.

5   Warburton, *Eastward!*, p. 20.

But, at that period, no provision had been made in America for a foreign mission, and for several months, after reading Buchanan, I found none among the students who viewed the subject as I did, and no minister in the place or neighborhood who gave me any encouragement; and I thought that I should be under the necessity of going to England and placing myself under foreign patronage.[6]

Given these discouraging factors, Judson could not help but second guess his own inclinations. But he continued to think and pray about the matter. Finally one day in February 1810, six months after initially reading "The Star in the East", he walked alone outdoors while once again contemplating whether or not he should devote himself to missionary service. He later described the simple yet definite circumstances that led to his reaching a settled decision that day:

It was during a solitary walk in the woods behind the college, while meditating and praying on the subject, and feeling half inclined to give it up, that the command of Christ, "Go ye into all the world and preach the Gospel to every creature" [Mark 16:15], was presented to my mind with such clearness and power, that I came to a full decision, and though great difficulties appeared in my way, resolved to obey the command at all events.[7]

Judson's commitment to become a missionary was severely tested when he spent the winter vacation of 1810 back home with his family in Plymouth. He was well aware of the ambitious career prospects his father cherished for him and felt "an exceedingly great reluctance" to share his missionary intentions, knowing they were not likely to be well received. One evening Rev. Judson dropped some hints of splendid prospects in his son's future. Judson's mother and sister added "smiling innuendos" that indicated their awareness of the secret. Alarmed, Judson asked his father to explain himself, stating that their views

6   Wayland, *Memoir*, vol. 1, p. 52.

7   ibid.

concerning his future might not coincide. The father stated his certainty there would be no difference of opinion on this matter. He then revealed that Dr Edward Griffin, Judson's instructor in Sacred Rhetoric at Andover, was about to assume the pastorate of the prestigious Park Street Church in Boston, the city's largest congregation. He desired Judson to become his assistant upon his graduation from seminary. Griffin had spoken early to Rev. Judson about the situation, so his son would not commit himself to another ministry. "And you will be so near home!" Mrs. Judson added.

Judson felt like his heart was breaking and for a moment he could make no response to his parents. But when Abigail joined in the conversation, he suddenly blurted out, "No, sister, I shall never live in Boston. I have much farther than that to go." He then related, calmly but fervently, his conviction that he was to become a missionary. His mother and sister responded to this stunning revelation with "very many tears", likely grieved that the family circle would be broken up, and fearing that such a venture would cost him his life. His father, though deeply disappointed, "scarcely offered a word of opposition" to what he probably sensed was inevitable.

Around the time Judson reached a settled determination to devote his life to missionary service, he was delighted to discover that a handful of other Andover students actually shared his earnest commitment to missions. The first to inform him of that was Samuel Nott, the son of a minister in Franklin, Connecticut, and a graduate of Union College in Schenectady, New York. After studying theology for a time under his father's tutelage following his graduation from Union, Nott had arrived at Andover the previous November. Though he had considered it his duty for more than a year to become a missionary, he hesitated to commit himself. But he now shared his heart on the matter with Judson, from whom he received enthusiastic encouragement. They were soon joined in their missionary determination by another senior, Samuel Newell. He had first started contemplating a missionary career while an undergraduate at Harvard but had not revealed his commitment until now.

During that same period these three seniors learned of three underclassmen who were similarly committed to vocational missionary service: Samuel J. Mills and James Richards, graduates of Williams College in Williamstown, Massachusetts, and Edward Warren, a graduate of Middlebury College in Middlebury, Vermont. Mills and Richards had both dedicated themselves to missions three and a half years earlier, in August of 1806, while freshmen at Williams. Mills's father was a minister in Torringford, Connecticut. Largely as a result of his mother's influence, young Mills had determined to become a missionary even before entering college.

On a sultry Saturday afternoon in August 1806, Mills, Richards and three other Williams students – Byram Green, Harvey Loomis and Francis L. Robbins – met for prayer in a maple grove known as "Sloane's Meadow" near the Hoosac River. When a thunderstorm suddenly came up they took cover under the overhanging sides of a nearby haystack. There they discussed Asia, which they had been studying about in a required geography class. Mills proposed that they take the Gospel "to the pagans of Asia and to the disciples of Mohammed", urging, "We can do it if we will!" There beneath the edges of the haystack they committed the matter to the Lord in earnest prayer.[8]

Two years later, in September 1808, five Williams students – Mills, Richards, Luther Rice, Ezra Fisk and John Seward – formed a society called "The Brethren", which had as its purpose "to effect, in the persons of its members, a mission or missions to the heathen". Those charter members signed the society's constitution, thereby pledging:

Each member shall keep himself absolutely free from every engagement which, after his prayerful attention, and after

---

8   In 1867 a stone monument was erected to commemorate the site of what has been immortalized as the Haystack Prayer Meeting. The monument bears the names of the five students who were at the historic, albeit impromptu, prayer meeting as well as the words: "The Birthplace of American Foreign Missions". Warburton, *Eastward!*, p. 26, contends Andover deserves that designation. Both locations rightly share in the honor: American foreign missions were conceived in prayer at Williamstown then birthed organizationally and practically at Andover.

consultation with his brethren, shall be deemed incompatible with the object of this society, and shall hold himself in readiness to go on a mission when and where duty may call.[9]

Richards arrived at Andover a year later, in September 1809, around the time Judson started "declaiming" about missions. Perhaps Richards was skeptical of Judson's excessive enthusiasm, or discouraged by the negative reception it received from other students, for he did not reveal his own interest in missions at that time. He did, however, write some of the Brethren from Williams about what he was observing.

Hearing of Judson's obvious interest in missions, Mills, who had begun studying theology at Yale, apparently concluded he would be better off at Andover. Consequently, on December 20, 1809, he wrote to another member of the Brethren – Gordon Hall, who was then preaching at Woodbury, Connecticut – stating his intention to transfer to Andover within four or five weeks. In that letter he also commented, interestingly:

> I heard previously of Mr. Judson. You say he thinks of offering himself as a missionary to the London Society, for the East Indies. What! Is England to support her own missionaries and ours likewise? ... I do not like this dependence on another nation, especially when they have done so much and we nothing.[10]

The death of Mills's mother delayed his arrival at Andover until late January or early February 1810. Given Mills's zeal for missions, it is likely Judson and he met and discussed their shared missionary passion soon after his arrival at Andover.

It is unknown whether or not Judson was aware of the missionary interest of these fellow students when he decisively committed his life to missions. In writing of his commitment, he gave no indication of any such awareness or its influence on his own decision. After discovering their mutual commitment to

9   Wayland, *Memoir*, vol. 1, p. 40.

10   ibid., p. 43.

missionary endeavor, the six Andover students began to discuss and pray together about where they might serve and how they could reach their destination. Initially the Williams men were inclined to work among Native Americans, although they had contemplated other possibilities in the past as well. But Judson's enthusiasm for a mission to the East soon influenced the entire group to join him in his determination to serve somewhere in the Orient should the Lord open a door of opportunity in that direction.

Judson, Nott and Newell would complete their seminary training and be available for service within half a year. Mills, Richards and Warren would not graduate for two years but in the meanwhile could throw their efforts into finding a way for the seniors, then later themselves, to be sent out to the foreign field as soon as possible. Sometime that spring of 1810 Luther Rice arrived from Williams as an underclassman at Andover, and immediately joined the others in enthusiastically supporting these efforts.

The students discussed their dreams and desires with their professors, especially Dr Edward Griffin. He agreed to write the London Missionary Society in their behalf but apparently was delayed in doing so by other pressing responsibilities. Eager for information, Judson took matters into his own hands by himself writing Dr David Bogue of the LMS on April 23:

> Rev. Sir: I have considered the subject of missions nearly a year[11], and have found my mind gradually tending to a deep conviction that it is my duty personally to engage in this service. Several of my brethren of this college may finally unite with me in my present resolution. On their as well as my own behalf, I take the liberty of addressing you this letter. My object is to obtain information on certain points – whether there is at present such a call for missionaries in India, Tartary[12], or any part of the *eastern* continent, as will induce

11 This being the case, he must have started thinking about missions, to one degree or another, at least a few months before he read Buchanan's "The Star in the East".

12 Tartary was then the common designation by Americans and Europeans for the vast region of northern and central Asia inhabited by Turkic and Mongol peoples, including the current areas of Siberia, Turkestan, Mongolia, Manchuria and Tibet.

the directors of the London Missionary Society to engage
new [American] missionaries; ... and whether, provided they
give satisfaction as to their fitness to undertake the work,
all their necessary expenses after arriving in England shall
be defrayed from the funds of the society, which funds will,
it is hoped, be ultimately reimbursed by supplies from the
American churches.[13]

While awaiting a reply, which in those days would take months to
arrive from England, the students did what they could to promote
their cause closer to home. They sometimes had opportunities
to preach in nearby towns and always sought to share their
missionary vision with influential local clergymen. Judson wrote
an impassioned article entitled "Concern for the Salvation of
the Heathen" for a Congregational publication, *The Panoplist and
Missionary Magazine United.*

Judson also penned a short letter to Gordon Hall, the interim
pastor at Woodbury, Connecticut, to inquire further about his
missions interest. Judson was probably unaware that Hall was
even then considering the call he had just received from the
Woodbury parishioners to settle as their permanent pastor with
an annual salary of 600 dollars. The morning after Hall received
Judson's letter he set out for Andover. Shortly after arriving there
he declined the pastoral opportunity at Woodbury and, instead,
enrolled at the seminary with plans to join the missionary
enterprise. His arrival late in June coincided with dramatic
developments that were just then unfolding in connection with
the fledgling missions cause.

13 Wayland, *Memoir*, vol. 1, p. 54.

4

"Devoted to This Work for Life"
(1810)

On Sunday, June 24, Samuel Nott preached a sermon in the Second Church of Newburyport, a flourishing seaport town eighteen miles northeast of Andover. The church was pastored by Dr Samuel Spring, a powerful advocate for missions. His son, Gardiner, was a classmate and good friend of Judson at Andover. While not sensing a divine leading to be a missionary himself, Gardiner Spring was a loyal supporter of the seven Andover students who did have that call and often spoke favorably of their intended undertakings to his father.

The day after preaching at Dr Spring's church, Nott rode with him to Andover. Along the way they discussed the annual meeting of the General Association of Massachusetts Proper, the recently organized consociation of the state's evangelical Congregationalists, which was to take place in Bradford beginning in the middle of that week. (Bradford was located midway between Newburyport and Andover, on the Merrimack River road.) Spring and Nott realized, as did others, that the General Association's annual meeting provided an ideal opportunity for the Andover mission students to present their aspirations to New England Congregationalists. An equally good opportunity would not come for at least another year.

That evening the student missionary band met in the home of Moses Stuart, one of their professors, to discuss their proposed venture with a number of ministers. In addition to Drs Stuart, Griffin and Spring, the meeting was attended by Dr Samuel Worcester, pastor of the prominent Tabernacle Church in Salem, who was another influential promoter of missions. At least three other pastors took part in the discussion that night as well. The prevailing opinion of those gathered was strongly in support of the students' undertaking and the council agreed the young men would be given the opportunity to present their proposal to the General Association that week.

Judson was selected to author the proposal and to read it at the conference. Doubtless with in-put from the others, he composed the written document on Tuesday, and six of them – Judson, Nott, Mills, Newell, Rice and Richards – signed it. That same day the ministerial delegates at Professor Stuart's home approved the document with one significant change. They thought the General Association would find the prospect of assuming the support of six missionaries overwhelming. After further discussion the names of Rice and Richards were omitted.

That Thursday morning the missionary students, accompanied by a few classmates from Andover, walked the nearly ten miles to Bradford, where the Association's meeting had gotten underway early that day. At two in the afternoon the students joined the conference delegates and guests as they reconvened, after lunch, in the First Church. Nineteen official delegates and nine guest ministers were seated in the box pews on the main floor. The public, with its lively interest in the proceedings, watched from the gallery. When the time came, Judson stepped forward in front of the pulpit to read the "Memorial" he had prepared. With his self-possessed manner and powerful public speaking voice he read:

> The undersigned, members of the Divinity College, respectfully request the attention of their reverend fathers, convened in the General Association at Bradford, to the following statement and inquiries:
>
> They beg leave to state that their minds have been long impressed with the duty and importance of personally attempting a mission to the heathen; that the impressions on their minds have induced a serious, and, as they trust, a prayerful consideration of the subject in its various attitudes, particularly in relation to the probable success

and the difficulties attending such an attempt; and that, after examining all the information which they can obtain, *they consider themselves as devoted to this work for life*, whenever God, in his providence, shall open the way.

They now offer the following inquiries, on which they solicit the opinion and advice of this association: Whether, with their present views and feelings, they ought to renounce the object of missions, as either visionary or impracticable; if not, whether they ought to direct their attention to the eastern or the western world; whether they may expect patronage and support from a missionary society in this country, or must commit themselves to the direction of a European society; and what preparatory measures they ought to take, previous to actual engagement.

The undersigned, feeling their youth and inexperience, look up to their fathers in the church, and respectfully solicit their advice, direction, and prayers.[1]

Judson and the three other students who had signed the Memorial each made a public statement of their "motives and intentions" with regard to their missionary aspirations. The sight of these fully-consecrated, well-educated young men publicly offering themselves for a lifetime of missionary service made a profound impression on the gathering. "Gray hairs were all weeping," one eye-witness related.[2]

The conference appointed a committee of three – Samuel Spring, Samuel Worcester and a Mr. Hale, secretary of the meeting – to consider the students' proposal and make a recommendation to the delegates the next day. When the committee presented its recommendations the following morning they were unanimously adopted by the conference. A nine-member Board of Commissioners for Foreign Missions was formed. Its members were to be jointly selected by the General Associations of Massachusetts and Connecticut. The delegates approved the following recommendation concerning the missionary candidates:

1 Wayland, *Memoir*, vol. 1, p. 55.
2 Warburton, *Eastward!*, p. 29.

That, fervently commending them to the grace of God, we advise the young gentlemen, whose request is before us, in the way of earnest prayer and diligent attention to suitable studies and means of information, and putting themselves under the patronage and direction of the Board of Commissioners for Foreign Missions, humbly to wait the openings and guidance of Providence in respect to their great and excellent design.[3]

In time the proposed mission board's official title was further specified as "The American Board of Commissioners for Foreign Missions". It became familiarly known, more simply, as "The American Board". For more than a century it was considered the father of all foreign missionary activities of American Congregational churches.

As Judson returned to Andover that Thursday with his companions, his mind was not wholly on their discussion concerning the conference's potential responses to their presentation. He was also thinking a great deal about a certain young lady he had met in Bradford early that afternoon, Ann Hasseltine. Their meeting took place in the home of her father, John Hasseltine, a deacon of Bradford's First Church. Deacon Hasseltine had hosted some of the Andover students and conference delegates to the noon meal at his house. Ann, or Nancy as she was then more commonly called, was helping to serve the dinner guests. She was an attractive, vivacious and intelligent young woman of twenty, sixteen months younger than Judson.

Reportedly, when Judson was first introduced to Ann that day, he was not only totally smitten with her but also struck nearly dumb. Normally he manifested an easy social grace and was an engaging conversationalist. But on this occasion he said little and scarcely looked up from his plate. Some of the assembled guests and host family members may have supposed him to be deep in thought about the presentation he was to make at the conference that afternoon. They would have been surprised to discover, instead, that an extemporaneous poem extolling the lovely Miss Hasseltine was then forming in his mind.

*   *   *

Ann Hasseltine was born in Bradford on December 22, 1789. She was the fourth daughter and fifth of seven children born to her parents, John and Rebecca Hasseltine. Her parents were good moral people and regular churchgoers but, according to their own later testimony, not genuine Christians when their children were young. Ann had a part in their coming to saving faith in Christ following her own conversion as a teen.

John Hasseltine was a well-to-do farmer and one of Bradford's leading citizens. His farm and large, comfortable house overlooked the Merrimack River valley to the north. He helped found Bradford Academy, located a short distance west of his property, at which all seven of his children were educated. About eighty students attended the academy during Ann's teen years there. The rear wing of the Hasseltines' home included a capacious second-floor room for games, entertainment and dancing. The Hasseltine "dance hall", as it was commonly called, was a social hub for Bradford's numerous youth.[4]

As a young girl, Ann Hasseltine possessed an active mind, "unusually ardent feelings" and a merry, exuberant spirit. She exhibited ingenuity of planning and indefatigable determination in achieving her wishes. Her mother, who sometimes wearied of needing to restrain young Ann's restless spirit, once told her, "I hope, my daughter, you will one day be satisfied with rambling." Though abundantly active, Ann also loved learning. A good book could entice her away from her cherished walks or a cheerful social gathering.

From an early age Ann's mother taught her to avoid common childhood vices such as lying, disobeying parents or stealing, and told her that if she were a good child she would escape going to

---

4   Courtney Anderson, *To the Golden Shore, The Life of Adoniram Judson* (Grand Rapids: Zondervan, 1972), pp. 73–4.

hell when she died.[5] Ann determined, therefore, to avoid those sins, to say her prayers each morning and evening and to abstain from her usual play on the Christian Sabbath. She was confident that such a course of good works would insure her salvation. But as a young teenager she became totally preoccupied with frivolous social opportunities and grew completely unconcerned about her spiritual welfare. For two or three years she hardly had an anxious thought concerning the salvation of her soul.

In the spring of 1806, however, when Ann was sixteen years old, a spirit of increased attention to spiritual matters began to stir in the Bradford parish and a series of religious meetings was held. Ann attended the special meetings regularly and often wept when hearing the minister and others emphasize the need to take advantage of the "present favorable season, to obtain an interest in Christ". Through the additional influences of an aunt who was herself under deep conviction and a consecrated Christian teacher at the academy, Ann was encouraged to be reconciled to God. By early July she came to have the peace and assurance that she had gained forgiveness and salvation through faith in Christ.

Ann's heart overflowed with her new-found Christian faith and she immediately started sharing freely with her friends and family members. She wrote letters to a number of friends, expressing earnest concern for their spiritual welfare and urging them to turn from sin to the Savior. God's Spirit doubtless used Ann's fervent witness to further the significant spiritual work He was bringing about in her immediate family at that time. Over the course of the next several months, Ann's parents and four of her siblings professed their faith in Jesus Christ.

Beginning at age seventeen and continuing for three years, Ann taught school in Haverhill (located just across the Merrimack from Bradford), Newbury and Salem. Two of her periodic diary entries, thought to be from March of 1809, reveal not only her desire to serve Christ but also her growing concern for the expansion of His Church, including among various "heathen"

---

5   James D. Knowles, *Memoir of Mrs. Ann H. Judson, Late Missionary to Burmah* (Boston: Lincoln & Edmands, 1829), pp. 12–19, records Ann's autobiographical account of her conversion process.

peoples. Though she would not meet Adoniram Judson for fifteen more months, these entries show the Lord was already at work in her heart, preparing her for the ministry which He would call her to share with Judson:

> *March* 17. Have had some enjoyment in reading the life of David Brainerd. It has a tendency to humble me, and excite desires to live as near to God, as that holy man did. Have spent this evening in prayer for quickening grace. Felt my heart enlarged to pray for spiritual blessings for myself, my friends, the church at large, the heathen world, and the African slaves. Felt a willingness to give myself away to Christ; to be disposed of as he pleases. ...

> [*March*] 24. ... I have at times felt engaged in prayer for the prosperity of the church, and for the conversion of the heathen and Jews.[6]

On July 28, 1810, one month to the day after first meeting Ann Hasseltine, Judson declared his intentions as a suitor in a letter he wrote her. She responded that her parents would have to give their consent before she could consider Judson. The zealous missionary candidate then penned a breathtaking letter to John Hasseltine, part of which read:

> I have now to ask, whether you can consent to part with your daughter early next spring, to see her no more in this world; whether you can consent to her departure for a heathen land, and her subjection to the hardships and sufferings of a missionary life: whether you can consent to her exposure to the dangers of the ocean; to the fatal influence of the southern climate of India; to every kind of want and distress; to degradation, insult, persecution, and perhaps a violent death. Can you consent to all this, for the sake of Him who left His heavenly home, and died for her and for you; for the sake of perishing immortal souls; for the sake of Zion, and the glory of God? Can you consent to all this, in hope of soon

6   ibid., p. 31.

meeting your daughter in the world of glory, with a crown of righteousness, brightened by the acclamations of praise which shall redound to her Savior from heathens saved, through her means, from eternal woe and despair?[7]

Ann's parents left the difficult decision to her. She recorded her initial response to the prospects facing her in her diary:

Aug. 8, 1810. Endeavored to commit myself entirely to God, to be disposed of, according to his pleasure. He is now trying my faith and confidence in him, by presenting dark and gloomy prospects, that I may be enabled, through divine grace, to gain an ascendancy over my selfish and rebellious spirit, and prefer the will of God to my own. I do not feel that his service is my delight. Might I but be the means of converting a single soul, it would be worth spending all my days to accomplish. Yes, I feel willing to be placed in that situation, in which I can do most good, *though it were to carry the Gospel to the distant, benighted heathen*.[8]

Exactly one month later Ann wrote to one of her girlhood confidantes, Lydia Kimball, who now lived in Salem:

I feel willing, and expect, if nothing in providence prevents, to spend my days in this world in heathen lands. Yes, Lydia, I have about come to the determination to give up all my comforts and enjoyments here, sacrifice my affection to relatives and friends, and go where God, in his providence, shall see fit to place me. My determinations are not hasty, or formed without viewing the dangers, trials, and hardships attendant on a missionary life. Nor were my determinations formed in consequence of an attachment to an earthly object; but with a sense of my obligations to God, and with a full conviction of its being a call in providence, and consequently my duty. My feelings have been *exquisite* in regard to the subject. Now my mind is settled and composed, and is

7   ibid., p. 42.
8   ibid., p. 37.

willing to leave the event with God – none can support one under trials and afflictions but him. In him alone I feel a disposition to confide.[9]

9   ibid., p. 43.

5

FRANCE AND ENGLAND
(1810-1811)

Judson graduated from Andover Seminary on September 24, 1810. Earlier that month, on September 5, he received the Master of Arts degree from Brown University. That same day the American Board met for the first time in Farmington, Connecticut. A three-member Prudential Committee was appointed "to obtain the best information in their power respecting the state of unevangelized nations on the western and eastern continents, and report at the next meeting of the board." The board also prepared a missions appeal and a subscription form to be printed and circulated among the churches.

While there was considerable interest on the part of the churches in the proposed missionary venture, it became increasingly apparent that it might be quite some time before the American Board would be able to raise the funds needed to send out the missionary volunteers. Consequently it was decided to approach the London Missionary Society to see if a partnership might be worked out whereby the American missionaries could be sent out in more timely fashion. On Christmas Day, 1810, the Prudential Committee interviewed Adoniram Judson, Samuel Newell, Samuel Nott and Gordon Hall and approved them as qualified candidates for missionary service. Judson was chosen to sail to England early in the New Year. He would personally represent the American Board in exploring the possibility of a joint mission venture with the LMS.

Judson sailed from Boston for Liverpool aboard the *Packet*, a British vessel, on Friday, January 11. He and two Spanish merchants were the only passengers aboard the ship. All went smoothly until one day a French privateer auspiciously named *L'Invincible Napoleon* came into sight. France and England were at war, so the privateer captured the British ship. The two Spaniards spoke French and were able to furnish a bribe so they were treated civilly. Judson could not speak French and possessed little money. Consequently he was placed in the hold of *L'Invincible Napoleon* along with the crew of the *Packet*. He reflexively shrank from the profane companions with whom he was detained and thought the confined air unendurable. Conditions became much worse, however, when the seas roughened, leaving Judson and several of the sailors excessively seasick. Before long the hold was a revolting mess.

Sick and discouraged, he began to feel sorry for himself and homesick. He thought of his beloved Ann in Bradford, of his family back home in Plymouth, even of "the biggest church in Boston" which he could have pastored had he chosen a different ministry vocation. He became alarmed at the strange feeling that crept over him and realized this was the first time he had experienced misgivings about his decision to become a missionary. As he became aware of the disconcerting feeling, he started praying against it, believing it to be a temptation from the Adversary. Judson also believed God was permitting him to undergo these difficulties as a trial of his faith. He determined to bear it with God's strength, as he doubtless would need to do with other trials in the future.

Having made that resolution, Judson searched about in the twilight of the hold until he located his Hebrew Bible. For a few minutes at a time he read from the Bible then mentally translated the Hebrew into Latin. In that way he kept his mind profitably occupied while not overstraining his eyes in the poor light. One day the ship's doctor spotted the Bible on Judson's pillow, picked it up and carried it to the gangway where he examined it. He then returned and addressed Judson in Latin. By means of that language Judson was able to explain who he was and why he, as an American, had been traveling on a British ship. Before long he was released from the hold, given a berth in the upper cabin and permitted to take his meals at the captain's table.

L'Invincible Napoleon docked at Le Passage, Spain, just long enough for the two Spanish merchants to disembark. It then continued on to Bayonne on the southwest coast of France. There, to Judson's surprise and indignation, he was marched through the streets as a prisoner with the crew of the *Packet*. He began to protest loudly, leading onlookers to regard him with differing degrees of curiosity, amusement and scorn. "Lower your voice!" a tall stranger suddenly commanded him.

"With the greatest pleasure possible," Judson responded. "I was only clamoring for a listener." He identified himself and explained his situation in a few hasty words. He also learned that the stranger was an American military officer from Philadelphia and received his promise of assistance.

"But you had better go on your way quietly now," advised his new acquaintance.

"Oh, I will be a perfect lamb," Judson complied, "since I have gained my object."

He and his fellow prisoners were led to a massive, gloomy prison where they were placed in a dank, chilly dungeon. A solitary lamp hanging from a column in the center of the room provided the chamber's only light. Rancid straw was heaped along the walls for bedding. The sailors soon settled down on it but Judson could not bring himself to do the same. Instead, he paced up and down the cell for what seemed like hours.

While he was resting momentarily against the chamber's center column, the cell door opened and the tall Philadelphian, wearing a voluminous military cloak, entered the room. The officer did not acknowledge or even look at Judson as he approached and removed the lamp from its post. Instead, holding out the lamp as he began making his way around the cell, he stated aloud, "Let me see if I know any of these poor fellows." Having carelessly looked over the room's occupants, he declared, "No, no friend of mine." As he replaced the lamp on the column he suddenly swung his immense cloak around Judson, concealing his slight form under yards of material. Judson immediately grasped the intended plan but doubted the clumsy subterfuge would work. The American officer, however, assured their success by placing some money into the jailer's hand as they exited the cell door, and by slipping another bribe to the guard at the prison's outer gate.

Judson's deliverer then led him hastily through the city streets to the wharf, where he was concealed on an American merchantman for the night. After that he was hidden away in the attic of a shipbuilder for a few days until the proper papers could be procured for him to be released on parole. Judson stayed six more weeks in Bayonne, boarding with an American woman who had spent most of her life in France.

During that period Judson did not disclose to his fellow boarders the fact that he was a Christian and a missionary appointee. Instead, in order to learn "as much as possible of the real state of French society ... [h]e attended various places of amusement with his fellow-boarders, pleading his ignorance of the language and customs of the country as an excuse for acting the spectator merely."[1] Judson continued this surreptitious course until finally:

> The last place of amusement he visited was a masked ball; and here his strong feelings quite overcame his caution, and he burst forth in his real character. He declared to his somewhat startled companions that he did not believe the infernal regions could furnish more complete specimens of depravity than he there beheld. He spoke in English, and at first addressed himself to the two or three standing near him, who understood the language; but his earnestness of manner and warmth of expression soon drew around him a large circle, who listened curiously and with apparent respect. ... He rapidly enumerated many of the evils which infidelity had brought upon France and upon the world, and then showed the only way of escape from those evils – the despised, but truly ennobling religion of Jesus Christ. Finally he sketched the character of man as it might have been in its original purity and nobleness, and then the wreck

1   Wayland, *Memoir*, vol. 1, p. 72.

    of soul and body to be ascribed to sin, and wound up all by
    a personal appeal to such as had not become too debased to
    think and feel.[2]

Most of the participants at the ball that night mistook Judson's "exhibition" as part of the evening's entertainment. But those who understood his remarks seemed confounded by his bold, unexpected onslaught. When he finished they stood aside and allowed him to pass from the room without a word.

In time Judson was introduced to some of Napoleon's officers and traveled with them through the country in one of the emperor's carriages. While in Paris he spent most of his time with those officers and other individuals to whom they introduced him. Generally he continued to carry out the same course of covert observation that he had in Bayonne.

Eventually Judson was able to obtain a passport from France to England. He arrived at Dartmouth on May 3 and three days later reached London. Four months had elapsed since he sailed from Boston for Liverpool. He was received respectfully and kindly by the London Missionary Society directors. At their meeting on May 20 the directors considered a letter the American Board's Prudential Committee had sent early in the year, requesting the cooperation of the LMS in sending out the four American missionary candidates.[3] They also read a letter of reference from the Andover Seminary faculty in behalf of those appointees. A committee was appointed to consider the matter further and to report its recommendations to the directors at their next meeting one week later.

During the intervening days the committee met with Judson. He stated that he and his colleagues were willing to consider themselves the missionaries of the LMS "in all respects the same as the other missionaries engaged by [it]". He also shared the desire of the four Americans to "be employed in forming a new station for missionary exertions, rather than be separated from each other among the several stations already occupied by the

2   ibid., pp. 72–3. This account was recorded by Judson's later wife, Emily.

3   A copy of the letter appears in Wayland, *Memoir*, vol. 1, pp. 65–8.

society." It soon became apparent that the American Board could pledge only minimal support for its own appointees. The LMS representatives seemed reluctant to consider the sending of the four candidates as a joint venture of the two mission boards. In the end, at their meeting on May 27, the LMS directors approved the committee's recommendation that the four Americans "be accepted as missionaries, to be employed by this society [the LMS] in India".[4]

While in London Judson made a much bigger impression than one would have expected from a young man of his slight stature and boyish appearance:

> He was at this time small and exceedingly delicate in figure, with a round, rosy face, which gave him the appearance of extreme youthfulness. His hair and eyes were of a dark shade of brown, in his French passport described as "chestnut". His voice, however, was far from what would be expected of such a person, and usually took the listeners by surprise. An instance of this occurred in London. He sat in the pulpit with a clergyman somewhat distinguished for his eccentricity, and at the close of the sermon was requested to read a hymn. When he had finished, the clergyman arose, and introduced his young brother to the congregation as a person who purposed devoting himself to the conversion of the heathen, adding, "And if his faith is proportioned to his voice, he will drive the devil from all India."[5]

4   The quotations in this paragraph are ibid., pp. 75–7.
5   ibid., p. 74, as recorded by Emily C. Judson.

6

COMMISSIONED AS MISSIONARIES
(1811-1812)

His mission in England completed, Judson sailed from Gravesend aboard the *Augustus* on June 18. He arrived in New York on August 17, eager to share his encouraging news from the London Missionary Society and to see his beloved Ann. He was also anxious to confirm a heartening financial report he had received from America shortly before sailing from England.

But before leaving New York he had a past wrong to set right. He had never been able to forget the period three years earlier when he had a part in bilking various landlords while associating with a traveling drama troupe in the New York City vicinity. To the contrary, at this time "the enormity of this vicious course rested with a depressing weight" on his mind.[1] Consequently he retraced his earlier steps and repaid all his debts. He was then able to set out for Massachusetts with a clean conscience.

Back in Andover, Judson learned more about the dramatic financial development that had taken place while he was still in England. Mrs. John Norris, the wealthy widow of one of the founding benefactors of Andover Seminary, had herself died in March, leaving a bequest of 30,000 dollars to the American Board for its missionary enterprises. Some of her heirs had tied up the estate in litigation but there was little doubt the funds would be available in time.

There was other significant news as well. Samuel Newell and Gordon Hall had gone to Philadelphia in June to spend several

---

1   Edward Judson, *The Life of Adoniram Judson*, p. 11.

months studying medicine as a further preparation for their future missionary service. Shortly before leaving for Philadelphia, Newell had become engaged to Ann Hasseltine's girlhood friend, Harriet Atwood of Haverhill. Ann was thrilled that not only another woman, but one of her long-time friends at that, would be part of their missionary party.

Judson and Samuel Nott met with the Commissioners of the American Board at their meeting in Worcester, Massachusetts, on September 18. The Commissioners were disappointed that the written response they had received from the London Missionary Society said nothing about the American Board's proposal that the two mission organizations jointly send out a delegation of American missionaries. They had learned from Judson that the LMS did not consider "a joint conduct of missions" practical. The LMS was willing to have the American missionaries under its patronage and would welcome assistance from American Christians in financially supporting them, but it did not think it workable for the American Board to share in the direction of the mission.

The American Board did not wish to surrender its missionaries to the LMS, especially in light of the substantial financial resources it hoped to have at its disposal soon. Some of the Commissioners were inclined to forge ahead in seeking to send out their appointees as quickly as possible. Others, including two wealthy merchants on the board, were more cautious. The embargo resulting from the war between England and France had crippled American maritime trade the past two or three years. To some it seemed an inopportune time to assume the financial responsibility of sending a group of missionaries to the Orient and maintaining them there.

Judson and Nott voiced the opposite opinion. They had already waited over a year to be sent. In addition, a war between America and England seemed imminent. Once it began, their departure might be delayed for years more. They should be sent at once, within a few weeks if possible. The Board's two prosperous merchants dismissed the notion of an imminent war, one of them even pledging his word that there would be no war at all.[2] At

2   Anderson, *To the Golden Shore*, pp. 99–100.

this Judson, backed by Nott, issued a virtual ultimatum. If the American Board could not send them out soon they would go out straightaway under the auspices of the London Missionary Society. Judson's ultimatum (and perhaps the spirit with which he issued it) rankled some of the Commissioners. They did not appreciate his "pertinacity" or his telling them what they needed to do rather than following their lead. Reportedly some Commissioners were ready to dismiss him on the spot.[3]

When the American Board reconvened its meeting the next day emotions had cooled. The Commissioners had likely reminded one another that the very qualities that sometimes made Judson difficult to deal with – ambition, drive, self-confidence, self-reliance, tenacity and the like – would help him succeed as a missionary in a foreign land where such characteristics would be needed. On that second day the Commissioners approved the following decisions:

> That this board do not advise Messrs Adoniram Judson, Jr, and Samuel Nott, Jr, to place themselves at present under the direction of the London Missionary Society, but to wait the further intimations of Providence relative to our means of furnishing them with the requisite support in the proposed foreign mission.
>
> Messrs Adoniram Judson, Jr, Samuel Nott, Jr, Samuel Newell, and Gordon Hall were appointed missionaries to labor under the direction of this board in Asia, either in the Burman empire, or in Surat, or in Prince of Wales Island, or elsewhere, as, in the view of the Prudential Committee, Providence shall open the most favorable door.[4]

Before the Commissioners adjourned their meeting that second day, however, they thought it necessary to issue a verbal reprimand to Judson. The exact content of the reproof is not known, but undoubtedly it had to do with some of the tensions already noted.

3   Anderson, *To the Golden Shore*, p. 100; Warburton, *Eastward!*, p. 36.

4   Wayland, *Memoir*, vol. 1, pp. 78–9. Surat is a city on the west coast of India. Prince of Wales Island (modern Penang Island) is in Malaysia.

Curiously enough, when this reprimand was made public some eight years later, Judson had no recollection of it and sincerely denied that it had ever taken place. Only after further affirmation from others and personal reflection on what transpired at this meeting did he realize that he had, indeed, been reprimanded. Judson later related that at the time of this meeting he was aware the Commissioners were annoyed with his obstinacy, though he thought their irritation with him was only temporary. He was unaware of any significant disapproval on the part of the Board toward him. Wayland comments further:

> He had no idea that any serious displeasure was intended; and every other thought was immediately swallowed up in the consideration that he and his brethren were now appointed missionaries to the heathen, and appointed by their American brethren. In his letters at this period he speaks of this event as the consummation of all his wishes. The board afterwards, until the time of his embarkation, gave him no reason to suppose that he had been subject to any serious displeasure; and the whole thing passed entirely out of his mind.[5]

The next great challenge, as autumn passed, proved to be locating a ship on which the missionary party could sail. France was not hesitant about seizing American ships; British cruisers began blocking American ports and no ships were sailing for India. The weeks began to drag by until one day in late January 1812, Newell and Hall appeared unexpectedly in Andover from Philadelphia. They brought the electrifying news that by special permission of the federal government the ship *Harmony*, under the command of Captain Brown, was to sail from Philadelphia for Calcutta in about two weeks and would take the missionaries.

The Prudential Committee met in Newburyport on Monday, January 27. It had less than one-quarter of the 5,000 dollars needed to send out the entire delegation amply supplied. Mrs.

---

5   Wayland, *Memoir*, vol. 1, p. 85. ibid., pp. 81–92, presents a full discussion of this incident.

John Norris's generous legacy was still tied up in litigation. Other options were considered. The missionaries could go initially without wives. Half the missionaries could seek support from the London Missionary Society and go out under its auspices. In the end, the Prudential Committee determined to forge ahead in the faith that God would supply the needed finances by blessing their redoubled fund-raising efforts.

Just at that seemingly inopportune time, a fifth missions enthusiast, Luther Rice, made application to the Prudential Committee to be sent out as part of the missionary delegation. Rice had originally signed the missions Memorial that the Andover students presented at the meeting of the General Conference in Bradford a year and a half earlier. Until recently he had been engaged to a young woman whom he had hoped would join him in his missionary aspirations. After a long delay she turned him down, their engagement was terminated and he immediately applied to the Prudential Committee.

Overwhelmed with their already existing obligations, the committee agreed to appoint him under one condition. The ordination service for the missionary appointees was to take place in just one week, on February 6. Rice could join the other missionaries in being ordained and sent out if he could raise his own support in the intervening six days. Rice instantly set out on horseback in the depth of the New England winter. Traveling day and night, he returned at the end of the allotted time with the necessary support in hand.

During that same week word arrived of another ship that would soon sail for Calcutta, this one from Salem. The brig *Caravan*, commanded by Captain Augustine Heard, could accommodate up to four passengers. It was tentatively scheduled to sail February 10, four days after the missionaries' ordination service. The Prudential Committee immediately decided that half the missionaries should travel on the *Caravan* in order to lessen the risk of tragedy befalling the entire delegation at sea.

Judson bid farewell to his parents at the family home in Plymouth the first weekend of February. On Monday, February 3, his brother, Elnathan, now eighteen years of age, accompanied him on horseback to Boston. Judson knew his brother had never made a profession of Christian faith and was deeply concerned for his spiritual welfare. Along the way that day they dismounted and knelt to pray beside the road. Judson poured out an earnest prayer for his brother, as he would for many years to come.

Two days later, on Wednesday, February 5, 1812, Judson and Ann were married in her parents' home in Bradford. Parson Allen, minister of Bradford's First Church and Ann's pastor throughout her girlhood, officiated the ceremony. He also delivered the sermon at a farewell service that was held for Ann and Harriet Atwood in the church in Haverhill that same day. The church was filled to overflowing with people who had watched these two young ladies grow up. (Ann was now twenty-two and Harriet only seventeen.) They came to wish them God's blessing and protection, and to say their final farewell since they supposed they very well might never see them again on earth.

The ordination service took place the following day at Samuel Worcester's Tabernacle Church in Salem.[6] A heavy snow had fallen the previous night and Thursday morning dawned clear and cold. People came on foot, on horseback and in sleighs from many surrounding towns and cities, some of them traveling a considerable distance. A group of boys from Phillips Academy at Andover and a delegation of students from the Theological Seminary trudged the full sixteen miles over drifted roads to Salem. In order to get to the church before the ceremonies started at eleven in the morning, the two groups of students had to set out long before dawn.

Despite the Tabernacle Church's considerable size, it could barely accommodate all the people who came. Attendance estimates ranged from fifteen hundred to two thousand. Every seat was filled and "the aisles could be traced only by the ridges or seams made by the people standing [in them]."[7] Members of the ordination council and various dignitaries completely filled

6   Many of the details of this service and day are from Anderson, *To the Golden Shore*, pp. 109–13.

7   James L. Hill, "The Immortal Seven" (Philadelphia, 1913), pp. 5–6, as cited in Warburton, *Eastward!*, p. 41.

the platform all around the high white pulpit. The five missionary candidates were seated on a wooden settee at the front of the auditorium, facing the pulpit. Ann sat just behind them in the aisle seat of the foremost box pew.

Dr Leonard Woods presented a fitting ordination message from Psalm 67 with its worldwide focus. When it came time for the prayer of consecration, the five missionaries and the entire audience knelt. Each of the ordaining ministers stood before one of the missionaries and placed both hands on his head. As the prayer was offered, sighing and weeping were heard throughout the sanctuary.

It was early afternoon when the service concluded and the attendees dispersed to return to their homes through the bitter cold. One of the Phillips Academy students, William Goodell, grew tired and apparently lagged behind his traveling companions. By nightfall, still some distance from Andover, he became so exhausted that he collapsed in the snow. He would have frozen to death had not a group of seminary students discovered him along the road. They took turns carrying him and managed to get him to a house on the outskirts of Andover, where he was placed under blankets on a mattress in front of a roaring fire. Goodell later went himself as a missionary to Turkey.

7

VOYAGE TO INDIA
(1812)

It had been decided that the Judsons and Newells would sail together on the *Caravan* from Salem. Consequently, after the ordination service, Judson and Ann went to stay with her sister and brother-in-law in Beverly, two miles north of Salem, across the bay. Rebecca Hasseltine had married Joseph Emerson, scholarly pastor of Beverly's Dane Street Church, two years earlier.

A flurry of activities and preparations continued in the days that immediately followed. On Friday, February 7, Judson made a brief trip to Boston to say a final farewell to his sister and brother, Abigail and Elnathan. Late in 1811 or early in 1812 Samuel Nott became engaged to Roxanna Peck, whom he had known since childhood. They were married on Saturday, February 8, then left immediately for Philadelphia, from which they were to sail with Gordon Hall and Luther Rice on the *Harmony*. Samuel Newell and Harriet Atwood were married in Haverhill on Sunday, February 9.

Meanwhile, an eleventh-hour fundraising blitz was taking place. The American Board had 1,200 dollars on hand the morning of the ordination. Another 220 dollars were received in a collection at that service. Reportedly: "Everywhere ministers and laymen were soliciting gifts. ... The appeal was irresistible. Even people who disbelieved in missions gave."[1] One evening while the Judsons and Emersons were visiting in the Beverly parsonage, someone opened the front door, tossed in a purse then fled without saying a word. The purse contained fifty dollars and

1   Anderson, *To the Golden Shore*, p. 115.

had a tag attached to it that read, "For Mr. Judson's private use." Before the *Caravan* and *Harmony* sailed, over 6,000 dollars had been contributed.

The *Caravan* was still being loaded on February 13, three days after its initial intended departure date. That day the Judsons relocated to the home of Eliphalet Kimball – the father of Lydia, Ann's girlhood friend and confidante – in Salem, to be closer at hand when the order came to board ship. The weather turned wet and stormy for a few days and a massive snowstorm on Monday, February 17, left the town buried in snow. Finally, the following morning, word suddenly came from Captain Heard that the missionaries should board as soon as possible. A fair west wind had sprung up and the captain desired to sail on the afternoon tide.

The Judsons and Newells, along with a number of friends who wished to see them off, hurried down to the wharf. The missionaries, accompanied by two especially solicitous friends, S. B. Ingersoll and Israel Putnam, were transported out to the ship which lay in the harbor. But then the wind died down and Captain Heard determined they would try to depart on the next morning's tide. As darkness began to fall the hardy missionary supporters, still waiting on the wharf, reluctantly made their way back to their homes. Ingersoll and Putnam offered to spend the night aboard the *Caravan*, to keep the missionaries company, a gesture that "much pleased" the Judsons and Newells. The ship set sail a little after sunrise the following morning. Six or eight miles out to sea, Putnam and Ingersoll left the ship to return to shore in the small pilot boat. The Judsons and Newells stood at the stern until first the pilot boat, then the entire New England coastline disappeared from view.

The *Caravan* was a modest-sized ship, just ninety feet long. As the ship rose and fell on the waves, Harriet and Ann quickly became seasick. Five days out to sea everyone aboard the vessel received a scare when the *Caravan* sprung a serious leak and began to sink despite the efforts of all hands at the pumps. Finally the hole was located and the leak stopped. Before long the weather moderated and the ladies' sickness diminished. Though the missionaries were able to spend considerable time on deck, some of them continued to feel somewhat poorly and found they had little appetite. Concluding that they were not getting adequate exercise within the confines of the small ship, they started jumping rope and dancing regularly in their cabin, with the results that soon they felt better and their appetites returned.

As had been prearranged, Thursday, February 27, was observed by the missionaries and their supporters back home as a day of fasting and prayer for the success of the mission. The twenty-seven-year-old Captain Heard proved to be "a young gentleman of an amiable disposition and pleasing manners". Beginning their second Sunday on board, March 1, the missionaries proposed that a weekly worship service be held in their cabin. The captain readily assented; he and two of his officers regularly joined the missionaries for the service. The missionary couples met each evening for prayer and scripture reading. Many evenings were devoted to "religious conversation". Much time was spent in reading and study as well. During the voyage Ann read the entire New Testament, two volumes of Thomas Scott's commentary on the Old Testament, works on the inspiration and prophecies of Scripture, a pair of biographies and a volume on the lives of the apostles and martyrs.

In the month of April, Adoniram Judson commenced an intensive study on the subject of baptism that was to have a profound impact on the course of his future ministry. While still in America, he had begun a translation of the New Testament from the original Greek. As he continued his translation work during the voyage, his attention was arrested concerning baptism. The word "baptism" itself as used in Scripture and other ancient literature always seemed to involve dipping or immersion rather than mere sprinkling. In the New Testament, people were commonly baptized in rivers where they were presumably immersed and not merely sprinkled. Further, it appeared from the New Testament that only those who had made a conscious commitment to Christ received Christian baptism and were considered members of the Christian Church.

As a Congregationalist, Judson had been raised with the assumed conviction of pedobaptism. Infants were baptized by sprinkling as a signification of their belonging to God's covenant people and looking forward to the time when those children would consciously profess faith in Christ Jesus for salvation. For Congregationalists, Christian baptism was basically the New Testament counterpart to circumcision for God's covenant people, the Jews, in the Old Testament. Abraham and his male descendants (as well as their male servants) were circumcised as the outward symbol of their belonging to God's covenant people. Similarly, those who professed faith in Christ and their children were baptized to symbolize their being numbered among God's covenant people who made up the Christian Church.

The American Board had instructed its missionaries to baptize "credible believers with their households".[2] But how was Judson to view and treat the children and household servants of new converts? Was he to baptize those children and servants and consider them as belonging to God's covenant people, though they themselves had made no profession of faith in Christ but were for all intents and purposes still "heathen"? Furthermore, Judson knew that initially in India he would be associating with Baptist missionaries from England. He wrongly assumed they would press him to defend his baptismal convictions. In this he was mistaken because as Joshua Marshman, one of the English Baptists serving in India, stated, "... we make it a point to guard against obtruding on missionary brethren of different sentiments any conversation relative to baptism."[3] Even beyond that concern, when nationals asked why Christians had divergent baptism practices, Judson wanted to be able to provide a strong biblical defense of his own convictions.

He confided his discoveries and doubts to Ann. She later revealed: "The more he examined, the more his doubts increased; and, unwilling as he was to admit it, he was *afraid* the Baptists were right and he wrong."[4] He continued to study and think much about the matter through the latter half of their voyage.

2   Wayland, *Memoir*, vol. 1, p. 110.

3   ibid., p. 112.

4   ibid., p. 105.

The weather turned "exceedingly hot" as they crossed the equator early in May. While going around South Africa's Cape of Good Hope they encountered twenty days of rough, rainy weather. The voyage progressed steadily until finally on the morning of Friday, June 12, after 114 days of seeing nothing but sea and sky, the joyful cry rang out, "Land, land!" They were about twenty miles off the coast of Orissa, an eastern state of India. That day all they could make out were "the towering mountains of Golconda" but by the next morning they could easily distinguish trees along the shoreline.

That Sunday they came alongside and were hailed by two ships, one American and the other British. The Judsons and Newells hoped the American vessel would prove to be the *Harmony* carrying their fellow missionaries but were disappointed to learn it was not. (As it turned out, the *Harmony* did not arrive in Calcutta for another eight weeks.) By day's end the *Caravan* was at anchor in the Bay of Bengal but dared not progress further that night without a pilot to guide the ship into the mouth of the Hooghly River.

A pilot vessel arrived at length on Monday. The pilot boarded the *Caravan* with his two servants, one of whom was the first Hindu the missionaries had ever seen. In a letter that Ann penned to her sister, Abigail, on Tuesday, she described the distressing events of the previous night:

> Last night was the most dangerous, and to me, by far the most unpleasant we have had. The navigation here being dangerous, on account of the sand-shoals, the pilot came to anchor before dark. The sea was high, and kept the vessel in continual motion. About ten the mate came down, and told us the cable had parted, and the anchor gone. I thought all hope of our safety was entirely gone, and immediately began to inquire into my preparedness for an entrance into another world. The thought of being shipwrecked was exceedingly distressing; and I could not but think the providence of God would preserve us, on account of this infant Mission. In him I confided, and he preserved us. They got the ship under

way; and the pilot being well acquainted with the shoals, we met with no difficulty. I slept none at all, in consequence of the continual noise, and profane language on deck. The Captain has never used any profane language since we have been with him; but the pilot, much more than we have ever heard before.[5]

The next two days proved to be as delightful as Monday night had been trying. Traveling up the Hooghly, a branch of the Ganges, they first passed the Sundarbans, islands at the mouths of the Ganges. "The smell which proceeds from them is fragrant beyond description," Ann wrote Abigail in telling her of the mango trees they saw along those banks. Ann's picturesque description continued on Wednesday:

> I have never, my dear sister, witnessed or read any thing so delightful as the present scene. On each side of the Hooghly, where we are now sailing, are the Hindu cottages, as thick together as the houses in our seaports. They are very small, and in the form of hay-stacks, without either chimneys or windows. They are situated in the midst of trees, which hang over them, and appear truly romantic. The grass and fields of rice are perfectly green, and herds of cattle are every where feeding on the banks of the river, and the natives are scattered about, differently employed. Some are fishing, some driving the team, and many are sitting indolently on the banks of the river. The pagodas we have passed are much handsomer and larger than the houses.[6]

As they neared Calcutta, Ann's heart was filled with praise: "O what reason we have to be thankful, for so pleasant, so prosperous a voyage. There is seldom a voyage so short as ours – we have not yet been out four months." Later that day the *Caravan* dropped anchor in the harbor at Calcutta. Numerous ships lay at anchor and hundreds of native Indians swarmed around the docks. "This city is by far the most elegant of any thing I have

5 Knowles, *Memoir of Mrs. Ann H. Judson*, pp. 53–4.

6 ibid., p. 54.

ever seen," Ann wrote from aboard the *Caravan*. Fresh fruit was brought on deck immediately. Of one type that Ann had never eaten before, she reported, "The bananas are a very delicious fruit; they taste much like a rich pear."[7]

While Ann and Harriet were relishing the first sights, sounds and even tastes of Calcutta, their husbands promptly went ashore. There a rather rude welcome awaited them.

7   ibid., pp. 54–5.

8

A CHANGE OF CONVICTION
(1812)

After going ashore Adoniram Judson and Samuel Newell made their way to the East India Company's local police station. All foreigners arriving in India were required to register with the powerful EIC, which jealously guarded its trade monopoly over the country. The EIC steadfastly opposed Christian missionary activity in the country, fearing it might stir up anti-foreign sentiment from the Hindu native population that would harm the company's profit-making capabilities. When Judson and Newell reported their intention to stay in India only until they could find a ship to Burma, they were strongly discouraged from going there due to the untenable and extremely dangerous conditions that awaited any foreigners attempting to settle in that country. But the missionaries were also bluntly informed that they almost certainly would not be allowed to remain long in India.[1]

The next day, Thursday, June 18, the Judsons and Newells made their way to the Calcutta residence of William Carey, founder and leader of the English Baptist mission in India. Having learned of the American missionaries' arrival, Carey had warmly extended his hospitality to them. Ann described Carey's large stone house:

---

1   One year later, during the summer of 1813, the East India Company's charter was reviewed by British Parliament, as occurred once each decade. Under tremendous pressure from the collective Christian community in Britain and led by influential MP William Wilberforce, Parliament sanctioned missionary activity throughout EIC territories. But when Judson and his missionary companions first arrived in Calcutta, the EIC still wielded its powerful, ironclad opposition to Christian missions in its domain.

His house is curiously constructed, as the other European houses are here. There are no chimneys or fire-places in them, the roofs are flat, the rooms twenty feet in height and proportionately large. Large windows, without glass, open from one room to another, that the air may freely circulate through the house. They are very convenient for this hot climate, and bear every mark of antiquity.[2]

When the Americans were shown into his study, Carey arose, shook hands with them and cordially welcomed them to his adopted country. He had been ministering in India for nearly nineteen years.

Due to the East India Company's strong opposition to missionary activity, when Carey first arrived in India he managed an indigo factory in Malda, nearly 300 miles north of Calcutta, for six years. During that time he also began translating the New Testament into Bengali. Early in 1800 Carey joined four other English Baptist missionaries who had recently settled in the Danish colony at Serampore, fifteen miles north of Calcutta. There they could carry out missionary activities without as much interference from the EIC. Within a year, two of the four new missionaries at Serampore died, leaving Carey, a schoolteacher named Joshua Marshman and a printer named William Ward to carry on the work. In 1801 Carey completed his translation of the Bengali New Testament and was appointed as a professor of Sanskrit and Bengali languages at Fort Williams College, a school in Calcutta that educated British civil servants. For a dozen years before the arrival of the Judsons and Newells, the Serampore Trio (as Carey, Marshman and Ward became famously known), aided by a few missionary reinforcements and a number of Indian assistants, steadily built up their ministries of evangelism, education and Bible translation in Serampore and Calcutta.

Carey and his ministry associates invited the Judsons and Newells to stay at the Serampore missionary compound while they awaited the arrival of the other American missionaries. Traveling upriver to Serampore that Friday afternoon, the Judsons and

2   Knowles, *Memoir of Mrs. Ann H. Judson*, pp. 56–7.

Newells were met at the water's edge by Marshman and Ward who led them to the mission complex with its scenic situation overlooking the river. The compound's central meeting place was a capacious stone building known as "the mission house". That structure contained a large chapel, a spacious dining hall, two good-sized libraries and roomy guest quarters. Marshman ran a school for local Indian boys while his wife had a separate school for "European young ladies" and the missionary children. Daily chapel services were held and Sunday worship services were provided in Bengali and English.

Adoniram Judson, with his intention of doing Bible translation work, was doubtless especially interested in the extensive Scripture translation and printing ministry that had developed at Serampore. By that time the Serampore Trio, assisted by Indian pundits, had translated and published not only the entire Bible into Bengali but also the New Testament into Sanskrit, Oriya, Hindi and Marathi. In addition, Carey was compiling grammars of various Indian languages as well as a massive polyglot Sanskrit dictionary,[3] all of which were intended to aid Bible translation and teaching ministries of missionaries for generations to come.

Tragically, on March 11, 1812, while the American missionaries were en route to India, a devastating fire of unknown origin gutted the building in which the Serampore printing operation was carried out. Material losses from the fire amounted to 10,000 English pounds. Far worse were the loss of: large portions of Scripture translations in seven Indian languages, including the entire New Testament in Kanarese; Carey's Telugu and Punjabi grammars; the considerable amount of material he had collected and compiled for his Sanskrit dictionary. Strengthened by God in the face of this seeming catastrophe, the indomitable Serampore missionaries immediately set about redoing the invaluable translation and printing work that had been destroyed. In their lifetime they would translate and publish the Bible, in whole or in part, into more than forty languages.

3   Sanskrit was the classic religious and literary language of India as well as the root language behind most of the country's modern vernaculars. Carey's polyglot dictionary was to include not only Sanskrit but also Hebrew and Greek.

Ten days after arriving at Serampore, Judson and Newell were summoned to Calcutta. There a government order was read to them, stating that they must leave the country immediately to return to America. They were to return on the *Caravan* and Captain Heard would not receive port clearance unless he took them. Thankfully, Heard did not plan to embark till August, so they still had a few weeks in which to see if other arrangements could be made.

The American Board had sent them out with instructions to establish their mission in Burma unless circumstances rendered it inexpedient to do so. But the opinion of missionaries and others in India was uniformly against attempting a work there. Foreigners in Burma were completely despised and lived at the mercy of a monarch and governors who were thoroughly despotic, capricious and corrupt. Burma's laws were said to be the bloodiest on earth. Two previous attempts by Protestant missionaries to establish a work in Burma had proved futile. William Carey's son, Felix, was currently living in Rangoon, Burma, as he had for four years. But he was able to remain there because he had married a Burmese woman. Recently he and a number of other English had been forced to take refuge in a British man-of-war lying in the Irrawaddy River when threatened with a general massacre.

In mid-July Judson and Newell were informed they could not undertake a mission in any British dominion or the territory of a British ally. But if they could prove they would be ministering outside British domain they would not have to return to America. Other countries they considered at that time as potential fields of service included China, Arabia, Turkey and Persia. Toward the end of July a heartening letter arrived from their fellow American missionaries who had traveled aboard the *Harmony*. They had reached Isle of France (modern Mauritius), east of Madagascar. The governor there was friendly toward missions and desired to see a missionary on both Isle of France and Madagascar. Although Isle of France was under British control, it was not part of the East India Company territory. Judson and Newell hastened back to Calcutta with the letter and were granted permission to proceed to Isle of France.

As it turned out, the ship *Colonel Gillespie* was set to sail there, leaving in just four days. But its commander, Captain Chimminant, was at first unwilling to take any passengers. After considerable persuasion by Judson, Chimminant finally agreed to transport two of the missionaries, not all four. It was decided that the Newells should go. Harriet was expecting a child in less than three months and should be settled back on land before giving birth. The Newells embarked from Calcutta on August 4.

Judson's mind continued to be uneasy over the issue of baptism, so some time in July he resumed his studies on that subject. Ann later wrote to a friend:

> I felt afraid he would become a Baptist, and frequently urged the unhappy consequences if he should. But he said his duty compelled him to satisfy his own mind, and embrace those sentiments which appeared most concordant with Scripture. I always took the Pedobaptist side in reasoning with him, even after I was as doubtful of the truth of their system as he.[4]

Ann even went so far as to frequently tell her husband that if he became a Baptist, she would not. When the Newells went to Calcutta to board the *Colonel Gillespie* late in July or early in August, the Judsons took up residence in the home of a Mr. Rolt in Calcutta. The library in the room where the Judsons stayed contained "many books on both sides" of the baptismal issue. Making free use of those works, both Judson and Ann gave themselves solely to the study of that subject for several days.

On Saturday, August 8, just four days after the Newells sailed for Isle of France, Samuel and Roxana Nott, Gordon Hall and Luther Rice finally reached Calcutta. Judson apparently was unable to keep to himself the matter that was weighing so heavily on his mind. Within three hours of Nott's arrival, Judson had "opened ... his whole mind" to him on the issue. Hall and Rice soon became aware of Judson's contemplations as well,

4   Wayland, *Memoir*, vol. 1, pp. 105–6.

and before a week passed, Nott, Hall and Rice had discussed the implications of the situation.

A letter that Judson afterward wrote to the Third Church in Plymouth, of which he had been a member for three years, revealed his heartache and determination in facing this wrenching issue:

> Must I, then, forsake my parents, the church with which I stand connected, the society under whose patronage I have come out, the companions of my missionary undertaking? Must I forfeit the good opinion of all my friends in my native land, occasioning grief to some, and provoking others to anger, and be regarded henceforth, by all my former dear acquaintances, as a weak, despicable Baptist, who has not sense enough to comprehend the connection between the Abrahamic and the Christian systems? All this was mortifying; it was hard to flesh and blood. But I thought again, it is better to be guided by the opinion of Christ, who is the truth, than by the opinion of men, however good, whom I know to be in an error. The praise of Christ is better than the praise of men. Let me cleave to Christ at all events, and prefer his favor above my chief joy.[5]

The last week of August, Ann came to share her husband's new conviction. On Thursday, August 27, Judson wrote Carey, Marshman and Ward, to whom he had not previously revealed "the late exercises of my mind on the subject of baptism". He now divulged the change of conviction he and Ann had come to have and stated their desire to be baptized by immersion.

The following Tuesday, Judson penned a letter to Samuel Worcester, Corresponding Secretary of the American Board, to inform him of these developments:

> My change of sentiments on the subject of baptism is considered by my missionary brethren as incompatible with my continuing their fellow-laborer in the mission which

5   ibid., p. 102. ibid., pp. 95–105, presents Judson's full and detailed explanation to the Third Church, in his own words, concerning his change of convictions on baptism.

they contemplate on the Island of Madagascar; and it will, I presume, be considered by the Board of Commissioners as equally incompatible with my continuing their missionary. ...

The dissolution of my connection with the Board of Commissioners, and a separation from my dear missionary brethren, I consider most distressing consequences of my late change of sentiments, and indeed, the most distressing events which have ever befallen me.[6]

That same day Judson wrote to Dr Lucius Bolles, pastor of the First Baptist Church of Salem, Massachusetts, with whom he had briefly discussed missionary enterprise before leaving America. Judson now made Bolles aware of the new situation and offered his services as a missionary of American Baptists should they choose to support him.

I recollect that, during a short interview I had with you in Salem, I suggested the formation of a society among the Baptists in America for the support of foreign missions, in imitation of the exertions of your English Brethren. Little did I then expect to be personally concerned in such an attempt. ... The missionaries at Serampore are exerted to the utmost of their ability in managing and supporting their extensive and complicated mission. Under these circumstances I look to you. Alone, in this foreign heathen land, I make my appeal to those whom, with their permission, I will call *my Baptist brethren* in the United States.[7]

Judson also corresponded with Dr Thomas Baldwin, pastor of the Second Baptist Church in Boston, thanking him for the benefit he had derived from a "Series of Letters" Baldwin had published on the topic of baptism. Judson sent Baldwin copies of the letters he had just written to the Serampore Trio and Samuel Worcester. Joshua Marshman sent a missive of his own to Baldwin in which the Englishman diplomatically encouraged American Baptists to take up the cause of supporting Judson:

6   ibid., p. 110.
7   ibid., p. 111.

It can scarcely be expected that the [American] Board of Commissioners will support a Baptist missionary, who cannot, of course, comply with their instructions, and baptize *whole households* on the parents' faith; and it is certain that the young man ought not to be left to perish for want, merely because he loved the truth more than father or mother; nor be compelled to give up missionary work for want of support therein. Now, though we [Serampore missionaries] should certainly interfere to prevent a circumstance like this happening, ... yet, to say nothing of the missionary concerns already lying on us, and constantly enlarging, it seems as though Providence itself were raising up this young man, that you might at least partake of the zeal of our Congregational missionary brethren around you. I would wish, then, that you should share in the glorious work, by supporting him. ... After God has thus given you a missionary of your own nation, faith, and order, without the help or knowledge of man, let me entreat you ... humbly to accept the gift.[8]

Adoniram and Ann Judson were baptized by immersion in the Baptist mission's Lal Bazar Chapel in Calcutta on September 6. William Ward conducted the ceremony. Later that month Judson preached a sermon on baptism in the same chapel. William Carey declared it the best sermon he had ever heard on the subject. It was subsequently published and widely circulated by Baptists in India, England and America.

8   ibid., pp. 112–13.

9

In Search of a Country
(1812-1813)

The Judsons realized it would take months for news of their change of baptismal conviction to reach America. Several more months would pass before it would be known if the Baptists there were willing to assume their support as missionaries. In the meanwhile, they soon needed to determine a country where they could serve in order to avoid deportation back to America.

Isle of France no longer seemed a possibility for them. The Newells were already en route there and the other American Congregational missionaries had obtained permission from the East India Company to go there as well. The Judsons gave consideration to Ceylon (modern Sri Lanka) off the southern coast of India, the islands of Java and Amboina in Indonesia, Japan and even Brazil. Many Portuguese lived in Calcutta and Judson started studying the Portuguese language for use in Brazil should the Lord direct their steps there.

Judson was still most attracted to the thought of serving in Burma with its immense population, then thought to be around 17 million, more than twice the size of the United States. (That estimate was later learned to be greatly exaggerated; the actual population of Burma at the time may have been only half that amount.) The Bible had not yet been translated into Burmese and the thought of translating the scriptures into the mother tongue of such a large nation appealed mightily to Judson.

Felix Carey arrived in Calcutta from Rangoon in September and Judson immediately made his acquaintance. Carey encouraged the Judsons to return with him to Rangoon and to take up the

Bible translation work he had just begun there. The Judsons could clearly see, however, that even Felix Carey's position in Burma was quite precarious, despite the fact that he was married to a Burmese woman. Furthermore, his responsibilities in Burma appeared to be more as a political ambassador than as a missionary. Fresh difficulties had arisen between the British and the Burmese government. Still, the Judsons were willing to go there should providence open the door for them to do so.

A great and unexpected encouragement came to the Judsons in the latter half of October when Luther Rice suddenly indicated that he, too, had come to have a change of conviction concerning baptism. He wished to be baptized by immersion and to partner with the Judsons in their missionary venture, wherever that would prove to be. This came as a considerable surprise because during the voyage to India on the *Harmony*, Rice had vociferously defended pedobaptism to a pair of English Baptist missionaries, Johns and Lawson, who sailed on the same ship. After Judson's change of perspective, Rice repeatedly tried to draw him into debate over the issue. Instead of arguing with Rice, Judson advised him to study the subject thoroughly for himself from Scripture. After thus becoming persuaded, Rice was immersed on Sunday, November 1.

Meanwhile Samuel and Roxana Nott and Gordon Hall, like the Judsons, had been considering various countries where they might serve. After enduring a month of illness following their arrival in Calcutta, the Notts and Hall booked passage to Isle of France on the ship *Adele*. When its departure was delayed week after week they received assurances that they would be permitted to go to Ceylon, a destination offering more promising missionary prospects. But by the time they discovered that no ship was likely to sail for Ceylon until early the next year, the *Adele* had already departed. Eventually they learned that the new Governor of Bombay, Sir Evan Nepean, was supportive of missions. Early in November the Notts and Hall found a ship, the *Commerce*, bound for Bombay, and received a pass from the police to sail on it.

But by then British officials had become deeply displeased, even suspicious, over the American missionaries' considerable delay in leaving Calcutta. On November 17 a peremptory order was issued that all the American missionaries were to leave Calcutta on a fleet that was about to sail for England. All their names were printed in the Calcutta papers as "passengers to England". Judson and Rice were summoned to the police station where they were given this order. Afterward a petty officer accompanied them back to Mr. Rolt's house, where they had been staying, and told them they could not leave it without permission.

The *Commerce* had received port clearance and was scheduled to embark any day. Since they did have a police pass to sail on the *Commerce* and their baggage was already on it, the Notts and Hall quietly boarded the ship in hopes of evading deportation to England. Just then the Judsons and Rice learned of a ship, *La Belle Creole*, slated to sail for Isle of France in two days. After the chief of police refused to issue them a pass to sail on the *Creole*, Judson and Rice approached the captain of the ship to ask if he would take them aboard without one. "There is my ship," he responded, "you may do as you please."

Mr. Rolt used his influence to get the dockyard gates unlocked at midnight on Saturday, November 21, so the missionaries could slip through them and onto the *Creole*. The next morning the ship began to move down the Hooghly River. Sunday passed without incident but near midnight on Monday the *Creole* was hailed and ordered to stop. A dispatch from Calcutta commanded the pilot to drop anchor and await further instructions because the vessel was thought to carry passengers who had been ordered to England.

Judson and Rice decided to lay low at an English tavern on shore about a mile from where the *Creole* was anchored in case authorities arrived to search the ship. Ann remained on the *Creole* with most of their baggage. Somewhat surprisingly, it was thought that her presence aboard the ship would not raise suspicions if the authorities came looking for the missionaries. Tuesday evening, however, she joined Judson and Rice at the tavern. Rice left that same night for Calcutta to try again to gain permission for them to remain aboard the *Creole*. He returned late Wednesday with the disheartening news that the request had been flatly refused. Early Thursday morning the *Creole*'s captain sent them word that he had received clearance to proceed but their belongings must be removed from the ship.

Hearing of another English tavern sixteen miles downriver at Fultah, the missionaries decided to go there to see what might be worked out. They had learned that a ship bound for Ceylon lay at anchor near Fultah. Rice again made his way to Calcutta, hoping to obtain permission for them to sail on that vessel. Ann returned to the *Creole* to look after the baggage. The captain agreed to transport their luggage as far as Fultah and invited Ann to stay aboard the ship till it arrived there. Judson intended to take a small rowboat downriver and to meet her there.

When the *Creole* came opposite the tavern at Fultah, Ann was taken ashore in the pilot's boat. After procuring a large boat to retrieve their belongings from the ship, she proceeded to the tavern, feeling very alone and vulnerable:

> I entered the tavern, a *stranger*, a *female*, and *unprotected*.
> I called for a room, and sat down to reflect on my disconsolate
> situation. I had nothing with me but a few rupees. I did
> not know if the boat which I sent after the vessel would
> overtake it, and if it did, whether it would ever return with
> our baggage; neither did I know where Mr. J. was, or when
> he would come, or with what treatment I should meet at
> the tavern. I thought of *home*, and said to myself, *These are
> some of the many trials attendant on a missionary life, and which I had
> anticipated.*[1]

Unknown to Ann, while she sat in the tavern, the *Commerce*, bearing the Notts and Gordon Hall toward their destination in Bombay, glided past quickly on the river. Thankfully, Judson arrived a few hours later and their baggage was returned toward nightfall.

Rice eventually rejoined them but with the disappointing report that they had been refused permission to take passage on the ship bound for Ceylon. Just as the dispirited trio sat down to

1   Knowles, *Memoir of Mrs. Ann H. Judson*, p. 72.

supper on Sunday, November 29, a letter was handed to them. They were astonished and overjoyed to discover that it contained a pass from the magistrate in Calcutta for them to sail aboard the *Creole*. "Who procured this pass for us, or in what way, we are still ignorant; we could only view the hand of God, and wonder," Ann afterward related.[2]

They feared that the *Creole*, which had continued downriver three days earlier, might already be out to sea. Their one hope was that the ship had anchored at Saugur, some seventy miles from their present location at Fultah, in order to take on supplies before heading out into the Bay of Bombay. They set out immediately in the boat that had brought their belongings from the *Creole*. Before dark the following night they arrived at Saugur where they were unspeakably relieved to find the *Creole* among the many ships lying at anchor.

The missionaries' seven week voyage to Isle of France was largely uneventful. They all invested considerable time studying the French language which they intended to use in their new ministry setting. Each evening they shared a time of Bible reading and prayer. Neither the *Creole*'s crew nor its five other passengers accepted the missionaries' invitations to join them for a weekly Sunday morning worship service.

Perhaps it was sometime during that voyage when Ann first realized she was pregnant. Doubtless she eagerly anticipated being reunited with Harriet Newell and seeing her newborn. Though there would be the sorrowful news to share of the decision to establish a separate mission, still for at least a short while Ann and Harriet could share their joys and concerns about motherhood and starting their families under such challenging circumstances.

The *Creole* reached Port Louis, Isle of France, on January 17, 1813. The ship had scarcely docked when the Judsons and Rice received the shocking and heart-wrenching news that Harriet and her baby were both dead! The next day a "disconsolate, brokenhearted" Samuel Newell came aboard the *Creole* and related to them what had happened. Shortly after the Newells left Calcutta aboard the *Gillespie*, the ship encountered contrary winds and storms. To make matters worse, Harriet, after recovering from a week of fever, was attacked with "severe pains in the stomach and bowels". The battered vessel began to leak dangerously and had to put in for repairs at a small town on India's eastern coast.

Harriet was fully recovered by the time the ship resumed its journey two weeks later. But because of the *Gillespie*'s continued slow progress, the Newells were still at sea when Harriet gave birth to a baby girl on October 8 – more than two months after leaving Calcutta and two days before the young mother's nineteenth birthday. Harriet bore the infant on the cabin floor with her husband as her only attendant. At first mother and newborn appeared to be doing well. But a day or two later a severe storm left everyone aboard drenched and chilled. Harriet and the baby both caught cold. The infant quickly developed pneumonia and died in her mother's arms just five days after birth.

Harriet continued to weaken and soon began to manifest signs of tuberculosis. After finally reaching Port Louis early in November, the Newells moved into a small house. Two doctors helped care for Harriet but were unable to save her life. Ann related of Harriet in her diary: "She frequently mentioned in her sickness that she had never repented leaving her native country, and that the consideration of having left it for the cause of Christ, now afforded her great consolation."[3] When one of the doctors informed Harriet the day before her death that she would not live another day, she raised her hands and exclaimed, "O glorious intelligence." She passed away late in the afternoon on Monday, November 30, and was buried the following day in the Port Louis cemetery.

Isle of France's Governor Farquhar was supportive of missionary service on the island. But the missionaries were soon disappointed to discover that their ministry efforts would be confined to British soldiers in the Port Louis army barracks and hospital. Most of the island's population was comprised of

3   ibid., p. 76.

slaves whose owners would not permit them to receive religious instruction.

Though the missionaries could do little to help the slaves, on one occasion Ann could not forbear from coming to the aid of a female slave who was being physically abused. On the evening of March 11, Ann heard a loud commotion in the yard of the house where they were staying, a yard that was shared with another family's residence. Going to the door, she saw a female slave with her hands tied behind her back; her mistress was beating her with a club "in a most dreadful manner". Ann approached the mistress and in broken French urged her to stop, adding, "What has your servant done?"

The angry woman immediately stopped beating the slave but answered angrily, "My servant is very bad. And recently she ran away." Ann continued to talk with the mistress till her anger appeared to have subsided. But she suddenly concluded her punishment by flinging her club at the slave. The cudgel struck the servant's head, causing blood to run down on her garment.

The slave's hands were left tied behind her all night. The next morning they were untied and she spent the day in labor. Ann supposed the servant would not be punished further. But that evening a chain, "as large and heavy as an ox chain", was brought into the yard. On one end of the chain was a ring, just large enough to fit around the slave's neck, which was to be fastened around her throat with a lock and key. Two pieces of iron were affixed to the ring and projected up on either side of the servant's face to prevent her from eating. The slave trembled in terror as they prepared to lock the ring around her throat. The weighty chain dangled from her neck to the ground.

At the sight of her servant, the mistress's rage was rekindled and she started beating her as she had the night before. Ann again intervened, begging the furious woman to desist. She did but so seethed with rage that she could barely speak. When her fury had abated somewhat, Ann asked her, "Could you not forgive your servant?" She then added, "Your slave has been very bad but it would be very good of you to forgive her."

"I will forgive her," the mistress reluctantly answered Ann, "but only because *you* have asked me to. I would not have my servant to think it is out of any favor to her." Turning to her slave she begrudgingly stated, "I forgive you because *she* requested it." The mistress then promised Ann that the chain with its collar would not be put on the servant and ordered it to be carried away.

The slave woman stepped forward, knelt before Ann, kissed her feet and repeated earnestly, "Mercy, madam – mercy, madam" (meaning "Thank you, madam"). Ann could hardly keep from weeping at the servant's fervent gratitude.

Since the missionaries could not minister to the general population on Isle of France they were unwilling to settle there. The much larger island of Madagascar to the west had earlier been considered as a potential field of service but was ruled out for the very pragmatic reason that its inhabitants usually imprisoned or killed all visitors. Newell desired to rejoin his fellow Congregationalists, so on February 24 he sailed from Port Louis on a Portuguese brig destined for Bombay.

Luther Rice had suffered from liver trouble in Calcutta and his condition worsened on Isle of France. It was feared that if he did not receive proper treatment in a more suitable climate his life might quickly come to an end. Encouraged by the Judsons to do so, Rice decided to return to America in order to fulfill a dual purpose; he would undergo liver treatment while at the same time promoting their infant mission to Baptist churches in the United States. Because war had broken out between Britain and the United States, no ships were sailing directly from Isle of France to the U.S. But in March a vessel docked at Port Louis en route to San Salvador, Central America. Rice sailed on it on March 13.

After further deliberation the Judsons determined to establish a mission on Penang Island in the Straits of Malacca, just off the western coast of Malaysia. As no ships ever sailed to Penang from Port Louis they decided to go to Madras, India, from which they hoped to find a vessel destined for Penang. By this time Ann was several months along in her pregnancy. If all worked out well, they might be able to reach Penang before the baby arrived. They accordingly embarked on the *Countess of Harcourt* on May 7 and arrived at Madras on June 4.

There they were warmly welcomed by an English Congregational missionary couple, Mr. and Mrs. Loveless. But the Judsons were disappointed to discover that no ships in Madras were headed for Penang. Having returned to India, they once again lived with the justifiable fear of being deported to England by the powerful East India Company. The likelihood of that fate befalling them increased with every passing day. After two weeks of anxious, fruitless searching for a ship bound for their desired destination, Judson learned of an intriguing alternative. A Portuguese ship, the *Georgiana* – "a crazy old vessel" as Judson described it – was intending to sail not to Penang but to Rangoon in Burma!

10

A Beginning in Burma
(1813)

Adoniram and Ann Judson were not long in deciding that perhaps they were being providentially directed back to their original country of choice in which to establish a mission work, despite all the uncertainties that still surrounded the prospect of seeking to do so. In a letter Judson wrote shortly after their arrival in Rangoon, he explained:

> A mission to Rangoon we had been accustomed to regard with feelings of horror. But it was now brought to a point. We must either venture there or be sent to Europe. All other paths were shut up; and thus situated, though dissuaded by all our friends at Madras, we commended ourselves to the care of God, and embarked the 22d of June.[1]

The Judsons hired a European woman to accompany them on the voyage. She would serve as midwife and nursemaid to Ann and the baby. The woman appeared to be in good health. But just as the ship was about to sail she had some sort of a seizure and fell to the floor. The Judsons did all they could to revive her but after a few gasps she died. There was no time to find her replacement before the *Georgiana* embarked.

The voyage quickly proved extremely trying. The ship was small, dirty and smelly. As the vessel sought to make its way across the Bay of Bengal it was battered about by strong winds and rough waters. The captain was the only other person aboard

1   Wayland, *Memoir*, vol. 1, pp. 119–20.

who spoke any English. The Judsons did not have a private cabin; the walls of their tiny apartment consisted only of canvas curtains. A few days out to sea Ann went into labor. Sadly, the infant was stillborn. Ann was exhausted by the delivery and from the continual pitching of the ship. Her strength ebbed away and for a time it was feared that she too would die.

The captain tried to steer the ship southeastward to the Nicobar Islands, above the northern coast of Sumatra, where he intended to pick up a cargo of coconuts. But the vessel was driven further north by the contrary winds, into a dangerous strait between two of the Andaman Islands. The water was calm in the sheltered strait but "black rocks" could be seen lying menacingly not far below the surface. In addition, as Judson afterward reported, they were attempting to make their way between "two savage coasts, where the captain had never been before, and where if we had been cast ashore, we should, according to all accounts, have been killed and eaten by the natives."[2] An unforeseen blessing of the passage through the "dangerous but quiet channel" was that Ann was finally able to rest peacefully and she began to recover her strength.

On the eastern side of the islands, the Andaman Sea was found to be peaceful. Giving up on his original idea of collecting coconuts, the captain instead let the ship be "gently wafted" along by the favorable south winds toward Rangoon. On Tuesday, July 13, three weeks after leaving Madras, the *Georgiana* glided into the wide entrance of the Rangoon River. The Rangoon was one of the many mouths of the much larger Irrawaddy River on Burma's south-central coastline.

Later in the day, a few miles upriver, they arrived at the bedraggled city of Rangoon. With its population of perhaps 10,000 residents, the town stretched out for about a mile along the river, being dissected by a number of muddy creeks that ran down to the shore. A high stockade of timbers, nearly twenty feet tall, surrounded the central part of town. Beyond the stockade could be seen two or three large brick houses, a pair of Catholic

2   ibid., p. 120.

churches, an Armenian church and scores of pointed spires on pagodas of various sizes. Most impressively, towering above the trees beyond the town, was the four-hundred-foot-high, gold-covered spire of the Shwe Dagon Pagoda. Shwe Dagon was the most eminent and venerated pagoda in all of Burma. By stark contrast, most of the houses in Rangoon were modest structures comprised of bamboo walls, teakwood floors and thatched roofs. Of their first impression of this new setting, Judson afterward wrote candidly:

> The prospect of Rangoon, as we approached, was quite disheartening. I went on shore, just at night, to take a view of the place, and the mission house; but so dark, and cheerless, and unpromising did all things appear, that the evening of that day, after my return to the ship, we have marked as the most gloomy and distressing that we ever passed. Instead of rejoicing, as we ought to have done, in having found a heathen land from which we were not immediately driven away, such were our weaknesses that we felt we had no portion left here below, and found consolation only in looking beyond our pilgrimage, which we tried to flatter ourselves would be short, to that peaceful region where the wicked cease from troubling and the weary are at rest. But if ever we commended ourselves sincerely, and without reserve, to the disposal of our heavenly Father, it was on this evening. And after some recollection and prayer, we experienced something of the presence of Him who cleaveth closer than a brother; something of the peace which our Savior bequeathed to His followers ...[3]

The next morning they left the ship to make their way to Felix Carey's house, which was half a mile outside the town's walls. As Ann was too weak to walk that distance, she was carried in a chair by four Burmese men. Upon reaching Carey's home, the Judsons discovered that he was away in Ava, Burma's capital city, 350 miles up the Irrawaddy from Rangoon. They were warmly

3   ibid., pp. 120–21.

welcomed by Mrs. Carey, though she spoke but little English. She was a young Eurasian woman in her mid-twenties. Her father was a British sea captain named Blackwell while her mother was Burmese.

The Baptist mission house was large and well-suited for that climate. While solidly constructed of teakwood, the inside of the house was unfinished with exposed beams and joists.[4] Two acres of enclosed gardens, full of various types of fruit trees, surrounded the residence. In this quiet, pleasant setting, Ann was able to rest and recoup her health. She and Judson enjoyed taking walks around the gardens and to some of the nearby villages.

Roman Catholic missionaries had first entered Burma in the sixteenth century. They gained a considerable following but were required by the government to limit their efforts to the remnants of early Portuguese settlers and those of mixed blood. The first Protestant missionaries to minister in Burma were English Baptists sent out by the Serampore Trio.[5] James Chater arrived at Calcutta in the summer of 1806. He was soon ordered back to England by East India Company officials but managed, instead, to make his way to Burma to explore the possibility of establishing a mission there. Felix Carey, then aged twenty-one, joined Chater in Rangoon in the latter half of 1807.

At first, circumstances were encouraging for the new missionary team. The whole city seemed friendly and even the Viceroy of Rangoon was interested in their mission. "The fact that the houses were miserably built, the streets filthy with vermin,

---

4 This was actually the second residence of Baptist missionaries since their coming to Rangoon in 1807: "The original mission house had stood not far from the place where the refuse of the city was thrown, with the public execution ground nearby, and the enclosure where dead bodies were burned. In 1809, however, a new house had been erected in a different location farther from the city" (Warburton, *Eastward!*, p. 64, citing S. Pearce Carey, in a letter to *The British Weekly*, July 2, 1931). Wayland, *Memoir*, vol. 1, p. 158, and Edward Judson, *The Life of Adoniram Judson*, p. 94, wrongly report the Judsons as living at the undesirable location of the original mission house.

5 The following summary of the inception of Protestant missionary endeavor in Burma is gleaned from: Knowles, *Memoir of Mrs. Ann H. Judson*, p. 101; Warburton, *Eastward!*, pp. 64–5; S. Pearce Carey, *William Carey, "The Father of Modern Missions"* (London: Wakeman, 2008), pp. 250–5, 270–71, 278.

the rents wickedly oppressive, the taxes absurdly high, and the punishments barbarous, only proved the country's urgent need of the Gospel together with Christianity's impulse toward social advance."[6] But young Carey was soon dealt a severe blow when he received news the following spring that his wife, whom he had temporarily left behind in Calcutta, had died in childbirth. Despite that shock, Felix remained at his new post in Rangoon.

Around that same time two missionaries sent out by the London Missionary Society, Pritchett and Brain, arrived in Rangoon. But Brain soon died and within a year Pritchett relocated to Vizagapatam (modern Visakhapatnam) on India's eastern coast. Chater remained in Rangoon four years and made considerable progress in the language. He translated the Gospel of Matthew into Burmese, a work that was later revised by Felix Carey and afterward printed at Serampore. In March 1811, after nearly three years as a widower, Felix Carey married Miss Blackwell, a twenty-two-year-old Eurasian woman from the town of Bassein on Burma's southwestern coast. Late that year Chater left Rangoon to go to Ceylon. Felix found his own time and attention increasingly absorbed by responsibilities laid on him by the Burmese government in Ava.

Immediately after their arrival at Rangoon, Judson procured a language teacher. Both he and Ann plunged into the study of Burmese, devoting twelve hours a day to it. Their instructor was an intelligent man and a Hindu. At first he was unwilling to instruct Ann as he held females in lowest estimation. But when he saw that Ann was determined to persevere in her studies and that Judson desired him to teach both of them, he became more attentive to her as well.

The process proved extremely difficult to begin with as neither teacher nor students understood each other's language. At first Adoniram and Ann simply pointed at various objects around the house and gardens. The instructor would name the objects and they would repeat the names back to him. They also started learning to write Burmese letters and words. This writing

6   S. Pearce Carey, *William Carey*, p. 271.

was done on dried palm leaves which were used in place of paper. Reading Burmese words and sentences proved especially challenging since they all ran together in one continuous stream. No spaces, punctuation marks or capital letters were used to separate or distinguish words, sentences and paragraphs. The only written aids they had to assist them in learning the language were the small portion of a Burmese grammar that Felix Carey had begun to compose and six chapters of Matthew's Gospel that he had translated.

The Judsons also began learning much about customs and conditions in Burma. Many years later Judson's future wife, Emily, provided a colorful description of the fashions and other characteristics of Burmese men, women and children. This description likely matched quite closely what Adoniram and Ann observed upon first arriving in Burma:

> The men invariably wear turbans ... The turban ... varies from several yards in size to a wisp twisted like a cable, or a small fillet confining the hair around the brow. It is usually white, though sometimes red ... The hair, which is allowed to grow – the longer the better – is ... confined in a knot or club on the top of the head, of the size of which they are very proud.
>
> The ears both of men and women have an immense hole bored in the soft part, through which a plug of gold the size of your finger, having a precious stone in each end, is thrust – that is, the wealthy wear this ornament; but the poorer classes use various substitutes, even to a roll of pasteboard or a bit of segar [cigar]. ... [T]he natives, generally, even those who are poorest to appearance, own jewelry more or less! Not merely for ornament's sake, but because it is convenient and portable, and they can raise money on it at any moment. Men shave more or less, and wear their beards ... in every variety of fashion.
>
> Their jacket or tunic (*engyee*, they call it), is usually of white long-cloth, with two or three pairs of strings in front by which it is confined at the throat and breast, and then allowed to follow its own way, parting and floating back ...

in a way very tasteful. ... Sometimes the tunic reaches only a little below the waist, sometimes down to the knees ... Men seldom wear this when at labor ...

The *waist cloth* is the great article of dress. And when I use this word for want of a better (the Burmans call it a *pa-tso*), I beg you will not think of the *bit rag* you usually see in pictures of the heathen. This cloth, which is usually a very gay-colored silk, is eight yards long when purchased. The only *making up* it requires is to sew the two sides together without cutting it, so that the width can cover the whole person from the waist to the heel ... This garment is worn in a great variety of ways. It is knotted up before; and sometimes falls over each leg like a pair of flowing trousers, sometimes hangs from the waist like a woman's skirt, and is sometimes twisted into as small a compass as possible to allow free play to the limbs. Very commonly one end is thrown foppishly over the shoulder. ... This silk is of Burmese manufacture, coarse, soft, of fast colors, and bears washing well. It is usually woven in checks or stripes. They have a way of making zig-zag stripes to appear like rays of light, a shading in of all the intermediate colors between pale lemon and deep crimson, which almost dazzles the eyes. ...

The Burmans never wear stockings or any thing of the kind about the ankles. The most common kind of shoe[s] or sandal[s] ... are variously embroidered and sometimes gilded. They have a piece of wood about an inch thick attached to the bottoms ... They manufacture umbrellas very much like those of the Chinese ... but rather coarser.

The betel-box is *always* carried, either by the person himself or a servant, just as an old lady at home carries her snuff-box. Chewing betel and smoking cigars is universal among men, women, and children as soon as they are weaned. ...

[Burmese women] are rather small of stature ... Their hair is straight and black; it is carefully oiled, combed directly back from the temples, and confined in a knot on the top of the head. They are fond of decorating the hair with flowers. They wear ear ornaments similar to those of the men, and those who are able to afford it wear a half dozen different necklaces, magnificent ornaments for the head, finger-rings, etc. The chief article of dress is the *ta-ming* ..., a species of petticoat, of the gayest colored silk, with a deep border at the bottom and a top of crimson cloth, which is gathered in folds about the breast. The *engyee* or tunic is very much like that worn by the men, though sometimes made of thinner material – jaconet, gold-sprigged lace, black lace, yellow gauze, etc. They usually fling a light scarf, silk handkerchief, or small shawl over one shoulder. Their sandals are mostly like those of the men. ...

The dress of the Burman women is pretty and coquettish, but decidedly objectionable on the score of modesty, if not of decency. ... The women are spirited, lively, fond of laughing and talking, and although shockingly quarrelsome as wives, in the main good-natured. They are as intelligent as could be expected in their circumstances. Boys are always taught to read – girls seldom.

Children seldom wear any kind of clothing till seven or eight years old, though they are profusely decorated with necklaces, bracelets, anklets, etc. I have seen children with rich silk velvet jackets just covering the hips, and no other article of dress, aside from jewelry.[7]

Practically no one in Burma drank alcohol or smoked opium. Dietary staples were rice, fish, fowl and tropical fruit. Most of the foods the Judsons were accustomed to eating in America, including white or wheat bread, butter, cheese, potatoes, beef, pork and mutton, were rarely if ever available. Due to the Burmans' Buddhist belief that humans could be reincarnated in various animal forms, the slaughter of animals for food was forbidden. Only animals that had died from sickness or by accident could be eaten.

7   A. C. Kendrick, *Life and Letters of Mrs. Emily C. Judson* (New York: Sheldon, 1860), pp. 312–16.

The vast majority of Burmese were Buddhist. Buddhist shrines and temples were everywhere. Burmans regularly worshiped at Buddhist temples and faithfully supported both temples and priests with their offerings. Saffron-robed priests were commonly seen in the streets and public squares, their eyes humbly downcast as they carried their baskets for begging rice. Many young males showed their devotion by serving as priests, though often only for a time before marrying. It was the priests who educated boys, teaching them to read and write.

Despite their outward religiosity, the Burmese were immersed in spiritual darkness. Their idolatry and false belief system were powerless to deliver them from all variety of evil. "But at present their situation is truly deplorable, for they are given to every sin", Ann recorded in her journal. "Lying is so common and universal among them, that they say, 'We cannot live without telling lies.' "[8]

No caste system existed in Burma. But an oppressive form of feudalism under Burma's despotic government made life difficult and dangerous for many Burmese. A serious food shortage that July made the situation even more desperate. As Ann reported, the despotism and famine resulted in lack of initiative, deep poverty, high inflation and serious crime:

> The country presents a rich and beautiful appearance, everywhere covered with vegetation and, if cultivated, would be one of the finest in the world. But the poor natives have little inducement to labor, or to accumulate property, as it would probably be taken from them by their oppressive rulers. Many of them live on leaves and vegetables, which grow spontaneously, and some actually die with hunger. At the present time there is quite a famine. Every article of provision is [priced] extremely high; therefore many are induced to steal whatever comes their way. There are constant robberies and murders committed. Scarcely a night passes, but houses are broken open and things stolen.[9]

---

8   Knowles, *Memoir of Mrs. Ann H. Judson*, p. 108.

9   Ann H. Judson, *An Account of the American Baptist Mission to the Burman Empire, In a Series of Letters Addressed to a Gentleman in London* (London: Joseph Butterworth,

Adoniram Judson tersely stated of Burma officialdom, "In all the affairs of this government, despotism and rapine are the order of the day."[10]

The current Viceroy of Rangoon and the surrounding province was a fierce, feared ruler named Mya-day-men. Life and death were determined by his nod. Judson determined to visit him in an effort to gain his favor or at least his tolerance. Such support would help the missionaries remain in the country or even protect their lives should threatening circumstances arise. But when Judson paid his visit, the Viceroy exhibited the typical disdain that Burmese rulers had for foreigners by scarcely deigning to look at him.

While English-speaking men were "no uncommon sight" in Burma in that day, a woman who spoke English was still "quite a curiosity". There were a few Frenchwomen in Rangoon at the time but Ann was the only female from America or Britain. Seeking to capitalize on her uniqueness, Ann sought an audience with the Viceroy's wife.

> My only object in visiting her was, that if we should get into any difficulty with the Burmans, I could have access to her, when perhaps it would not be possible for Mr. Judson to get access to the viceroy. One can obtain almost any favor from her by making a small present.[11]

Ann made her visit on Saturday, December 11, being accompanied by a Frenchwoman who had frequently visited the Vicereine before:

> When we first arrived at the government-house, she was not up, consequently we had to wait some time. But the inferior wives of the viceroy diverted us much by their curiosity, in minutely examining every thing we had on, and by trying on our gloves and bonnets, etc. At last her highness made her appearance, dressed richly in the Burman fashion, with a long silver pipe in her mouth, smoking. At her appearance,

1827), pp. 18–19.

10   Wayland, *Memoir*, vol. 1, p. 168.

11   ibid., p. 165.

all the other wives took their seats at a respectful distance, and sat in a crouching posture, without speaking. She received me very politely, took me by the hand, seated me upon a mat, and herself by me. She excused herself for not coming in sooner, saying she was unwell. One of the women brought her a bunch of flowers, of which she took several and ornamented my cap. She was very inquisitive whether I had a husband and children, whether I was my husband's first wife – meaning by this, whether I was the highest among them, supposing that Mr. Judson, like the Burmans, had many wives – and whether I intended tarrying long in this country.

When the Viceroy came in I really trembled; for I never before beheld such a savage looking creature. His long robe and enormous spear not a little increased my dread. He spoke to me, however, very condescendingly, and asked if I would drink some rum or wine. When I arose to go, her highness again took my hand, told me she was happy to see me, that I must come to see her every day. She led me to the door; I made my *salaam*, and departed.[12]

---

12 Ann Judson, *An Account*, p. 23.

11

TRAGEDY AND ENCOURAGEMENT
(1814-15)

Felix Carey returned briefly to Rangoon from Ava as 1813 drew to a close. In a private letter that Judson wrote to his brother-in-law, Joseph Emerson, on January 7, 1814, he reported:

> There has yet been but very little effected in this country to any real missionary purpose. Brother Carey's time is greatly occupied in government matters. The emperor has given him a title, and requires him to reside in the capital. He is just now going to Bengal on his majesty's business, and expects, after his return, to reside at Ava. Not a single Burman has yet been brought to a knowledge of the truth, or even to serious inquiry.

But not at all despairing, he added: "We have this consolation, that it was the evident dispensation of God which brought us to this country; and still further, that if the world was all before us, where to choose our place of rest, we should not desire to leave Burma."[1]

A few days later the Judsons moved from the mission house to a residence within the city walls. They did this partly on account of the bands of robbers in the country that recently had been "very numerous and daring". Viceroy Mya-day-men was about to be recalled to Ava. The Judsons anticipated that conditions throughout the province would be in confusion during the interim period before a new Viceroy was installed. In addition,

---

1   Wayland, *Memoir*, vol. 1, pp. 167–8.

by living in the city they could more readily observe the customs of the local residents and would hear Burmese spoken more often, thus aiding in their learning of the language.

Barely one week after the Judsons' relocation, a group of some twenty robbers looted a house nearby the missions premises and stabbed the homeowner. As a deterrent to similar attacks Mya-day-men had seven thieves executed and exposed as a gruesome object lesson: "They were tied up by the hands and feet, and then cut open, and left with their bowels hanging out. They are to remain a spectacle to others for three days, and then be buried."[2]

One Sunday the following March the Judsons ventured out to spend a quiet Sabbath at the mission house. They had just arrived when a servant informed them that a fire was burning near the city. Investigating, they found several houses in flames in a line that led directly to the city. They hastened to safely remove all their belongings back to the mission residence. The conflagration continued to rage throughout the day, destroying "almost all" the city's houses and walls. Thousands were left homeless. After that the mission house became the Judsons' permanent residence as long as they were at Rangoon.

Felix Carey returned from Calcutta in mid-April. He brought with him copies of the Gospel of Matthew in the Burmese language that had been printed at Serampore. Burma's King Bodawpaya had invited him to establish a mission station, complete with printing press, in Ava. Felix had received some medical training in Calcutta and doubtless the monarch was most interested in some of the medical and literary benefits Carey could offer his family and country. Consequently, on August 20 he, his family and servants, and all their possessions set out on a government brig for Ava. Disaster struck ten days upriver when the ship overturned in a squall. After being catapulted into the Irrawaddy:

> Felix held up his wife and babe, till he sank, exhausted. When he came to the surface again, they had vanished. He thought he saw his little boy at a distance, but, strive as he would, could not reach him. He himself struggled to the

2   Ann Judson, *An Account*, p. 25.

river bank, where, still in much danger, he was rescued by *lascars* (sailors).[3]

In addition to Carey's wife, baby and three-year-old son, all the female servants and some of the male servants were drowned. All their possessions, including the printing press, the Burmese copies of Matthew's Gospel and a Burmese dictionary manuscript Felix had been compiling, were lost.

The Judsons received the "dreadful intelligence" of this tragic event on September 3. Despite the shattering blow, Felix Carey resolutely continued on to Ava to take up his intended service there. King Bodawpaya remunerated Felix for his financial losses but the tragedy affected him mentally and spiritually. In time he resigned from the mission, plunged into debt and drink, then became something of an aimless wanderer along the border between Burma and Assam, a state in northeast India, on the edge of the Himalayas. Eventually, at the end of 1818, William Ward persuaded Felix to return to live once again at Serampore, to the solace of the entire missionary staff there.[4]

Adoniram and Ann Judson continued to prosecute their study of the Burmese language with diligence. Shortly after Felix Carey returned from Calcutta to Rangoon in April 1814, Ann reported to a friend in a letter:

> Our progress in the language is slow, as it is peculiarly hard of acquisition. We can, however, read, write, and converse with tolerable ease, and frequently spend whole evenings very pleasantly in conversing with our Burman friends. We have been very fortunate in procuring good teachers. Mr. Judson's teacher is a very learned man, was formerly a [Buddhist] priest, and resided at court. He has a thorough knowledge of the grammatical construction of the [common] language, likewise of the Pali, the learned language of the Burmans.[5]

3   S. Pearce Carey, *William Carey*, pp. 320–1.

4   A fuller summary of this period in Felix Carey's life is recorded, ibid., pp. 321–3.

5   Wayland, *Memoir*, vol. 1, pp. 165–7.

The following September Ann related to another correspondent:

> As it respects ourselves, we are busily employed all day long. I can assure you that we find much pleasure in our employment. Could you look into a large open room, which we call a verandah, you would see Mr. Judson bent over his table, covered with Burman books, with his teacher at his side, a venerable looking man in his sixtieth year, with a cloth wrapped round his middle, and a handkerchief on his head. They talk and chatter all day long, with hardly any cessation.
>
> My mornings are busily employed in giving directions to the servants, providing food for the family, etc.
>
> At ten my teacher comes, when, were you present, you might see me in an inner room, at one side of my study table, and my teacher at the other, reading Burman, writing, talking, etc. I have many more interruptions than Mr. Judson, as I have the entire management of the family. This I took on myself, for the sake of Mr. Judson's attending more closely to the study of the language; yet I have found, by a year's experience, that it is the most direct way I could have taken to acquire the language; as I am frequently obliged to speak Burman all day. I can talk and understand others better than Mr. Judson, though he knows more about the nature and construction of the language.[6]

Around that same time a new Viceroy arrived in Rangoon. Unlike his fierce, feared predecessor, this Viceroy was, according to Ann, "much beloved and respected by the people". Shortly after his arrival in Rangoon he visited the Judsons at their home and invited them to come "very often" to his government residence. When they did so they found that they were treated with even greater respect than were the Burmese.

By early the following year, 1815, Ann's health had seriously deteriorated. She thought it necessary to seek medical treatment in Madras since none was available in Rangoon. In addition, she

6   Ann Judson, *An Account*, pp. 29–30.

may very well have begun to suspect what was indeed the case, that she was pregnant again. She insisted, however, that her husband must not leave his language studies for a few months to accompany her on the voyage. Instead, they went together to ask the Viceroy to permit a Burmese woman to serve as Ann's companion on the trip. They were not at all sure the request would be granted as Burman law generally forbade any female to leave the country. Upon hearing their petition, however, the governor not only granted it but also stipulated that the traveling companion was to be provided at no expense to the Judsons.

Ann left for Madras on January 25. She resided with the Lovelesses the six weeks she was in Madras and they gave her "every attention". Just before returning to Rangoon she sent seventy rupees to the physician who had attended her in Madras. He promptly returned the payment, saying he was happy if he had been of service to her. Ann arrived back in Rangoon on April 13. She brought with her a seven-year-old orphan girl named Emily Van Someren. Little is known of Emily except that she was a member of the Judsons' household for six and a half years before returning to Madras as a young teen.

On September 5 the Judsons were enormously encouraged to receive letters from America. These represented the first contact they had had with any Americans since Luther Rice left them at Isle of France nearly two and a half years earlier. The war between America and Britain had ended early in 1815, allowing the line of communication to be restored between the Judsons and their acquaintances in the States.

Through these newly arrived missives the Judsons learned of the considerable support that had been developing among Baptist congregations in America in their behalf.[7] The Baptists responded with immediate enthusiasm when news reached America in January 1813, that the Judsons wished to come under their patronage. Several influential ministers in Massachusetts gathered at the home of Dr Thomas Baldwin in Boston and

---

7 The following summary of the Baptist response is taken from Wayland, *Memoir*, vol. 1, pp. 122–7; Edward Judson, *The Life of Adoniram Judson*, pp. 53–4; and Anderson, *To the Golden Shore*, p. 184.

organized "The Baptist Society for Propagating the Gospel in India and Other Foreign Parts". The leaders of this infant organization promptly corresponded with the Baptist Missionary Society in London, proposing that the Judsons come under the direction of the Serampore mission and that Baptists in England and America should cooperate in the work of foreign missions. This proposal, however, was respectfully declined by the English Baptists. As soon as Luther Rice arrived in America:

> He was immediately requested to visit the various parts of the country, organize societies, and promote the formation of a general association. This object he performed with eminent success. Every where he was received almost with acclamation. Societies in aid of the cause were formed almost at his bidding. Contributions, in amounts unprecedented, were made to the object. Christians of all denominations in many cases extended liberal aid.[8]

"The greatest enthusiasm was aroused and missionary societies similar to the one in Boston sprang up in the Middle and Southern States."[9] On May 14, 1814, delegates from various societies throughout the country assembled at the First Baptist Church of Philadelphia, Pennsylvania, and formed "The General Missionary Convention of the Baptist Denomination in the United States of America for Foreign Missions".

A Board of Managers was elected and Thomas Baldwin was made its President. Judson and Rice were officially appointed as missionaries. But the latter was asked to remain in the United States for a time to further promote the setting up of new missionary societies and the raising of funds. Some months later the Managers appointed another missionary, George Hough, a printer. He and his wife, Phebe, were already making preparations to sail for Calcutta, from which they would seek passage to Rangoon. Of these heartening reports Adoniram Judson wrote:

8   Wayland, *Memoir*, vol. 1, p. 126.
9   Edward Judson, *The Life of Adoniram Judson*, pp. 53–4.

These accounts from my dear native land were so interesting as to banish from my mind all thoughts of study. This general movement among the Baptist churches in America is particularly encouraging, as it affords an additional indication of God's merciful designs in favor of the poor heathen. ... Thanks be to God, not only for "rivers of endless joys above," but for "rills of comfort here below".[10]

The following Monday, September 11, Ann gave birth to a son. As had been the case with her first delivery, she had no physician and her husband was her only attendant. They named the boy Roger Williams after the founding pastor of the first-ever Baptist church in America, at Providence, Rhode Island. Williams established Providence as a refuge of religious liberty. Of the infant, Ann wrote her family two weeks later: "He is a sprightly boy, and already begins to be very playful. We hope his life may be preserved and his heart sanctified, that he may become a Missionary among the Burmans."[11] Concerning herself, Ann revealed: "Since the birth of our little son, my health has been much better than for two years before. I feel now almost in a new state of existence."[12]

That same letter revealed that the Judsons were finding it difficult to communicate "the least truth to the dark mind of a heathen, particularly those heathen who have a conceited notion of their own wisdom and knowledge, and the superior excellence of their own religious system." To Ann's attempts to share the truths of Christianity with Burmese women, they had sometimes responded, "Your religion is good for you, ours for us. You will be rewarded for your good deeds in your way – we in our way." When Judson sought to explain the doctrine of the atonement through Christ to various Burmese they put him off with statements like, "Our minds are stiff. We do not yet believe."

10   Ann Judson, *An Account*, p. 38.

11   Knowles, *Memoir of Mrs. Ann H. Judson*, p. 118.

12   ibid., p. 117.

12

"O MAY WE NOT SUFFER IN VAIN!"
(1815-1816)

Since July the Judsons had been working with a new language teacher. His name was Oo Oungmeng and he was forty-seven years old. Judson described him as "the most sensible, learned, and candid man that I have ever found among the Burmans."[1]

Judson recorded a significant exchange he had with Oungmeng on September 30. This dialogue revealed that Judson had already gained a considerable degree of proficiency and skill in discussing religious matters with the Burmans. Judson started the conversation by commenting of a man they had both known, "Mr. J. is dead."

"I have heard so."

"His soul is lost, I think."

"Why so?"

"He was not a disciple of Christ."

"How do you know that? You could not see his soul."

"How do you know whether the root of the mango tree is good? You cannot see it; but you can judge by the fruit on its branches. Thus I know that Mr. J. was not a disciple of Christ, because his words and actions were not such as indicate the disciple."

---

1 Ann Judson, *An Account*, p. 39. Anderson, *To the Golden Shore*, p. 185: "His name would probably be spelled today as U Aung Min, but Adoniram, spelling words as they sounded to his ear ..., wrote it variously as Oungmen, Oo Oungmen, and Oo Oungmeng." Anderson, p. 188: "His very title 'U' meant that he had position or prestige, or at least merited respect."

"And so all who are not disciples of Christ are lost?"

"Yes, all, whether Burmans or foreigners."

"That is hard."

"Yes, it is hard, indeed; otherwise I should not have come all this way, and left parents and all, to tell you of Christ."

Oungmeng seemed to sense the force of that statement and was silent a moment before asking, "How is it that the disciples of Christ are so fortunate above all men?"

"Are not all men sinners, and deserving of punishment in a future state?"

"Yes, all must suffer in some future state for the sins they commit. The punishment follows the crime, as surely as the wheel of a cart follows the footsteps of the ox."

"Now, according to the Burman system, there is no escape. According to the Christian system there is. Jesus Christ has died in the place of sinners; has borne their sins. And now those who believe on him, and become his disciples, are released from the punishment they deserve. At death they are received into heaven, and are happy for ever."

"That I will never believe. My mind is very stiff on this one point, namely, that all existence involves in itself principles of misery and destruction. The whole universe is only destruction and reproduction. It therefore becomes a wise man to raise his desires above all things that exist, and aspire to *nikban*, the state where there is no existence."

"Teacher, there are two evil futurities, and one good. A miserable future existence is evil, and annihilation or *nikban* is an evil, a fearful evil. A happy future existence is alone good."

"I admit that it is best, if it could be perpetual; but it cannot be. Whatever is, is liable to change, and misery, and destruction. *Nikban* is the only permanent good, and that good has been attained by Gautama, the last diety."

"If there be no eternal being, you cannot account for any thing. Whence this world, and all that we see?"

"Fate."

"Fate! The cause must always be equal to the effect. See, I raise the table; see also, that ant under it. Suppose I were invisible; would a wise man say the ant raised it? Now fate is not even an ant. Fate is a word, that is all. It is not an agent, not a thing. What is fate?"

"The fate of creatures is the influence which their good or bad deeds have on their future existence."

"If influence be exerted, there must be an exerter. If there be a determination, there must be a determiner."

"No; there is no determiner. There cannot be an eternal Being."

"Consider this point. It is a main point of true wisdom. Whenever there is an execution of a purpose, there must be an agent."

Oungmeng paused briefly, as if contemplating Judson's assertion, then stated, "I must say that my mind is very decided and hard, and unless you tell me something more to the purpose, I shall never believe."

"Well, teacher, I wish you to believe, not for my profit, but for yours. I daily pray the true God to give you light, that you may believe. Whether you will ever believe in this world I don't know; but when you die I know you will believe what I now say. You will then appear before the God you now deny."

"I don't know that," Oungmeng concluded simply.

Judson had started compiling notes for a Burmese grammar and words for a Burmese-English dictionary. His study of Burmese had convinced him of the need to learn another language as well, Pali, which was commonly employed only by Burman scholars. Buddhism had been brought to Burma in the Pali tongue nearly 2,000 years earlier and the sacred writings taught by Burmese priests were still largely in that language. The common Burmese vernacular lacked words to convey the kind of ethical and theological concepts that were needed to effectively translate the

New Testament and communicate Christian doctrine. Burma's scholars used some such terms that had been adopted from Pali, a language related to Sanskrit. Readily perceiving how essential an understanding of Pali would be to the success of Bible translation and Christian teaching ministries, Judson devoted considerable time to studying it throughout the latter half of 1815. On January 1, 1816, he related:

> The greater part of my time, for the last six months, has been occupied in studying and transcribing, in alphabetical arrangement, the Pali Abigdan, or dictionary of the Pali language, affixing to the Pali terms the interpretation in Burman, and again transferring the Burman words to a dictionary, Burman and English. With the close of the year, I have brought this tedious work to a close, and find that the number of Pali words collected amounts to about four thousand. It has grieved me to spend so much time on the Pali, but the constant occurrence of Pali terms in every Burman book make it absolutely necessary.[2]

In a letter written two weeks later he further reported: "... I am beginning to translate the New Testament, being extremely anxious to get some parts of Scripture, at least, into an intelligible shape, if for no other purpose than to read, as occasion offers, to the Burmans I meet with."[3] In addition to working on his own Burmese translation of Matthew, Judson began composing a tract that would provide Burmans with a summary of the Christian religion in their language.

Baby Roger was an unspeakable joy to them. Ann described to her family:

> He was a remarkably pleasant child, – never cried except when in pain, and what we often observed to each other was the most singular, he never ... manifested the least anger or resentment at any thing. ... Whenever I or his father passed his cradle without taking him, he would follow us with his

2   Wayland, *Memoir*, vol. 1, p. 174.
3   ibid., p. 177.

eyes to the door, when they would fill with tears, and his countenance so expressive of grief, though perfectly silent, that it would force us back to him, which would cause his little heart to be as joyful as it had been before sorrowful. He would lie hours on a mat by his papa's study table, or by the side of his chair on the floor, if he could only see his face. When we had finished study, or the business of the day, it was our exercise and amusement to carry him round the house or garden, and though we were alone, we felt not our solitude when he was with us.[4]

As the only Caucasian infant in Rangoon, Roger was "quite a curiosity" to the Burmans. Ann once visited the Viceroy's wife with her baby. (By that time Mya-day-men, the former, feared Viceroy had returned to govern Rangoon.) The Vicereine placed Roger on the velvet cushion upon which she normally sat and exclaimed, "What a child! How white!" When her husband entered the room, she again exclaimed, "Look, my Lord, see what a child!" Pointing out the baby's pudgy appendages, she added, "Look at his feet; look at his hands." The Viceroy, who had "at least twenty or thirty children" of his own by his wives and concubines, smiled down on the infant. He asked a few questions about the baby before taking his leave.

Early in March Ann became alarmed when Little Roger began running a slight fever and sweating heavily every night. But since he seemed fine during the daytime and maintained a good appetite, she hoped his difficulties would pass once he started teething. At the beginning of April Adoniram Judson's health gave way: "I was seized with a distressing weakness and pain in my eyes and head, which put a stop to all my delightful [study] pursuits, and reduced me to a pitiable state indeed."[5] For months he would be able only intermittently to read, write or otherwise exert himself in the least.

The morning of Tuesday, April 30, little Roger had a violent coughing fit that lasted for half an hour and brought on a fever.

4   Knowles, *Memoir of Mrs. Ann H. Judson*, p. 123.

5   Wayland, *Memoir*, vol. 1, p. 180.

Wednesday morning the fever abated, the babe slept quietly through the day and had his usual good appetite. When his cough and fever returned the next day the concerned parents sent for a Portuguese priest, the only individual in Rangoon who knew anything about medicine. His treatment of "a little rhubarb and gascoign powder" failed to ease the baby's cough or loud breathing, which could be heard at some distance.

Ann sat up with her infant son till two in the morning on Saturday, May 4. Exhausted, she went to bed as Judson took over caring for the baby. Roger eagerly drank the milk Judson offered him. After the babe was laid back in his cradle, he slept peacefully for half an hour. But then, without struggle or warning, his breathing stopped and he was gone.

In that hot climate burials could not be delayed. So late in the afternoon that same day the stunned and grieving parents buried their son's body in a small grove of mango trees on the far side of the garden. Forty or fifty Burmese and Portuguese acquaintances accompanied them to the gravesite and sought to console them in their loss.

Adoniram and Ann were overwhelmed with grief. Even in the midst of their heartache they sought to honor God by submitting themselves to His will in the trial He had brought upon them. To Mr. Lawson, one of the English missionaries at Serampore, Judson wrote three days after the funeral:

> O may we not suffer in vain! May this bereavement be sanctified to our souls! and for this I hope we have your prayers.
>
> How is Mrs. Lawson, and your little *ones*? We had only *one*. Might not this have been spared? It was almost all our comfort and amusement in this dreary place. But, "the Lord gave," etc. [Job 1:21][6]

That same day Ann wrote her parents:

> Death, regardless of our lonely situation, has entered our dwelling, and made one of the happiest families wretched.

6   Edward Judson, *The Life of Adoniram Judson*, p. 97.

Our little Roger Williams, our only little darling boy, was three days ago laid in the silent grave. Eight months we enjoyed the precious little gift, in which time he had so completely entwined himself around his parents' hearts, that his existence seemed necessary to their own. But God has taught us by afflictions, what we would not learn by mercies – that our hearts are his exclusive property, and whatever rival intrudes, he will tear it away.

But what shall I say about the improvement we are to make of this heavy affliction? We do not feel a disposition to murmur, or to inquire of our Sovereign why he has done this. We wish rather, to sit down submissively under the rod and bear the smart, till the end for which the affliction was sent, shall be accomplished. Our hearts were bound up in this child; we felt he was our earthly all, our only source of innocent recreation in this heathen land. But God saw it was necessary to remind us of our error, and to strip us of our only little all. O may it not be in vain that he has done it. May we so improve it, that he will stay his hand and say, "It is enough" [2 Sam. 24:16; 1 Chron. 21:15].[7]

The Viceroy's wife learned of little Roger's death a few days later. She immediately paid the Judsons a visit "in all her state" to console them in their loss. She was accompanied by a retinue of some 200 attendants and officers of state. Smiting her breast, she asked Ann, "Why did you not send me word, that I might have come to his funeral?" "I did not think of anything, my distress was so great," Ann answered truthfully.

A few days later the Vicereine went even further in the Judsons' behalf by inviting them to accompany her on a ride into the country, both for their health and, as she said, that their minds "might become cool". She sent an elephant to convey them; the Judsons rode in an ornately decorated house-like howdah atop the beast. A guard of thirty men, armed with guns and spears and wearing red caps on their heads, led the procession into the jungle. Next came two elephants, lumbering side by side. One carried the

7   Knowles, *Memoir of Mrs. Ann H. Judson*, pp. 122, 124.

Judsons while the larger of the two animals carried the governor's wife in her gilt howdah. Three or four other elephants, carrying the Viceroy's son and a few high-ranking government officials, followed them. Two or three hundred male and female retainers brought up the rear of the procession.

The party proceeded on a three or four-mile jaunt through the dense jungle. The route for the trek had been planned so that it terminated in one of the Viceroy's gardens. It was "a wildly beautiful spot" where fruit trees of various varieties grew largely untended. There the many attendants hastened to spread mats on which the attentive hostess and her honored guests were seated. Ann afterward wrote:

> Nothing could exceed the endeavors of the vicereine to make our excursion agreeable. She gathered fruit and pared it; culled flowers and knotted them, and presented them with her own hands, which was a mark of her condescension. At dinner she had her cloth spread by ours, nor did she refuse to partake of whatever we presented her.[8]

That evening, Ann further related, the missionary couple returned to their home "fatigued with riding on the elephant, delighted with the country and the hospitality of the Burmans, and dejected and depressed with their superstition and idolatry – their darkness and ignorance of the true God."

8   Ann Judson, *An Account*, p. 52.

13

A HELPFUL COLLEAGUE AND A SERIOUS INQUIRER
(1816-1817)

The following month – June 1816 – a pious sea captain named Kidd came to stay for a time with the Judsons at the missions house. He was in the habit of riding horseback for exercise and suggested Judson try it in an effort to restore his health. Though painful at first, Judson soon found his health improving. He eventually bought his own horse and rode each morning before sunrise.

For a time Judson also considered returning to Calcutta to seek medical treatment to further promote his recovery. He and Ann, in fact, had already booked passage for such a voyage when news came that the Houghs had arrived in Calcutta from America and should be joining the Judsons in Rangoon before long. In addition, the Serampore brethren were sending a generous and strategic gift – a printing press and sets of type – to assist the Burma missionaries in launching their literature ministry. After receiving this news the Judsons decided to postpone indefinitely their journey to Bengal.

As Judson gradually recovered, he was able to compile all the notes he had been collecting about the language into a concise, helpful grammar to aid future missionaries in learning Burmese. On July 13, three years to the day after he first arrived in Burma, he completed a modest manuscript that he entitled *Grammatical Notices of the Burman Language*. When the work was published some twenty years later it comprised seventy-six pages. The *Calcutta Review* praised its "lucid, comprehensive conciseness".[1]

1   Wayland, *Memoir*, vol. 1, p. 159.

By the end of July Judson also finished the Burmese tract he had started composing before his illness. Bearing the title "A View of the Christian Religion, in three parts, Historic, Didactic, and Preceptive", the treatise was printed as a seven-page pamphlet several months later.[2] Ann also kept herself busy that summer by beginning a small school for young girls and by starting to compose a simple catechism in Burmese.

The Houghs and their two children arrived in Rangoon on October 15. They settled with the Judsons in the missionary house. The missionaries also converted one of the rooms into a temporary printing office. George Hough soon learned enough about the Burmese language to begin his printing work. By the end of January 1817, he had printed 1,000 copies of Judson's seven-page tract. In the first part of February he printed 3,000 copies of the six-page catechism that Ann had completed. Hough also set to work printing 800 copies of Matthew's Gospel, producing it in sections as Judson completed subsequent chapters, ten of which were translated by early March.

Hough was stunned by the spiritually-unresponsive, morally degraded, oppressive and barbaric conditions he observed in Burma:

> I can say truly, I had no idea of a state of heathenism before I saw it. ... The few [Burmans] with whom brother Judson has conversed, since I have been here, appear inaccessible to truth. They sit unaffected, and go away unimpressed with what they have heard. They are unconvinced by arguments, and unmoved by love; and the conversion of a Burman, or even the excitement of a thought towards the truth, must and will be a sovereign act of Divine power. ...
>
> Although the Burmans have every motive, according to their system of religion, to practice good works, yet no people can be worse. Their religious motives are wholly inadequate to the production of any good, or to maintain private and public morality. It may be said of the Burmans, as

2   A translation of the original Burmese tract is recorded in Edward Judson, *The Life of Adoniram Judson*, pp. 568–71.

of every other pagan religion, there is no power in it to make men better ... The Burmans are subtle, thievish, mercenary, addicted to robbery and fraud; truth and honesty are not known among them as virtues. They are excessively prone to gambling and sporting.

The government of the country is in the will of the Sovereign, who considers his subjects as slaves; in short, every person coming into the country, reports himself "the king's most willing slave". The viceroy of Rangoon acts with a power limited only by the King. He punishes criminals with severity. ... Reprieves from extreme desert, however, are often purchased with money; but when a malefactor is destitute of friends and money, he dies without mercy.[3]

Decapitation by sword was the mildest form of execution. On January 26 Judson and Hough witnessed the gruesome aftermath of an execution by disemboweling of four thieves who had been caught tunneling under a pagoda for the treasures buried beneath it. On February 7 the two missionaries observed another execution in which five criminals were beheaded and one was shot to death. Another man was to be shot on that same occasion and a bull's-eye had even been painted on his stomach. But after four separate shots failed to hit him he was released. At each shot "a loud peal of laughter" went up from the crowd of spectators. Everyone knew that he had paid a handsome bribe in order to save his own life. Hough afterward related: "He is now considered to be a wonderful man, and that a bullet cannot prove him mortal. ... He is now raised to a *high* rank among the governor's attendants."[4]

In the midst of such difficult and discouraging circumstances, God mercifully brought a timely and significant encouragement to the faithful missionaries. On March 7, as Judson sat with his teacher on the verandah of the mission house, a respectable looking Burman, accompanied by his servant, ascended the steps and sat down beside the missionary. The visitor's name was Maung Yah. When Judson asked, as he customarily did

3   Ann Judson, *An Account*, pp. 64, 67–8.
4   ibid., p. 70.

with newcomers, where he was from, the man did not offer an explicit answer. Judson began to suspect he had come from the government house "to enforce a trifling request" they had declined earlier in the day. But presently the missionary was astonished to hear the stranger ask, "How long a time will it take me to learn the religion of Jesus?"

"Such a question cannot be answered," Judson responded. "If God gives light and wisdom, the religion of Jesus is soon learned. But without God a man might study all his life long and make no proficiency." He then asked, "But how came you to know any thing of Jesus? Have you ever been here before?"

"No."

"Have you seen any writing concerning Jesus?"

"I have seen two little books."

"Who is Jesus?"

"He is the Son of God, who, pitying creatures, came into the world, and suffered death in their stead."

"Who is God?"

"He is a being without beginning or end, who is not subject to old age and death, but always is."

Judson's heart thrilled at these declarations. This was the first time he had ever heard a Burman acknowledge the existence of an eternal God. He realized immediately that the visitor was quoting statements from the tract he had written. He handed the man a tract and a catechism, both of which he instantly recognized. Maung Yah read excerpts from them, occasionally remarking to the servant who accompanied him, "This is the true God" or "This is the right way."

Judson attempted to explain to Maung Yah some further truths about God, Christ and himself as a human being. But he paid little attention and seemed interested only in getting another book. "I have finished no other book," Judson reiterated for the second or third time. "But in two or three months I will give you a larger one that I am now daily employed in translating."

"But have you not a little of that book done, which you will graciously give me now?".

Judson, "beginning to think that God's time is better than man's", folded and gave him the first two half sheets of Matthew's Gospel that had been printed thus far. They contained the first five chapters of Matthew. Upon receiving them, Maung Yah immediately stood, as though his intended business were completed. After Judson invited him to come again, he departed with his servant. Later that same day Judson wrote the Corresponding Secretary of his mission board:

> I have this day been visited by the first inquirer after religion that I have ever seen in Burma. For, although in the course of the last two years I have preached the gospel to many, and though some have visited me several times, and conversed on the subject of religion, yet I have never had much reason to believe that their visits originated in a spirit of sincere inquiry. Conversations on religion have always been of my proposing, and, though I have sometimes been encouraged to hope that truth had made some impression, never, till to-day, have I met with one who was fairly entitled to the epithet of *inquirer*.[5]

Two and a half weeks later, Judson reported further: "We have not yet seen our inquirer; but to-day we met with one of his acquaintances, who says that he reads our books all the day, and shows them to all that call upon him. We told him to ask his friend to come and see us again."[6]

Judson finished his translation of Matthew's Gospel late in May then promptly set to work compiling a Burmese dictionary. He knew the latter would be another valuable tool to assist future missionaries in more easily learning and using the language. In recent months Ann had been holding Sunday services for females and by this time fifteen to twenty women and girls attended the weekly meetings. An increased number of visitors had been stopping by the mission house to converse with Judson.

5   Wayland, *Memoir*, vol. 1, p. 187.
6   Ann Judson, *An Account*, p. 74.

But that summer brought a sudden decline in the flow of visitors. The missionaries realized the Burmese feared persecution if they were suspected of being interested in the foreigners' religion. Judson related in an August 26 letter to the President of his mission board:

> Sometimes persons who have been conversing with me on religion have been surprised by [the arrival of] others, on which I have observed that they were disconcerted, remained silent, and got off as soon as possible. They all tell me that it would ruin a Burman to adopt the new religion. My teacher was lately threatened in public for having assisted a foreigner in making books subversive of the religion of the country. He replied that he merely taught me the language, and had no concern in the publication.[7]

Those circumstances set Judson to contemplating a bold new strategy to gain greater tolerance for their missionary work:

> Then [early next year] it may be thought best for one of us to go up to Ava, and introduce the matter gradually and gently to the knowledge of the emperor. I am fully persuaded that he has never yet got the idea that an attempt is being made to introduce a new religion among his slaves. How the idea will strike him it is impossible to foresee. He may be enraged, and order off the heads of all concerned. The urbanity, however, with which he treats all foreigners, and his known hatred of the present order of Buddhist priests, render such a supposition improbable. And if he should only be indifferent, should discover [reveal] no hostility, especially if he should treat the missionaries with complacency, it would be a great point gained. No local government would dare to persecute the espousers of a new religion if it was known that they had friends at court.[8]

Sixteen eventful months would pass, however, before Judson would actually attempt to carry out such a risky undertaking.

7   Wayland, *Memoir*, vol. 1, p. 191.
8   ibid., pp. 191–2.

14

A TRYING EXCURSION
(1818)

As 1817 drew to a close, Judson completed the work he had been doing on compiling a small Burmese dictionary. This appears to have been something of an unfinished project that he ended up setting aside in light of higher priorities and more pressing demands. He also settled on the pursuit of a new expedient to help promote the effectiveness of their mission work. He had heard that in Chittagong, eastern Bengal, there was a small group of Burmese-speaking nationals who had become Christians through the recent efforts of an English Baptist missionary. Chittagong was the coastal region north of Burma's mountainous western province of Arakan. Judson wished to meet these Chittagong Christians and to see about bringing one or two of them to assist him with evangelism in Rangoon.

Chittagong was a ten or twelve-day voyage from Rangoon. Ships almost never sailed directly there and back within a period of a few short weeks. But Judson had discovered a small vessel, the *Two Brothers*, that was intending to make just such a compact roundtrip. He sailed aboard the ship when it embarked from Rangoon on Christmas Day, intending to return in not more than three months.

The *Two Brothers* proved unmanageable as, battered by contrary winds, it slowly made its way up the western coast of Burma. After a full month at sea the ship was still far from its original destination. The captain decided to change course and to sail southwest across the Bay of Bengal to Madras. Judson later revealed: "It was with the most bitter feelings that I witnessed the entire failure of my undertaking, and saw the summits of the mountains of Arakan ... sinking in the horizon, and the ship stretching away to a distant part of India, which I had no wish to visit, and where I had no object to obtain."[1]

When the vessel neared the Coromandel coast, strong winds and currents prevented its progress toward Madras. By then another month had elapsed and for some time all aboard the ship had been reduced to subsisting on nothing more than rice and water. The decision was made to go instead to Masulipatam, some 300 miles north of Madras. During those final three or four weeks, those aboard the ship were sometimes "in great distress" and counted themselves fortunate when they were able to acquire a bag of moldy rice or a few buckets of water from any native vessel that happened by. Under these hardships Judson's physical health weakened, bringing about a return of the disorder of his head and eyes that he had experienced two years earlier. Eventually he became so weak and disheartened by starvation, pain and filth that he was unable to leave his berth. He developed a fever that left him with no appetite and a devouring thirst.

The *Two Brothers* finally reached Masulipatam on March 18, twelve weeks after leaving Rangoon. The small ship came to anchor in the mud, two or three miles from the town's uninviting beach. When Judson was informed they were near shore he roused himself enough to pencil a note, addressed to "any English resident of Masulipatam", requesting only a place on land to die. A while later he spotted from the window of his cabin a small boat approaching from the shore in which he could readily distinguish the red coats of British soldiers and the white jackets of well-dressed civilians. Overcome with relief and rekindled hope, he fell to his knees and wept. When the Englishmen entered his cabin a short while later they were shocked at his wretched condition. He was haggard, unshaven, dirty and so weak he could barely support his own weight. One of the officers took him to his own house where he provided him with generous hospitality, clothes from his personal wardrobe and a nurse to help care for him.

1   Wayland, *Memoir*, vol. 1, pp. 193–4.

A few days after arriving at Masulipatam it was announced that the *Two Brothers* would offload its cargo and remain there for several months. That season of the year no ships were sailing to Madras, the only port from which Judson could hope to find a vessel bound for Rangoon. Weak as he was, he needed to hire a palanquin and bearers to transport him by land to Madras. Arriving there on April 8, he was again deeply disappointed to learn that, due to unsettled conditions that had recently developed in Burma, no vessels were likely to venture there for some time to come. As it turned out, he had to remain in Madras for three and a half months. Throughout that time he was the object of "great kindness and hospitality" in the homes of Chaplain Thompson of the East India Company and the Lovelesses. But the time of unproductive weakness and enforced waiting was "almost insupportable" for Judson. He struggled to submit himself to God's will in allowing these circumstances.

Seven more weeks crept past before Judson, on July 20, was able to embark on an English ship bound for Rangoon. When the vessel anchored at the mouth of Rangoon River on August 2, Judson had been away for just over seven months. Throughout that time there had been no reliable means of communication between himself and Ann or the Houghs. The next morning a pilot boarded the ship to guide it upriver to Rangoon. Judson was stunned when the very first thing the pilot announced to him was that, due to the development of a dangerous state of affairs, the mission had been broken up and Ann and the Houghs had taken passage for Bengal! Great was the missionary's relief when the pilot further revealed that Ann's reluctance to leave the place had led her to return alone to the mission house. The Houghs had not yet left either because their ship, having been found unfit for sea travel, was still detained. Ann and George Hough met Judson at the Rangoon wharf later that day. Ann was radiant with delight at her husband's safe return after so many months of uncertainty. She was optimistic about the mission's future success now that he had returned. Hough, however, was more reserved and still determined to leave the country as soon as opportunity presented itself.

For a few weeks after Judson's departure from Rangoon the mission work had progressed smoothly. The Vicereine continued to show her goodwill by more than once inviting the missionaries to join her for elephant rides. She accepted from Ann a copy of the tract, the catechism and Matthew's Gospel. Maung Yah, Judson's first serious inquirer, returned to visit at the mission house. He had not returned sooner because he had been appointed governor of a group of villages in the Pegu region, northeast of Rangoon. When Ann asked if he had become a Christian, he replied, "Not yet, but I am thinking and reading in order to become one. ... Tell the great teacher when he returns that I wish to see him, though I am not yet a disciple of Christ." Ann gave him a completed copy of Matthew's Gospel and distributed tracts and catechisms to the members of his retinue.

Scarcely a month after Judson left Rangoon, Ann was shocked to receive word that the primary leader among the professing Christians at Chittagong had reportedly murdered the missionary who had been ministering there! In March, around the time Ann was anticipating Judson's return, a boat arrived from Chittagong with the report that neither he nor the *Two Brothers* had ever arrived there. Shortly thereafter Ann received letters from friends in Bengal stating that the ship had not been reported anywhere.

That same month, March of 1818, a new Viceroy came to govern Rangoon. He was completely unknown to the Judsons and, as he had come without his wife, Ann had no way of gaining a friendly hearing in his court should that prove necessary. Just a few days later George Hough received a peremptory order, "couched in the most menacing language, to appear immediately at the court-house, to give an account of himself". When Hough promptly complied, the lesser government officials who interrogated him stated menacingly that if he did not reveal everything about why he was in Burma "they would write with his heart's blood".[2] Hough spent two full days at the courthouse answering hundreds of questions, with all his answers being carefully recorded.

2   Knowles, *Memoir of Mrs. Ann H. Judson*, p. 139.

Ann and Hough rightly suspected that lower officials were operating without the Viceroy's awareness and had chosen this time while Judson was away to pressure the mission in hopes of extorting a bribe from it. Aided by Ann's teacher, she and Hough were able to make an appeal directly to the Viceroy who immediately put a stop to the harassment. Unfortunately, the incident had an immediate chilling effect on the work of the mission. After these events very few Burmese men came to the mission house and attendances at Ann's Sunday services for women and girls plummeted from over thirty to only ten or twelve.

Around that same time, in March and April, Burma experienced its first ever cholera outbreak. The epidemic swept like wildfire through Rangoon, claiming the lives of countless individuals of all ages. The terrified population thought the mortal sickness was caused by malicious spirits. For three successive nights local residents raised a tremendous tumult, by firing canons and beating on their houses with clubs, in an effort to scare the spirits away. The misguided effort, of course, proved futile and the deadly sickness continued until the rainy season came several weeks later.

To make matters worse, just when the epidemic was at its height, an alarming rumor began to circulate that Britain would soon invade Burma. For years tensions had existed between the British and Burmese governments due to periodic incursions by Burman forces into British-controlled territory along Burma's borders. No British ship had arrived in Rangoon for months. The few foreign vessels still in the city were all making preparations to leave.

In the face of all those uncertain and threatening circumstances, Hough concluded it was his duty to take his family to Bengal. They would be safe and he could continue to carry out his printing ministry there. When the Houghs urged Ann to go with them, she at first refused. But by late June, when only one foreign ship remained at Rangoon and it was to leave soon, she finally relented. She had actually boarded the ship with the Houghs when it was discovered the boat had been improperly loaded and its cargo would have to be shifted before it could safely set out across the Bay of Bengal.

At that point Ann determined to return to the mission house, continue her language studies there and "leave the event with God". The *Two Brothers* arrived back in Rangoon in mid-July with the news of Adoniram Judson's having left Masulipatam for Madras, from which he hoped to find passage back to Rangoon. On July 25 the Houghs joined Ann back at the mission house as their ship would not be able to sail for several weeks. Eight days later the joyous intelligence was received that Judson had just arrived on a vessel at the mouth of the river.

15

FIRST CONVERT
(1818-1819)

In the weeks that followed Adoniram Judson's return to Rangoon, the threat of war subsided and the cholera epidemic gradually passed. The Judsons were greatly heartened by the arrival in mid-September of two new Baptist missionary couples from Boston, Massachusetts. Edward and Eliza Wheelock were twenty-two and twenty years old respectively while Mr. and Mrs. James Colman were also in their early twenties.

For a time the mission house, with its six rooms for living quarters and a hall that was used as a chapel and meeting place, was uncomfortably crowded. But the eight adults and three children (the Houghs' two and Emily Van Someren) sought to handle the situation good-naturedly. After the Houghs left for Calcutta on November 1, taking the printing press with them, each of the three remaining couples had two rooms for their private living quarters. Still, the situation was less than ideal.

Shortly after Edward Wheelock and James Colman's arrival, it became apparent that their health was quite feeble. Of the manifestation of their tuberculosis, Judson wrote: "They have both a slight return of bleeding at the lungs, an old complaint, to which they were subject in America. May the Lord graciously restore and preserve them."[1] Wheelock and Colman immediately launched into their study of the Burmese language but before long had to lay it aside when their health gave out. By the beginning

---

1   Wayland, *Memoir*, vol. 1, p. 196.

of 1819 Colman had almost fully recovered but Wheelock continued to decline.

Judson had long considered the location of the mission house too secluded for effective public ministry. He was delighted, therefore, with an opportunity that arose around that time to purchase a long piece of property at the back of the mission house garden. The new property fronted on the highly-trafficked "Pagoda Road", some 200 yards from the mission compound. That road was the main thoroughfare from town to the famed Shwe Dagon Pagoda. Four times per month thousands thronged the road to Burma's pre-eminent pagoda; during annual festivals those numbers swelled to tens of thousands.

Pagoda Road was lined with numerous pagodas and zayats of various sizes. Buddhist priests lived at the pagodas and lay people gathered to worship at them. The zayats were buildings where men gathered to dialogue, travelers could rest and Buddhist lay teachers offered instruction. Priests taught at zayats only on special occasions. Some zayats were small and simple while others were large and elaborate with numerous roofs towering up one over another.

On the Pagoda Road side of their newly-acquired property Judson superintended the construction of a zayat that would serve as a Christian meeting house and a place where they could minister to passers-by. The unpretentious structure was eighteen feet wide and twenty-seven feet long. Like virtually all the other buildings in Rangoon, it stood on posts about four feet above the ground. The zayat's front ten feet consisted of a thatched bamboo porch where visitors could comfortably rest and visit. The enclosed part of the building was "a large airy room" with four doors and four windows. Here public worship would be held and men could gather to study. The rear of the zayat was a small room in which the women could study; it was also an entryway leading into the mission garden. Judson was able to purchase the new land and have the zayat built at a total cost of 200 dollars.

On Sunday, April 4, even before the front porch was completed, the missionaries held their first public worship service at the zayat. About fifteen adults from the neighborhood attended the service as well as a number of children. Though the service was conducted in Burmese, Judson recorded of his indigenous audience, "Much disorder and inattention prevailed, most of them not having been accustomed to attend Burman worship."[2] Though a humble beginning, still Judson saw this commencement of Burmese worship services as "a new, and I hope important era in the mission".

Two evenings later the Judsons attended a Buddhist service at one of the nearby zayats, perhaps to learn more about how local worship and teaching services were conducted. About one hundred people gathered and sat on mats, men and women on opposite sides of the room. The speaker, a popular lay teacher of about forty-five years of age, sat on a low platform in the center of the zayat. As the Judsons entered, they overheard some saying, "There come some wild foreigners." But when they sat down properly and took off their shoes, the estimation of them changed to, "No, they are not wild; they are civilized." Some recognized Judson and said, "It is the English teacher." The Buddhist lay teacher approached and pleasantly welcomed them. But when he learned that Judson was a missionary, "his countenance fell and he said no more".

When it was time for the service to begin, an appointed individual called three times for silence and attention. Each member of the audience except the Judsons placed flowers and leaves which had been distributed to them between their fingers. They raised these to their heads and held them in a respectful, motionless posture throughout the duration of the half-hour service that followed. The teacher closed his eyes and recited, in "soft, mellifluent tones", a portion from the Buddhist scriptures that related the conversion and subsequent promotion to glory of the two chief disciples of Gautama. When the discourse was completed, the entire congregation suddenly "burst out" in a short, united prayer, after which all rose and exited the zayat.

In the following weeks the Judsons ministered at the mission zayat daily, Adoniram to the male visitors and Ann to the female.

2   Ann Judson, *An Account*, p. 121.

Judson regularly sat on the open front porch and hailed passers-by with scriptural invitations such as, "Ho! Every one that thirsteth, come ye to the waters" (Isa. 55:1). He informally discussed spiritual matters with visitors who stopped by during the week and conducted a more formal public worship and preaching service on Sundays.

Ann held a meeting for Burmese women each Wednesday evening. In addition, for a year and a half, aided by her teacher, Ann had been studying the Siamese language along with her ongoing study of Burmese. Several thousand Siamese "who speak and write the pure language of Siam" lived in Rangoon at that time. With the help of her teacher, a scholar of both the Siamese and Burmese languages, she had translated the Burman catechism, tract and Gospel of Matthew into Siamese.[3]

A number of individuals from Rangoon and other towns visited the zayat, some of them repeatedly. Many manifested idle curiosity in the foreigners and their religion. The Burmese commonly raised "numberless cavils and objections" to Christianity. Others expressed doubts about the truthfulness of Buddhism. Several seemed genuinely interested in Christianity or even close to embracing it. But one hopeful inquirer after another, after showing earnest interest for a time, suddenly stopped returning to the mission zayat.

On Friday, April 30, a quiet, reserved Burmese man in his mid-thirties, Maung Nau, visited the zayat for the first time. (Maung was a Burmese title that indicated a young man.) Maung Nau listened in silence for several hours as Judson interacted with other visitors. Due to the young man's extreme reserve, Judson at first paid Maung Nau little attention and had nearly no hope that he would prove to be a serious seeker. But that outlook rapidly changed when the Burman returned the next two days to continue his intent, though silent, consideration of Christian teaching.

The following Wednesday proved to be a red-letter day for Judson and the Baptist mission in Burma. After nearly six years of ministry in Burma Judson was at last able to record in his journal:

3   Knowles, *Memoir of Mrs. Ann H. Judson*, p. 147.

May 5. Maung Nau has been with me several hours. I begin to think that the grace of God has reached his heart. He expresses sentiments of repentance for his sins, and faith in the Savior. The substance of his profession is, that from all the darkness, and uncleannesses and sins of his whole life, he has found no other Savior but Jesus Christ; no where else can he look for salvation; and therefore he proposes to adhere to Christ, and worship him all his life long.

It seems almost too much to believe that God has begun to manifest his grace to the Burmans; but this day I could not resist the delightful conviction that this is really the case. PRAISE AND GLORY BE TO HIS NAME FOREVERMORE. Amen.[4]

Maung Nau had no family, was of "middling abilities" and quite poor. Though he needed to work hard for his living, he was so eager to learn further spiritual truth that he continued to visit the zayat daily. "He ... manifests a teachable, humble spirit, ready to believe all that Christ has said, and obey all that he has commanded." The Saturday after Judson concluded Maung Nau had become a genuine believer, the missionary zayat was thronged with visitors for nearly eight hours, that being a Burman day of worship. "Maung Nau was with me a great part of the day," Judson related, "and assisted me much in explaining things to new comers." The next day, following a Christian worship service attended by thirty people, Maung Nau "declared himself a disciple of Christ, in presence of a considerable number".[5]

Four weeks later, on Sunday, June 6, the missionaries considered Maung Nau's written testimony as well as his request to be baptized. For some time they had all been satisfied with the genuineness of his Christian profession, so they agreed to baptize him the following Sunday and to welcome him into official church membership.

As it turned out, Maung Nau's baptism needed to be delayed till the end of the month due to a period of governmental instability,

4   Ann Judson, *An Account*, pp. 131–2.
5   ibid., pp. 132–3.

even crisis, in Burma that was just then being felt in Rangoon. For the Baptist mission the first indication of such instability had been the sudden imposition of a number of taxes and "several other molestations" from petty government officials in recent weeks. By mid-June Rangoon was in a state of consternation over recent governmental developments. Two days after the city's Viceroy departed for the capital, Judson reported in his journal:

> June 21. The town is in the utmost anxiety and alarm. Order after order has reached our viceroy, to hasten his return to Ava, with all the troops under arms. Great news is whispered. Some say there is a rebellion; some say the king is sick, some that he is dead. But none dare to say this plainly. It would be a crime of the first magnitude; for the *"lord of land and water"* is called immortal. The eldest son of his eldest son (his father being dead) has long been declared the heir of the crown; but he [the heir apparent] has two very powerful uncles, who, it is supposed, will contest his right; and in all probability the whole country will soon be a scene of anarchy and civil war.[6]

The following day, a Tuesday, Judson was "out all morning, listening for news". Around 10 a.m. a royal dispatch boat arrived from upriver and throngs of people followed "the sacred messengers" to the government building where an imperial edict was read aloud:

> Listen ye: The immortal king, wearied, it would seem, with the fatigues of royalty, has gone up to amuse himself in the celestial regions. His grandson, the heir apparent, is seated on the throne. The young monarch enjoins on all to remain quiet, and wait his imperial orders.[7]

King Bodawpaya had already been dead for two weeks and his grandson, Bagyidaw, was the new monarch.

In customary fashion for a new Burmese emperor, in an effort to assure that his reign would be long and peaceful, the new king

6   ibid., pp. 141–2.
7   ibid., p. 142.

132

had executed a number of potential rivals to the throne along with their relatives and other supporters. Bagyidaw had his own brother and all the members of the brother's family sewn up in red sacks, befitting royalty, and drowned. One of Bagyidaw's uncles was strangled after his bones were crushed on the rack. One of the prime ministers, governor of the Western Provinces, suffered the same fate. Their property was seized and devoted to the support of the new emperor's army. In all, some 1,400 members of the upper classes were put to death along with as many as 15,000 commoners.[8]

The following Sunday, June 27, saw just over thirty people, including several strangers, in attendance at the worship service in the missionary zayat. At the close of the service, Judson invited Maung Nau to come forward. After reading and commenting on a fitting portion of Scripture, Judson asked the new believer several questions about his Christian faith, hope and love, and then offered the baptismal prayer. The small gathering made its way to a large pond nearby where an enormous statue of Buddha brooded over the bank. There in the presence of the lifeless, helpless image that epitomized Burma's prevailing spiritual deception, Judson baptized the first Burman to have found true spiritual life through faith in Jesus Christ.

One week later the missionaries had the first-time "pleasure" of sharing communion with a Burmese Christian. "And it was my privilege," commented Judson, "a privilege to which I have been looking forward with desire for many years, to administer the Lord's Supper in two languages."[9]

Throughout the year, Edward Wheelock's health had continued to deteriorate. His wife, Eliza, became convinced that she must take him to Calcutta as his only hope of recovery. It was the roughest season of the year for sea travel and the other members of the mission feared the journey would likely hasten his death rather than prolong his life. Though they shared their concerns with Eliza she would not be dissuaded. She embarked

8   Anderson, *To the Golden Shore*, p. 227.
9   Ann Judson, *An Account*, p. 144.

with her husband on August 7. The voyage proved to be even more tragic than their fellow missionaries feared it might. As the journey progressed Wheelock became feverish then delirious. On the thirteenth day of the voyage, in a fit of delirium, he stumbled out of his cabin and threw himself overboard. The sea was so rough no attempt could be made to rescue him. Eliza continued on alone to Bengal. She chose to remain there and subsequently married a Mr. Jones of Calcutta.

16

FRUITFUL EVANGELISM
(1819)

Two days after Maung Nau's baptism was the beginning of Burman Lent. That same day all of Rangoon's government officials gathered at the Shwe Dagon Pagoda and took an oath of allegiance to the new emperor, King Bagyidaw. Fired with fresh religious and patriotic fervor, a large group of Burmese came to the mission zayat that evening, "all disposed to condemn and ridicule and persecute" the foreigners with their contrary religion. The local protestors were led by one "very virulent opposer", an influential Buddhist instructor known as "the Mangen teacher". He had visited the zayat and argued with Judson on at least one previous occasion. Despite this unsettling exhibition of opposition, a good number of visitors continued to come to the mission zayat in the weeks that followed.

For the past few months several Burmese had been living in temporary dwellings which they had erected on the mission's somewhat spacious premises. One of those, a young man named Maung Thahlah, began to visit about spiritual matters with Judson or Maung Nau for an hour or two nearly every day. Maung Thahlah possessed superior abilities and had read much more widely than most Burmese. He appeared to be truly earnest about becoming a disciple of Christ. On August 24 Judson was able to report in his ministry journal:

> [I had] Another conversation with Maung Thahlah, which at length forces me to admit the conviction that he is a real convert; and I venture to set him down the second disciple

of Christ among the Burmans. He appears to have all the characteristics of a new-born soul, and though rather timid in regard to an open profession, has, I feel satisfied, that love to Christ which will increase and bring him forward in due time.[1]

Two days later a distinguished teacher of formidable debating skills, Maung Shway-gnong, visited Judson at the zayat. Though he worshiped at the pagodas and conformed to prevailing Burmese customs, Maung Shway-gnong seemed to Judson to be "half deist and half skeptic". He returned the following day and stayed from noon until it was quite dark. "We conversed incessantly the whole time," Judson related, "but I fear that no real impression is made on his proud, skeptical heart."[2]

Around that same time a poor fisherman named Maung Ing visited the zayat five or six days in a row. As Judson was busily occupied with other visitors, Maung Ing at first conversed primarily with Maung Nau and read the Gospel of Matthew. He revealed to Maung Nau that he had long been searching for the true religion and declared he would have preferred to be born a brute beast rather than to die in spiritual delusion and go to hell. The last Sunday of August he listened attentively during the worship service and Judson was able to visit with him at length afterwards. "He is quite sensible of his sins, and of the utter inefficacy of the Buddhist religion," the missionary reported, "but is yet in the dark concerning the way of salvation, and says, that he wants to know more of Christ, that he may love him more."[3]

The following Friday, September 3, the teacher Maung Shway-gnong, accompanied by several of his followers, spent nearly the entire day debating with Judson. Of the day's discussion and a surprising revelation from Maung Shway-gnong at its conclusion, Judson wrote:

1   Ann Judson, *An Account*, p. 154.

2   ibid., p. 155.

3   ibid., p. 156.

He is a complete Proteus in religion, and I never know where to find him. We went over a vast deal of ground, and ended where we began, in apparent incredulity. After his adherents, however, were all gone, he conversed with some feeling; owned that he knew nothing, and wished me to instruct him; and when he departed, he prostrated himself and performed the *sheeko*, an act of homage which a Burman never performs but to an acknowledged superior.[4]

Maung Ing had been listening to the discussion throughout the day and followed Judson home that evening. After conversing with the lowly fisherman all that evening, Judson testified of him: "... his expressions have satisfied us all, that he is one of God's chosen people. His exercises have been of a much stronger character than those of the others, and he expresses himself in the most decided manner."[5] Maung Ing stated his desire to become a public disciple of Jesus and declared his readiness to suffer persecution and death for the love of Christ. Judson reminded him of the danger to which he was exposing himself and asked, "Do you love Christ better than your own life?"

Very deliberately and solemnly the Burman responded, "When I meditate on this religion, I know not what it is to love my own life."

Three days later Judson wrote for the first time of another Burmese inquirer, Maung Byaay. He and his family had lived on the mission property for some time and regularly attended the worship services. The missionaries had started an evening school at the zayat a few weeks earlier. Though fifty years old, Maung Byaay was an "indefatigable" student at the school and had learned to read. He was remarkably moral and appeared to put great stock in his good works. But he sincerely desired to know and embrace the truth. "The greater part of the evening was spent in discussing his erroneous views," Judson related. "Towards the close, however, he seemed to obtain some evangelical discoveries, and to receive the humbling truths of the gospel, in a manner

4   ibid., p. 157. Proteus was a Greek sea god capable of assuming different forms.
5   ibid.

which encourages us to hope that the Spirit of God has begun to teach him." Even at that time Maung Byaay professed "a full belief in the eternal God, and his Son Jesus Christ".[6]

Half a dozen Burmese men and several women attended the evening school. The men studied in the main meeting room of the zayat while the women did so in the smaller room at the rear of the building. Each student sat with his or her "torch" for light and an improvised slate. After learning to spell and read aloud basic letter and word combinations, the pupils applied them in reading the catechism that Ann had written. Maung Byaay actually committed the catechism to memory as he read and considered it.

Prior to Maung Ing's first coming to the missionary zayat he had been hired to work on a boat that was planning to go to sea soon. For a full week immediately following his definite profession of faith in Christ, he was confined aboard the ship with preparations for the imminent voyage. The night before the vessel was to sail he gained permission to go ashore and hastened back to the zayat. Of him Judson wrote:

> He appears very well indeed. He is quite distressed that he has so far engaged himself; and appears desirous of getting off, and returning to us, if possible; but I have very little hope of his succeeding. I believe, however, that he is a real Christian, and that, whenever he dies, his immortal soul will be safe, and that he will praise God forever for his transient acquaintance with us. The Lord go with him and keep him.[7]

On Sunday, September 19, Maung Shway-gnong again remained at the zayat following public worship, discussing religious and spiritual matters till nightfall. Two and a half weeks later, on October 7, he and Judson spent the entire day together, uninterrupted by any other company. The scholarly Burman's perspectives swung like a pendulum:

6   ibid., p. 158.
7   ibid., p. 159.

In the forenoon, he was as crabbed as possible – sometimes
a Berkeleian – sometimes a Humeite, or complete skeptic.[8]
But in the afternoon he got to be more reasonable, and
before he left, he obtained a more complete idea of the
atonement than I have commonly been able to communicate
to a Burman. He exclaimed, "That is suitable – that is as it
should be," etc. But whether this conviction resulted from
a mere philosophic view of the propriety and adaptedness
of the way of salvation through Jesus Christ, or from the
gracious operations of the Holy Spirit, time must discover.[9]

On Saturday, October 23, Maung Thahlah and Maung Byaay
presented a paper to Judson and Colman in which they professed
their faith in Jesus and requested to be baptized, but in private.
After the missionaries visited with the young believers, Judson
reported: "They appear to have experienced divine grace; but we
advised them, as they had so little love to Christ as not to dare to
die for his cause, to wait and reconsider the matter."[10]

Three weeks and a day passed between Maung Shway-gnong's
visit to the mission zayat early in the month and his return to it on
Friday, October 29. To Judson the esteemed teacher "appears to
be quite another man". At the instigation of the mission's "virulent
opposer", the Mangen teacher, it was reported to the Viceroy
that Maung Shway-gnong had renounced the religion of the
country. The Viceroy merely replied, "Inquire further about him."
When Maung Shway-gnong received news of that intimidating
directive, he immediately went to the Mangen teacher to explain
and defend himself. "He denies that he really recanted, and I hope
he did not," Judson commented. "But he is evidently falling

8   George Berkeley (1685–1753) was an Irish philosopher who advanced a theory
     he termed "immaterialism". He denied the existence of material substance and
     contended that physical objects are only ideas in the minds of perceivers, so
     cannot exist without being perceived. Scottish philosopher David Hume (1711–
     1776) was known especially for his philosophical empiricism and skepticism. He
     concluded humans have knowledge only of things they directly experience.

9   Ann Judson, *An Account*, p. 162.

10   ibid., p. 163.

off from the investigation of the Christian religion."[11] On that occasion Maung Shway-gnong stayed only a short while at the zayat then took his leave as soon as he decently could.

The following Monday was "one of the greatest festivals in the year" and the crowds on Pagoda Road were "truly immense and overwhelming". Judson explained the missionaries' rationale for staying away from their zayat that day: "We vacated the Zayat, as we have ..., of late, beg[u]n to question whether it is prudent to go on boldly, in proclaiming a new religion, at the hazard of incensing the government, and drawing down such persecution, as may deter all who know us from any inquiry."[12] The next day was the birthday and official coronation of King Bagyidaw.

At the end of that week, on Saturday, November 6, Maung Thahlah and Maung Byaay presented another written request to be baptized. This time they asked to be baptized "not absolutely in private, but about sunset, away from public observation". After Judson and Colman spent "some hours" in again discussing the matter with the two new Christians:

> We felt satisfied that they were humble disciples of Jesus, and were desirous of receiving this ordinance purely out of regard to his command, and their own spiritual welfare; ... we were convinced that they were influenced rather by desires of avoiding unnecessary exposure, than by that sinful fear, which would plunge them into apostasy, in the hour of trial; and when they assured us that, if actually brought before government, they could not think of denying their Savior, we could not conscientiously refuse their request, and therefore agreed to have them baptized to-morrow at sunset.[13]

The following day they held their usual worship service at the zayat, after which the attendees dispersed to their homes. About half an hour before sunset Maung Thahlah and Maung Byaay returned to the zayat, accompanied by three or four of their

11 ibid.
12 ibid.
13 ibid., p. 164.

friends. After a short prayer the small group made its way to the same pond where Maung Nau had been baptized earlier. Judson afterward recorded his mixed perspectives on the ceremony:

> The sun was not allowed to look upon the humble, timid profession. No wondering crowd crowned the overshadowing hill. No hymn of praise expressed the exultant feelings of joyous hearts. Stillness and solemnity pervaded the scene. We felt, on the banks of the water, as a little, feeble, solitary band. But perhaps some hovering angels took note of the event, with more interest than they witnessed the late coronation; perhaps Jesus looked down on us, pitied and forgave our weaknesses, and marked us for his own; perhaps, if we deny him not, he will acknowledge us another day, more publicly than we venture at present to acknowledge him.[14]

That same evening missionaries and Burmese Christians shared in a communion service together. Three days later Judson met with the three new converts for "the first Burman prayer meeting that was ever held". "We agreed to meet for this purpose," Judson reported, "every Tuesday and Friday evening, immediately after family worship, which in the evening has for some time been conducted in Burman and English, and which these people, and occasionally some others, have attended." The following Sunday, November 14, Judson was delighted to record in his journal with added emphasis: "Have been much gratified to find, that this evening the THREE CONVERTS REPAIRED TO THE ZAYAT, AND HELD A PRAYER MEETING OF THEIR OWN ACCORD."[15]

14   ibid., p. 166.
15   ibid.

17

APPEAL TO THE EMPEROR
(1819-1820)

On the morning of Friday, November 26, Adoniram and Ann Judson were riding on horseback to a mineral pond on the outskirts of town where they regularly bathed. The road on which they traveled was one of several that passed by the Shwe Dagon Pagoda. Suddenly they were "accosted" by their implacable opponent, the Mangen teacher, who doubtless was accompanied by his retinue. He peremptorily forbade them to ride there again and stated that they would be punished with a beating if they did.

When the Judsons looked into the matter they learned that the Viceroy, influenced by the Mangen teacher, had recently issued an order that no person wearing a hat or shoes, carrying an umbrella or mounted on a horse could be on the sacred grounds belonging to Burma's pre-eminent pagoda. The pagoda's property extended half a mile on some sides and all the principal roads led to it. This new directive was obviously aimed primarily at foreigners.

The same day they were confronted by the Mangen teacher, Judson recorded in his journal recent developments in Burma and at the missionary zayat. As well as a risky step those developments were leading him to reconsider:

> Since the death of the old king, who was known to be in heart hostile to religion, people have been more engaged than ever, in building pagodas, making sacred offerings, and performing the public duties of religion. ...

Ever since the affair of Maung Shway-gnong, there has been an entire falling off [of visitors] at the Zayat. I sometimes sit there whole days, without a single visitor, although it is the finest part of the year, and many are constantly passing. We and our object are now well known throughout Rangoon. None wish to call, as formerly, out of curiosity; and none dare to call from a principle of religious inquiry. ...

Our business must be fairly laid before the emperor. If he frowns upon us, all missionary attempts within his dominions will be out of the question. If he favor us, none of our enemies, during the continuance of his favor, can touch a hair of our heads. But there is a greater than the emperor, before whose throne we desire daily and constantly to lay the business. Oh! Lord Jesus, look upon us in our low estate, and guide us in our dangerous course![1]

Judson and Colman reached a definite decision the very next day that they would proceed to Ava without delay and seek to introduce their endeavors to King Bagyidaw.

Maung Shway-gnong returned to pay Judson a lengthy visit on Saturday, December 5. After "several hours spent in metaphysical cavils", the Burmese teacher admitted he did not believe any of the trivial objections he had been raising. He revealed that he had been testing Judson and his religion because he was determined to embrace only what he found "unobjectionable and impregnable". He also declared that he really did believe in God, his Son Jesus Christ, the atonement and other key Christian doctrines.

Judson was aware of one vital aspect of Christian belief that Maung Shway-gnong might still be unwilling to accept. So he asked, "Do you believe all that is contained in the book of St Matthew that I have given you? In particular, do you believe that the Son of God died on a cross?"

"Ah, you have caught me now," Maung Shway-gnong acknowledged. "I believe he suffered death. But I cannot admit that he suffered the shameful death of the cross."

1   Ann Judson, *An Account*, pp. 167–8.

"Therefore, you are not a disciple of Christ," Judson declared frankly. "A true disciple inquires not whether a fact is agreeable to his own reason, but whether it is in the book. His pride has yielded to the Divine testimony. Teacher, your pride is still unbroken. Break down your pride and yield to the word of God."

After reflecting a moment, Maung Shway-gnong responded, "As you utter these words, I see my error: I have been trusting in my own reason, not in the word of God." Their conversation was briefly interrupted and when it resumed the Burmese teacher reiterated, "This day is different from all the days on which I have visited you. I see my error in trusting in my own reason. And I now believe the crucifixion of Christ because it is contained in the Scripture." Some time later in the discussion, while speaking of the uncertainty of life, Maung Shway-gnong declared, "I do not think that I shall be lost, even if I die suddenly."

"Why?" Judson questioned.

"Because I love Jesus Christ."

"Do you really love him?"

"No one that really knows him can help loving him," Maung Shway-gnong replied with personal conviction.

Five days later Judson and Colman sought the Viceroy's permission "to go up to the golden feet, and lift up our eyes to the golden face". Such were the common Burmese expressions for seeking an audience with the emperor. The Viceroy was apparently pleased with their request and granted it "in very polite terms".

In preparation for their journey the missionaries had purchased a boat and had it fitted out. The craft was six feet wide in the middle and forty feet long. A temporary bamboo deck was laid the entire length of the vessel. At the rear of the boat two low rooms were constructed with thin wooden walls and a roof of thatch and mats. The missionaries' crew included a headman (who carried "a little authority from government" for the expedition), ten oarsmen, a steersman, a cook (their own convert, Maung Nau), a washerman and a man in charge of "several guns and blunderbusses". The firearms were considered indispensable due to the prevalence of robbers on the river.

After puzzling over what to present as a fitting gift to the king, the missionaries finally settled on a handsome edition of the English Bible in six volumes. They had each volume covered in gold leaf in Burman style, then placed each in "a rich wrapper". They also took pieces of fine cloth and other articles as presents for other government officials.

The journey got underway on Tuesday, December 21. Two days later they entered the Irrawaddy River on which they would travel the remainder of the distance to Ava. Practically every day they heard new reports of recent robberies in nearby locations along the river. By January 2, 1820, they reached Prome, 120 miles from Rangoon. Once the seat of an ancient dynasty of Burmese kings, the city was now in a dilapidated state. There they learned of "a most daring robbery" that had recently taken place a few miles upriver. A governor traveling to Ava with about fifty men and 7,000 ticals (equaling around 4,500 dollars) was attacked. The governor was shot and all the treasure was carried off.

Late in the evening on January 20, they moored at Gnah-hmyah-gnay, "a solitary and dangerous place" some 300 miles north of Rangoon. Suddenly a large boat full of men rounded the river bend and bore down on the missionaries' vessel. Judson's headman warned off the encroaching craft but it kept coming straight toward them. When the headman fired a gun over their heads, they "called out to forbear and sheered off ".

Finally, on Tuesday, January 25, five weeks after leaving Rangoon, they passed Old Ava, "the seat of the dynasty immediately preceding the present", and about noon pulled ashore at O-ding-mau, the southern boat-landing for New Ava, residence of the current emperor. New Ava, more commonly known as Amarapura, was six miles north of Old Ava and about 350 miles from Rangoon.[2]

Early the next morning Judson and Colman set out for Amarapura. On the outskirts of the city they stopped to pay visits

---

2   "Today's Mandalay, second largest city in Burma, is just a few miles upriver from the two Avas of Adoniram [Judson]'s time" (Anderson, *To the Golden Shore*, p. 245). Mandalay was founded in 1857.

at the residences of two Englishmen, a Mr. Gibson and a Mr. Rodgers, whom they had first met in Rangoon. Both Gibson and Rodgers had become Burmese subjects and entered the king's service. Gibson had recently served as port collector of Rangoon while Rodgers, another former collector, was presently out of favor at the royal court.

Entering Ava, Judson and Colman went to the residence of Mya-day-men, the former Viceroy of Rangoon whose wife had treated Ann with such extraordinary kindness. Mya-day-men was now one of the eight highest ranking officials in the emperor's service:

> As a Wungyi, Mya-day-men was one of the four high Burmese officials who made up the Hlutdau, the great council of state, which discharged at the emperor's pleasure all the administrative, executive, legislative and judicial functions of the state. Only the four Atwinwuns who composed the emperor's privy council enjoyed comparable power; and it was always a matter of debate among Burmans whether Wungyis or Atwinwuns really had the higher rank.[3]

The missionaries presented Mya-day-men and his wife with valuable gifts and were received "very kindly" by both of them. They requested the powerful Wungyi's permission "to behold the golden face" but did not disclose their precise objective in seeking an audience with the king. Mya-day-men promptly instructed one of his favorite officials, Maung Yo, to introduce Judson and Colman to Maung Zah, one of the influential Atwinwuns, with the requisite orders needed for a visit with the emperor. That evening Judson recorded in his journal:

> We lie down in sleepless anxiety. Tomorrow's dawn will usher in the most eventful day of our lives. Tomorrow's even will close on the bloom or the blight of our fondest hopes. Yet it is consoling to commit this business into the hands of our heavenly Father – to feel that the work is His, not ours; that the heart of the monarch, before whom we are to

3   ibid.

appear, is under the control of Omnipotence; and that the event will be ordered in the manner most conducive to the divine glory and the greatest good. God may, for the wisest purposes, suffer our hopes to be disappointed; and if so, why should short-sighted, mortal man repine? Thy will, O God, be ever done; for thy will is inevitably the wisest and the best![4]

Thursday morning Maung Yo, "as a matter of form", first led the missionaries back to Mya-day-men. There they learned that the king had been privately apprised of their arrival and responded, "Let them be introduced." After reaching the outer gate of the palace and presenting a gift for Maung Zah, the powerful privy council member, they were shown to his apartments in the palace yard. He received them pleasantly and invited them to be seated in front of several "governors and petty kings" who were also awaiting an audience with the influential official. Judson and Colman informed Maung Zah that they were "propagators of religion" (missionaries) and that they wished to appear before the emperor in order to present their sacred books along with a petition. The Atwinwun took and read about half the petition, then asked several questions about their God and religion.

Just then someone announced that "the golden foot was about to advance". Maung Zah instantly arose and began putting on his robes of state, saying that he must seize the moment to present them to the emperor. It was then that the missionaries learned they were about to be introduced to King Bagyidaw at "an unpropitious time". In recent weeks 30,000 troops had marched from Ava to successfully quell a rebellion that had taken place in the Cassay region, north of Burma, at the accession of the new monarch. This was the day that that recent victory was being celebrated and the very hour when the king was coming forth to witness the grand display made on the special occasion.

Maung Zah led them through "various splendor and parade", up a flight of stairs and into "a most magnificent hall". He directed Judson and Colman where to sit and took his place on one side of

4   Ann Judson, *An Account*, pp. 184–5.

them while Maung Yo and another officer of Mya-day-men sat a little behind them. "The scene to which we were now introduced really surpassed our expectation," Judson afterward reported. "The spacious extent of the hall, the number and magnitude of the pillars, the height of the dome, the whole completely covered with gold, presented a most grand and imposing spectacle."

After more than five minutes of anxious waiting had passed, Maung Yo suddenly whispered that his majesty had entered. Judson later related:

> We looked through the hall as far as the pillars would allow, and presently caught sight of this modern Ahasuerus. He came forward, unattended – in solitary grandeur, exhibiting the proud gait and majesty of an eastern monarch. His dress was rich, but not distinctive; and he carried in his hand the gold-sheathed sword, which seems to have taken the place of the scepter of ancient times.[5]

As the king approached, every Burman in the hall (only high-ranking officials being present) prostrated himself with his head to the ground. Judson and Colman remained kneeling with their hands folded and their eyes fixed on the monarch. In an effort to present themselves to the emperor in garb indicating their role as religious teachers, the missionaries had elected to wear white robes, like a surplice, on this occasion. The sight of the foreigners caught King Bagyidaw's attention as he drew near. He stopped, partly turned toward them and asked, "Who are these?"

"The teachers, great king," Judson immediately replied.

"What, you speak Burman – the priests that I heard of last night?" the emperor responded with surprise. He then proceeded to ask a number of other questions: "When did you arrive? Are you teachers of religion? Are you like the Portuguese Priest? Are you married? Why do you dress so?" Judson briefly answered these and similar queries.

The king appeared pleased with them and sat down on an elevated seat that was provided for him. His hand rested on the

5   ibid., p. 186.

hilt of his sword and he continued to look at them intently. As he did, Maung Zah proceeded to read their formal petition:

> The American teachers present themselves to receive the favor of the excellent king, the sovereign of land and sea. Hearing that, on account of the greatness of the royal power, the royal country was in a quiet and prosperous state, we arrived at the town of Rangoon, within the royal dominions, and having obtained leave of the governor of that town, to come up and behold the golden face, we have ascended, and reached the bottom of the golden feet. In the great country of America, we sustain the character of teachers and explainers of the contents of the sacred Scriptures of our religion. And since it is contained in those Scriptures that, if we pass to other countries, and preach and propagate religion, great good will result, and both those who teach, and those who receive the religion, will be freed from future punishment, and enjoy, without decay or death, the eternal felicity of heaven, – [in order] that royal permission be given, that we, taking refuge in the royal power, may preach our religion in these dominions, and that those who are pleased with our preaching, and wish to listen to and be guided by it, whether foreigners or Burmans, may be exempt from government molestation, they present themselves to receive the favor of the excellent king, the sovereign of land and sea.[6]

Having listened to the petition, the monarch stretched out his hand. Maung Zah crawled forward and presented it to him. The king deliberately read back through it. As he did, Judson gave Maung Zah a carefully abridged version of their tract, A View of the Christian Religion. After perusing the petition, King Bagyidaw handed it back to Maung Zah without saying a word and took the tract. But upon reading only the first two or three sentences, the emperor, "with an air of indifference, perhaps disdain, ... dashed it down to the ground!"[7]

6   ibid., pp. 187–8.
7   ibid., p. 188.

Maung Zah stooped forward, picked up the pamphlet and handed it back to the missionaries. Maung Yo made a slight attempt in their behalf by unfolding one of the biblical volumes and displaying its attractiveness to the king. But in a massive hall entirely coated in gold, King Bagyidaw took no notice of one more gold-coated book. After a few uncomfortable seconds, Maung Zah interpreted his sovereign's will by declaring, "In regard to the objects of your petition, his majesty gives no order. In regard to your sacred books, his majesty has no use for them. Take them away."

King Bagyidaw promptly rose from his seat, strode to the end of the hall and lounged down on a cushion where he lay listening to the music and gazing at the parade spread out before him in the palace courtyard below. Judson and Colman were unceremoniously hustled out of the palace. Maung Yo conducted them back to Mya-day-men's house where the official reported to his superior the reception the missionaries had received from the king "in as favorable terms as possible".

Early Friday morning Gibson visited Judson and Colman at their boat. He had heard of the response they had received from the king but encouraged them not to give up hope. He was "perfectly acquainted" with Maung Zah and offered to accompany them to the high official's house a little before sunset that evening. Gibson thought the influential Antwinwun would be accessible then and they could present their case more fully to him in private. But when they arrived at Maung Zah's home he received them "with great coldness and reserve". Gibson advanced a number of arguments in favor of the missionaries. The only suggestion that seemed to carry any weight was that if the missionaries obtained royal favor, other foreigners would settle in the empire and trade would be greatly benefited. "Looking out from the cloud which covered his face", Maung Zah at last offered that if they would wait some time, he would seek to speak to the emperor about them.

Saturday morning the missionaries wrote down their request for religious tolerance "in the most concise and moderate terms" and sent it to Gibson with a message. They asked him to once more approach Maung Zah, present the paper to him and ascertain "unequivocally" if there was any possibility of gaining their request by waiting several months. Gibson returned to them on Monday, January 31. "I have shown your paper to Maung Zah," he reported, "and begged him not to deceive you, but to say distinctly what hopes you might be allowed to entertain. He replied, 'Tell them that there is not the least possibility of obtaining the object stated in this paper, should they wait ever so long.'"

Judson and Colman went to pay another visit to Rodgers. He told them of a distinguished Burmese teacher who, some fifteen years earlier, had embraced Catholicism. The teacher's own nephew accused him of having renounced the national religion and, at King Bodawpaya's orders, had him imprisoned and tortured, eventually with an iron mall. "With this instrument," Judson reported, "he was gradually beaten, from the ends of his feet up to his breast, until his body was little else but one livid wound." When he was near death, an appeal for mercy was made to the king on the basis that the teacher was a madman. The appeal was granted and the teacher was taken to Bengal where he died.

Ever after that the Catholic priests, of whom there were currently only four in all of Burma, never sought to proselyte the Burmese but confined their efforts to the Portuguese. Rodgers revealed that the nephew who had subjected his uncle to torture was now one of the four powerful Atwinwuns who formed the king's private government council. He outranked even Maung Zah. In addition, the present queen, who exerted tremendous influence on the king, was zealously committed to Buddhism.

Returning to their boat, Judson and Colman ordered their crew to sell off all superfluous supplies and to be ready to embark for Rangoon as soon as their passport could be obtained. The following day, Tuesday, they applied to Mya-day-men for the necessary permission. He seemed willing to oblige them but said they would need to make formal application to Maung Zah.

Thursday, after sending their headman to Maung Zah with a petition for the passport, Judson and Colman called on Gibson. They learned that, since seeing him last, Gibson had been summoned before King Bagyidaw. Among other matters, the monarch inquired about the foreign teachers. Gibson told him more about the American missionaries' country, their character and their objectives in coming to Burma. King Bagyidaw divulged that the Portuguese priest had told him very different things about them – specifically, that they were "a sect of Zandees (a race very obnoxious to former emperors)". Gibson sought to vindicate the missionaries' character but the ruler seemed unwilling to hear anything in their favor. In conclusion the king had laughed incredulously as he declared, "What, they have come presuming to convert us to their religion! Let them leave our capital. We have no desire to receive their instructions. Perhaps they may find some of their countrymen in Rangoon who may be willing to listen to them."

At last on Saturday, February 5, after five days of effort and dispensing gifts totaling thirty dollars in value to various officials, Judson and Colman received the desired passport from Maung Zah. They were relieved to set out the next morning on the return trip to Rangoon.

18

"The Emperor Himself Cannot Stop It" (1820)

Judson and Colman's trip back toward Rangoon progressed quickly. After traveling 230 miles in the first six days, they arrived at Pyee. There they were greatly surprised to meet the teacher, Maung Shway-gnong, who had come upriver to visit an acquaintance who had fallen dangerously ill. Judson and Colman told him of their rebuff by the king, the resulting danger of professing and propagating Christian belief as well as the story of the iron mall. Maung Shway-gnong seemed less affected and intimidated by all this than the missionaries had expected. "Indeed," commented Judson, "his language was rather too high for the occasion."

Rather bluntly, Judson said to Maung Shway-gnong, "It is not for you that we are concerned but for those who have become disciples of Christ. When they are accused and persecuted, they cannot worship at the pagodas or recant before the Mangen teacher." When Maung Shway-gnong started to explain his past conduct, Judson cut him off, "Say nothing. One thing you know to be true – that when formerly accused, if you had not in some way or other satisfied the mind of the Mangen teacher, your life would not now be remaining in your body."

"Then if I must die," Maung Shway-gnong responded, "I shall die in a good cause. I know it is the cause of truth." He then stated "with considerable emphasis" the primary points of his present beliefs, "I believe in the Eternal God, in His Son Jesus Christ, in the atonement which Christ has made, and in the writings of the apostles, as the true and only word of God." Continuing on, he further related:

Perhaps you may not remember that during one of my last visits you told me that I was trusting in my own understanding rather than in the Divine word. From that time I have seen my error and endeavored to renounce it. You explained to me also the evil of worshiping at pagodas, though I told you that my heart did not partake in the worship. Since you left Rangoon I have not lifted up my folded hands before a pagoda. It is true, I sometimes follow the crowd on days of worship in order to avoid persecution. But I walk up one side of the pagoda and walk down the other. Now, you say that I am not a disciple. What lack I yet?

Judson softened slightly. "Teacher, you may be a disciple of Christ in heart but you are not a full disciple. You have not faith and resolution enough to keep all the commands of Christ, particularly that which requires you to be baptized, though in the face of persecution and death. Consider the words of Jesus, just before he returned to heaven, 'He that believeth and is baptized shall be saved' [Mark 16:16]."[1] Judson then hinted that the missionaries were considering leaving Rangoon since King Bagyidaw had virtually prohibited the propagation of Christianity, and no Burman under such circumstances would dare to investigate, much less embrace it.

"Say not so," Maung Shway-gnong immediately responded. "There are some who will investigate, notwithstanding. Rather than have you quit Rangoon, I will go myself to the Mangen teacher and have a public dispute. I know I can silence him. I know the truth is on my side."

"Ah, you may have a tongue to silence him," Judson replied, "but he has a pair of fetters and an iron mall to subdue you! Remember that."

Six more days brought the missionaries back to Rangoon. Two days after their arrival, on the evening of Sunday, February 20, 1820, Judson and Colman met with the three baptized Burmese

1 Adoniram Judson did not espouse baptismal regeneration. But he saw baptism as an essential act of obedience and a mandatory outward affirmation of the faith of a truly regenerate believer.

Christians. They provided them with a full account of all that had happened in Ava, so they would clearly understand the danger of their present circumstances and the reasons for the missionaries' intended departure from Rangoon.

"But whither are the teachers going?" the young believers asked anxiously. The missionaries sought to assure them that it was their intention never to desert Burma. However, due to the king's intolerance, they thought it necessary to leave for a time those parts of the empire directly under his dominion. They shared their plan to go for a time to Chittagong to minister to the Arakanese Christians living there.

Judson and Colman then asked the Burmese Christians individually what they would do. Maung Nau reiterated what he had previously told them, he would follow them to any part of the world. His only fear was that, not knowing another language, he might not be able to earn his living in a strange land and could be a burden to the missionaries.

"As for me," Maung Thahlah declared, "I go where preaching is to be had."

Maung Byaay was silent and thoughtful for a time. At length he said, "Since no Burman woman is allowed to leave the country, I cannot, on account of my wife, follow the teachers." He added earnestly, "But if I must be left here alone, I shall remain performing the duties of Jesus Christ's religion; no other shall I think of."

The following Thursday evening Maung Byaay visited Judson with his brother-in-law, Maung Myat-yah, who had also lived on the missionary property for several months and attended worship services at the mission zayat. "I have come," said Maung Byaay, "to petition that you will not leave Rangoon at present."

"I think that it is useless to remain under present circumstances," Judson responded. "We cannot open the zayat; we cannot have public worship. No Burman will dare to examine this religion. And if none examine, none can be expected to embrace it."

"Teacher," Maung Byaay replied, "my mind is distressed. I can neither eat nor sleep since I find you are going away. I have been around among those who live near us, and I find some who are even now examining the new religion. Brother Myat-yah is one of them, and he unites with me in my petitions." After Maung Myat-yah assented that it was so, Maung Byaay continued, "Do stay with us a few months. Do stay till there are eight or ten disciples. Then appoint one to be the teacher of the rest. ... Though you should leave the country, the religion will spread of itself. The emperor himself cannot stop it. But if you go now and take the two disciples that can follow, I shall be left alone. I cannot baptize those who may wish to embrace this religion. What can I do?"

Just then Maung Nau arrived and expressed similar sentiments. He thought that, despite all opposition, several would yet become Christian disciples and that it was best for the missionaries to stay awhile longer. Upon hearing these perspectives, the Judsons could not restrain their tears. "As we live only for the promotion of the cause of Christ among the Burmans," Judson told them, "if there is any prospect of success in Rangoon, we have no desire to go to another place and will, therefore, reconsider the matter."

The missionaries concluded that under these "interesting circumstances" they could not all leave the Christians and inquirers in Rangoon. At the same time they thought it very important that the small band of believers in Chittagong should not be neglected. In the end they decided that the Colmans should proceed immediately to Chittagong. If persecution against Christians became too strong in Rangoon, the Judsons, accompanied by as many Burmans as could join them, would flee to Chittagong.

During the next couple of weeks Judson had repeated opportunities to dialogue with Maung Shway-gnong and an acquaintance of his, Oo Yan.[2] The latter was an elderly doctor who had previously attended one worship service at the mission house shortly before Judson and Colman left for Ava. Like Maung Shway-gnong, Oo Yan possessed "a very acute, discriminating mind" and exceptional debating skills. While he was ready to admit that Buddhism was untenable, he held to the same system of belief that Maung Shway-gnong had previously espoused.[3]

2   Concerning the spelling and meaning of the title Oo, see chapter 12, footnote 1.
3   Maung Shway-gnong's former beliefs are described in chapter 16.

Maung Shway-gnong at this time inquired about and seemed reluctant to embrace the "outward rules" that he would be expected to observe should he become a professing Christian. Judson listed only three such public requirements – baptism, assembling each Lord's Day for worship and periodically observing communion. Maung Shway-gnong's reluctance to embrace such public practices doubtless stemmed from his fear of persecution.

On Tuesday, March 21, Maung Thahlah introduced one of his relatives, Maung Shway-bay, to Judson, stating that he desired to consider the Christian religion. That evening and the next the missionary had extended conversations with the earnest inquirer. Thursday morning Maung Thahlah informed Judson that he and Maung Shway-bay had sat up most of the previous night in the zayat, reading, conversing and praying. In the afternoon Maung Shway-bay came to Judson with surprisingly strong expressions of personal Christian belief. "It only seems strange to us," Judson commented, "that a work of grace should be carried on so rapidly, in the soul of an ignorant heathen."[4]

Maung Shway-bay also presented a written statement of his Christian faith along with "an urgent request" to be baptized the following Lord's Day. After spending all Friday evening with Maung Shway-bay, Judson wrote further of him: "Feel satisfied that he has experienced a work of Divine grace."[5] However, the missionary thought it best to defer Maung Shway-bay's baptism for a week in order to give him more time to reflect on his new-found beliefs. After dark on Sunday, April 2, Maung Shway-bay was baptized at the same pond where his fellow countrymen had earlier been immersed. Afterwards he joined the Judsons and the other three Burmese believers in observing the Lord's Supper.

The Colmans left for Bengal, and ultimately Chittagong, on March 27. One of the rooms they had occupied in the mission house was converted into a small chapel for Sunday and nightly worship services as well as conversations with believers and

4   Ann Judson, *An Account*, p. 208.
5   ibid., p. 209.

inquirers living on the mission premises. The mission zayat, where they had met for Sunday worship behind closed doors since returning from Ava, was abandoned for a time.

Since mid-March, a trio of women had been visiting the mission house and attending a worship service about once a week. Their leader, Mah Men-lay,[6] was an acquaintance of the teacher Maung Shway-gnong. She was also the wife of Maung Myat-lah, one of two friends who commonly accompanied the doctor Oo Yan when he visited Judson. On Friday, April 14, those three women spent most of the day with Ann. Adoniram Judson stated of that visit, "it has afforded pretty satisfactory evidence that ... Mah Men-lay has experienced Divine grace."[7]

After a month away from the mission house, Maung Shway-gnong returned on Sunday, April 16. He indicated that all his reservations to obeying the positive outward commands of Christ had been removed and that he desired to be a full disciple. But when Judson questioned him closely on the subject, Maung Shway-gnong intimated that his wife and friends opposed his making a decided commitment, and that if he did he would be "exposed to imminent danger of persecution and death". Judson's heart went out to this distressed would-be follower of Christ:

> He mentioned these things with so much feeling, and such evident consciousness of simple weakness, as completely disarmed me. My heart was wrung with pity. I sincerely sympathized with him, in his evident mental trials. I could not deny the truth of what he said; but gently hinted, "as thy day is, thy strength shall be" [Deut. 33:25], and proposed the example of the apostles and martyrs, the glory of suffering for Christ, etc. But the thought of the iron mall, and a secret suspicion, that if I was in his circumstances, I should perhaps have no more courage, restrained my tongue.[8]

6   Mah was a common Burmese title denoting a younger woman.

7   Ann Judson, *An Account*, p. 216.

8   ibid., pp. 217–18.

The following Thursday Mah Men-lay and her friends again spent the entire day with Ann. Afterward Judson reported of the Burmese woman:

> She gives increasing evidence of being a real disciple; but is extremely timid, through fear of persecution. One of her remarks deserves notice, as a natural expression of true Christian feeling. "I am surprised," said she, "to find this religion has such an effect on my mind, as to make me love the disciples of Christ more than my dearest natural relations."[9]

That same day Judson completed a Burmese translation of the epistle to the Ephesians. He had started translating the book before going to Ava but was able to work on it only intermittently due to recurring eye trouble. "It is with real joy that I put this precious writing into the hands of the disciples," Judson commented. "It is a great accession to their scanty stock of Scripture, for they have had nothing hitherto but St Matthew. Intend to give them the Acts, as fast as my eyes will allow."[10]

By the first week of May, the Judsons had good reason to hope that Mah Men-lay's husband, Maung Myat-lah, had become a genuine believer. In addition, Maung Myat-lah's friend, Maung Thah-ay, who often accompanied him and Oo Yan when they visited Judson, was giving equally good evidence of having become a true disciple. Maung Thah-ay, a former government official, had amassed a considerable fortune, which he previously spent primarily in building pagodas and presenting offerings. Despite his obvious devotion to Buddhism, Judson testified of Maung Thah-ay: "But he obtained no satisfaction, found no resting place for his soul, until he became acquainted with the religion of Jesus. He now rests in this religion with conscious security – believes and loves all that he hears of it ..."[11]

Maung Myat-yah (Maung Byaay's brother-in-law) had first started considering Christianity three months earlier, late in

9   ibid., p. 218.
10   ibid., pp. 218–19.
11   ibid., p. 221.

February. On Sunday, March 26, he told the missionaries, "Set me down for a disciple. I have fully made up my mind, in regard to this religion. I love Jesus Christ. But I am not yet quite ready for baptism." Now on Sunday evening, May 28, he requested to be baptized. Joining him in making that request was Maung Thah-yah, another resident on the mission property. Maung Thah-yah faithfully attended nightly worship at the mission house and had been slowly progressing in his knowledge and love of Divine truth. Both men were baptized the following Lord's Day.

Since the middle of April Ann Judson had been suffering from liver trouble and had undergone two courses of salivation treatment. By the end of June her health was failing so rapidly that the Judsons decided they must sail to Bengal to seek further treatment. At the news that the missionaries would soon be leaving for a time, two other Burmese men who had been attending evening worship at the mission for several weeks, Maung Nyo-dway and Maung Gway, requested baptism. Judson, partly to test their sincerity, suggested that it might be better to delay their baptism till after his return. The two Burmans were distressed at that proposal. They asserted that, as they had fully embraced Christianity in their hearts, they could not be at peace without following Christ's command to be baptized. They also pointed out that no one knew for sure whether or not Judson would ever return once he left. They asked to be baptized in a small pond near the mission house. Judson granted their request by baptizing them on Sunday evening, July 16.

The next morning Maung Shway-gnong returned to visit Judson after an absence of a few weeks. Judson at first received him with reserve but soon learned that both the teacher and his family had been ill with fever for some time. The missionary related:

> He gradually wore away my reserve; and we had not been together two hours, before I felt more satisfied than ever, from his account of his mental trials, his struggles with sin, his strivings to be holy, his penitence, his faith, his exercises in secret prayer, that he is a subject of the special operations of the Holy Spirit, that he is indeed a true disciple.[12]

12   ibid., p. 227–8.

Maung Shway-gnong stayed at the mission house throughout the entire day. In the afternoon the doctor Oo Yan and several other inquirers arrived and "much interesting conversation" about spiritual matters ensued. Toward the end of the visit, Maung Shway-gnong, "as if to bring things to a crisis", declared to Judson, "My lord teacher, there are now several of us present, who have long considered this religion. I hope that we are all believers in Jesus Christ."

> "I am afraid to say that," Judson responded. "However, it is easily ascertained. And let me begin with you, teacher. I have heretofore thought that you fully believed in the eternal God. But I have had some doubt whether you fully believed in the Son of God and the atonement he has made."
>
> "I assure you that I am as fully persuaded of the latter as of the former."
>
> "Do you believe then that none but the disciples of Christ will be saved from sin and hell?"
>
> "None but his disciples."
>
> "How then can you remain without taking the oath of allegiance to Jesus Christ, and becoming his full disciple, in body and soul?"
>
> "It is my earnest desire to do so by receiving baptism. And for the very purpose of expressing that desire I have come here today."
>
> "You say you are desirous of receiving baptism. May I ask *when* you desire to receive it?"
>
> "At any time you will please to give it. Now – this moment, if you please."
>
> "Do you wish to receive baptism in public or in private?"
>
> "I will receive it at any time and in any circumstance that you please to direct."
>
> "Teacher, I am satisfied from your conversation this forenoon that you are a true disciple. And I reply, therefore, that I am as desirous of giving you baptism as you are of receiving it."

The Christians listening to this exchange rejoiced at the step of commitment Maung Shway-gnong was ready to make while the others present were astonished at it. Turning next to Maung Thah-ay, Judson asked him, "Are you willing to take the oath of allegiance to Jesus Christ?"

"If the teacher Maung Shway-gnong consents, why should I hesitate?"

"And if he does not consent, what then?"

"I must wait a little longer."

"Stand by. You trust in Maung Shway-gnong rather than in Jesus Christ. You are not worthy of being baptized."

Judson "similarly interrogated" Oo Yan, Maung Myat-lah and the latter's wife, Mah Men-lay. The two men were not ready to commit to baptism while Mah Men-lay, "probably on account of her husband's having just declined", expressed such hesitant desire that Judson deemed her response "not satisfactory".

At nightfall the following day, Tuesday, Judson baptized Maung Shway-gnong at "the accustomed place", the pond nearby the mission zayat. When Judson returned to the mission residence, Ann told him that as soon as Mah Men-lay saw that Maung Shway-gnong had actually gone to be baptized, she exclaimed, "Ah! he has now gone to obey the command of Jesus Christ, while I remain without obeying. I shall not be able to sleep this night. I must go home and consult my husband and return."

The small Christian band, accompanied by its newest member Maung Shway-gnong, had just finished partaking of the Lord's Supper when, about 9 p.m., Mah Men-lay returned. She immediately requested to be baptized and all the believers present gave their assent. Judson led a small procession out to the pond near the mission house where he baptized her. She was the tenth Burman convert and the first Burmese woman to be baptized. Judson testified of her: "Mah Men-lay is fifty-one years old, of most extensive acquaintance through the place [area], of much strength of mind, decision of character, and consequent influence over others. She is, indeed, among women, what Maung Shway-gnong is among men."[13]

13   ibid., p. 231.

19

A PAINFUL SEPARATION
(1820-1822)

At noon the next day, July 19, nearly one hundred local residents accompanied the Judsons to their ship – "the women crying aloud, in the Burman manner, and almost all deeply affected." The vessel on which the Judsons traveled arrived in Calcutta on August 18. Nine days later they removed to Serampore with its "more healthful climate". There they stayed with the George Houghs, not far from the Baptist mission premises.

Throughout the Judsons' "very quiet and happy sojourn" there, Ann's physical condition alternately improved and declined. Her attending physician, a Dr Chalmers, stated his opinion that her ailment was a chronic liver condition which could only be corrected through extended treatment in either Bengal or America. The last day of October the Judsons returned to Calcutta, having decided that Adoniram must proceed alone to Rangoon for the foreseeable future. In Calcutta they consulted another eminent physician, a Dr Macwhirter, who affirmed Chalmers's basic diagnosis. But Macwhirter thought he could provide Ann with appropriate prescriptions that would render her return to Rangoon "less dangerous" than initially thought.

Consequently, Adoniram and Ann Judson sailed together from Calcutta for Rangoon on November 23. After arriving there on January 3, 1821, Ann recorded of their return trip to Burma:

> Our voyage was tedious and distressing above any that we had ever taken. The brig was so small and so filled with native passengers that we were unable to obtain the least

exercise by walking on deck, and was so full of scorpions and centipedes that we never dared to shut our eyes to sleep without completely enclosing ourselves with curtains. In addition to these inconveniences, we had a strong contrary wind and frequently violent squalls, with the most terrific thunder and lightning we had ever witnessed. We were six weeks in making a passage which is generally made in ten or fifteen days.[1]

The Judsons were heartened to learn that Mya-day-men had returned as Rangoon's Viceroy. They were hopeful he would show greater toleration to their mission work and the Burmans associated with it. During the Judsons' absence of five and a half months, some of the Burmese Christians had found it necessary to hide out in the woods in order to avoid "heavy extortion and oppression from petty officers of government". Despite that fact, all of them remained "firm in their faith and attachment to the cause".

Shortly after Mya-day-men's return to Rangoon, while the Judsons were still away, all the officials and Buddhist priests of Maung Shway-gnong's village conspired to destroy him. A high ranking official complained to the Viceroy that Maung Shway-gnong was "making every endeavor to turn the priest's rice-pot bottom upwards". "What consequence?" Mya-day-men replied. "Let the priests turn it back again." His simple, disinterested statement was all it took to blast the hopes of the conspirators and to assure the Burmese Christians that he would grant them toleration.

Judson immediately recommended regular worship services and prayer meetings as well as personal interaction with the steady stream of individuals who stopped by the mission house to discuss spiritual matters. Maung Ing, the fisherman and the third Burman convert, returned to visit the Judsons in the middle of February, nearly a year and a half since his departure from Rangoon. He had been living in Mergui,[2] a town far down the

1   Edward Judson, *The Life of Adoniram Judson*, p. 183.
2   Modern Myeik. In Judson's day it was also called Bike.

southeastern coast of Burma. There he sought to evangelize both Burmans and Portuguese. He now requested to be baptized and was on Sunday afternoon, March 4. A week later he left to return to Mergui, taking with him a supply of Christian literature.

Toward the end of April Judson reopened the missionary zayat. At first it attracted few visitors but before long their numbers increased. On Monday, June 4, Judson hired Maung Shway-bay to assist him with ministry responsibilities at the zayat . He was to be paid "a small allowance" of seven or eight rupees (equaling about five dollars) per month. Judson viewed this as an initial step toward Maung Shway-bay eventually becoming an official Gospel minister. Of his selection for this important responsibility, Judson wrote:

> I have this day taken Maung Shway-bay into the service of the mission. He bids fairer than any other member of the church to be qualified, in due time, for the ministry; for though inferior to Maung Thah-lah in fluency of speech, and to Maung Shway-gnong in genius and address, he is superior to the former in consistency of character, and gravity of deportment, and to the latter in experimental acquaintance with Divine things, and devotedness to the cause. But the principal trait of character which distinguishes him from the rest, and affords considerable evidence that he is called by higher authority than that of man to the Christian ministry, is his *humble* and *persevering* desire for that office – a desire which sprung up in his heart soon after his conversion, and has been growing ever since.[3]

The following Lord's day, June 10, Mah Myat-lay requested to be baptized. She was the sister of Mah Men-lay and had regularly accompanied her in attending worship services. "The evidences of her piety are of the most satisfactory kind," Judson commented. "We esteem her quite as highly as her sister Mah Men-lay, though she is far inferior in external qualifications." Originally Mah Myat-lay's baptism was set for the next Sunday. But news of the

3   Ann Judson, *An Account*, p. 250.

intended event caused "a great uproar" among her neighbors. "She is not, however, disheartened," Judson reported, "but rather wishes that her baptism may not be deferred until Sunday, lest some measures be taken to prevent it."[4] Judson accordingly baptized her two days earlier, on Friday, June 15.

With the help of Maung Shway-gnong, Judson spent several weeks, beginning in March, thoroughly revising his translation of Ephesians and the opening chapters of Acts. In mid-May those improved works were sent to George Hough in Serampore to have 600 copies of each printed. By the middle of July Judson had finished translating the Gospel and Epistles of John, "those exquisitely sweet and precious portions of the New Testament", and was working on the latter section of Acts.

Shortly thereafter Adoniram and Ann were struck by cholera morbus and fever. For several days they were too weak and sick to help each other but managed to get their own medicines periodically. They had only their adopted daughter, Emily, now aged thirteen, to assist them in their distress. Despite ongoing salivation treatments with blue mercury pills, Ann's health had continued to decline and she had suffered severely from her liver ailment. Early in August they reached "a final conclusion" that she must return to America in hopes of recovering her health. On August 21 Ann embarked for Calcutta on the first leg of the journey to her homeland. Emily Van Someren accompanied her to Calcutta, from which the young teen returned to her former home in Madras. She had been part of the Judsons' household for six years.

In an era when commitment to one's ministry often trumped personal and family considerations, the Judsons made the wrenching decision that Adoniram would carry on in Burma while Ann sought to recoup her health in America. They anticipated being apart at least two years. Comments that Judson made in a letter to George Hough on August 13 give some idea how agonizing this decision was for the missionary:

> I feel as if I was on the scaffold, and signing, as it were, my
> own death warrant. However, two years will pass away at

4   ibid., pp. 251–2.

last. Time and tide wait for no man, heedless alike of our joys and sorrows. ... For ten days or a fortnight we were laid by with fever, unable to help one another ...; and since we became convalescent, I have been occupied in making up my mind to have my right arm amputated, and my right eye extracted, which the doctors say are necessary in order to prevent a decay and mortification of the whole body conjugal.[5]

Not long after Ann's departure, the leader of Maung Shway-gnong's village, in union with several Buddhist priests, presented written charges against him to Viceroy Mya-day-men. Maung Shway-gnong's opponents accused him of having embraced sentiments that aimed at destroying the Buddhist religion and that were prejudicial against the existing authorities. This time Mya-day-men responded that if their assertions were true, Maung Shway-gnong was deserving of death. Upon learning of this, the teacher fled upriver with his family where they settled in the town of Shway-doung, about one hundred miles from Rangoon. Maung Shway-gnong took with him a supply of printed tracts and Scripture portions. He continued to actively share his Christian beliefs and consequently stirred up considerable commotion among Shway-doung residents.

In a letter that Judson wrote to Ann at that time, he revealed both his discouragements and his ongoing consecration:

September 12. Company continued with me until after three o'clock; and then I found myself alone, and, for a few hours, was very desolate and unhappy. But about sunset, the time mentioned in your last letter for mutual prayer, I felt more comfortable.

I wish I could always feel as I did last evening, and have this morning. At first, on hearing Maung Shway-gnong's story, I felt much disheartened, and thought how pleasant it would be if we could find some quiet resting-place on earth, where we might spend the rest of our days together in peace,

5 Wayland, *Memoir*, vol. 1, p. 302.

and perform the ordinary services of religion. But I fled to Jesus, and all such thoughts soon passed away. Life is short. Happiness consists not in outward circumstances. Millions of Burmans are perishing. I am almost the only person on earth who has attained their language to such a degree as to be able to communicate the way of salvation. How great are my obligations to spend and be spent for Christ! What a privilege to be allowed to serve Him in such interesting circumstances, and to suffer for Him! The heavenly glory is at hand. O, let me travel through this country, and bear testimony to the truth all the way from Rangoon to Ava, and show the path to that glory which I am anticipating. O, if Christ will only sanctify me and strengthen me, I feel that I can do all things. But in myself I am absolute nothingness; and when through grace I get a glimpse of divine things, I tremble lest the next moment will snatch it quite away.

Let us pray especially for one another's growth in grace. Let me pray that the trials which we respectively are called to endure may wean us from the world, and rivet our hearts on things above. Soon we shall be in heaven. O, let us live as we shall then wish we had done. Let us be humble, unaspiring, indifferent equally to worldly comfort and the applause of men, absorbed in Christ, the uncreated Fountain of all excellence and glory.[6]

Following Maung Shway-gnong's difficulties, Burmese Christians came "as privately as possible" to the mission house for worship and religious instruction while former inquirers withdrew almost entirely. Judson found it necessary to close the zayat again. For a time he was disheartened and unsure how to proceed. But soon after seeking the Lord's guidance "with some uncommon feelings of faith", "my mind became more settled on pursuing the [Bible] translations, as being the most honorable to God, the most beneficial to my own soul, and the most conducive to the real interest of the mission."[7]

6   Edward Judson, *The Life of Adoniram Judson*, pp. 194–5.

7   Ann Judson, *An Account*, p. 256.

Around that same time Maung Ing returned from Mergui. He and Maung Shway-bay spent every evening reading the Scriptures together. As they made their way through the book of Acts, they used a map that Judson had made for them to locate the places where the apostles had preached. Early in November, Maung Thahlah, the second Burmese convert, passed away very suddenly. Though he was a young man in "perfect health", he contracted cholera and died less than nineteen hours later. Judson did not learn of Maung Thahlah's illness until he had already lost consciousness. His death was considered "a heavy loss" to the mission. He was one of the few Burmans willing to lead in public prayer, and he did so in a manner that was both apt and edifying. In addition to possessing "fine talents" and "superior education", he had an arresting manner of communicating spiritual truths.

On December 13 Judson was delighted to welcome Dr and Mrs. Jonathan Price to Rangoon as new missionary colleagues. Immediately after they arrived with their infant daughter, Price set about learning the Burmese language and establishing his medical practice. Word of his medical proficiency, including his ability to restore sight by removing cataracts, spread quickly. That news was not long in reaching the Golden Ears in Ava. "Another season of rejoicing" was occasioned on January 20, 1822, by the return of the Houghs to Rangoon. But tragedy struck three and a half months later when Mrs. Price died of dysentery on May 2.

Judson remained primarily focused on his Bible translation work. By the middle of March he had finished a new revision of Matthew as well as first-time translations of Mark and Luke. Having translated John and Acts earlier, he next moved on to Romans. In late May or early June his progress was interrupted by a return of a debilitating fever and an attack of cholera morbus, as he had experienced the previous July and August. Then on July 20, 1822, he recorded in his journal:

> My hopes of finishing the New Testament without interruption, all blasted, by the arrival of an order from the king, summoning brother Price to Ava, on account of his medical skill. I must of course accompany him, and endeavor

to take advantage of the circumstance, to gain some footing in the capital and the palace. But it is most repugnant to my feelings to leave my present pursuits and prospects in Rangoon. May the Lord direct!

Attendances at the mission's Sunday worship services had built back up to nearly thirty people, including a number of active inquirers. By the time Judson and Price left for Ava on August 28, five more Burmese – four women and one man – were baptized and received into church membership. That brought the total number of baptized Burman believers to eighteen. Judson was quite certain that two others had been regenerated. But they both hesitated to be baptized for fear of persecution.

20

ENCOURAGEMENT IN AVA
(1822-1823)

Judson and Price's departure to Ava was delayed a few days by the death of Viceroy Mya-day-men on August 20. The two missionaries left Rangoon eight days later and arrived at the capital on September 27. By this time Old Ava had once again become the capital city, with the royal family and highest government officials residing there rather than at Amarapura. Members of the royal family were living in temporary housing while a new palace was being built. Some 40,000 homes had been moved from Amarapura as a result of this relocation of the capital back to Old Ava and Judson estimated the current population of the restored capital to be around 700,000.[1]

As soon as they arrived they were introduced to the emperor. King Bagyidaw received Price very graciously and asked many questions about his medical knowledge and skill. The monarch took no notice of Judson except as interpreter. But Maung Zah, the Atwinwun who had introduced Judson to the emperor on his previous visit, immediately recognized the missionary and

---

1   Ann Judson explained the situation in a later correspondence: "As there has been much misunderstanding relative to Ava and Amarapoora [Amarapura], both being called the capital of the Burmese empire, I will here remark, that the present Ava was formerly the seat of government; but soon after the old king [Bodawpaya, Bagyidaw's grandfather] had ascended to the throne, it was forsaken, and a new palace built at Amarapoora, about six miles from Ava, in which he remained during his life. In the fourth year of the reign of the present king [Bagyidaw], Amarapoora was in its turn forsaken, and a new and beautiful palace built at Ava, which was then in ruins, but is now the capital of the Burmese empire" (Wayland, *Memoir*, vol. 1, pp. 335–6).

asked about his welfare in the king's presence. After Bagyidaw withdrew, Maung Zah conversed a little on religious subjects with Judson and privately encouraged him to remain at the capital.

On the first day of October the two missionaries appeared again before the emperor. After making some further inquiries of Price, King Bagyidaw suddenly turned his attention to Judson, who was wearing a typical American-style suit, and asked, "And you in black, what are you – a medical man, too?"

"Not a medical man, but a teacher of religion, your majesty," Judson responded.

After asking a few questions about Judson's religion, the king suddenly raised an alarming query, "Have any embraced your religion?"

"Not here," Judson replied evasively.

"Are there any in Rangoon?" Bagyidaw persisted.

"There are a few."

"Are they foreigners?"

Judson later related: "I trembled for the consequences of an answer, which might involve the little church in ruin; but the truth must be sacrificed or the consequences hazarded, and I therefore replied, 'There are some foreigners, and some Burmans.' " The monarch was silent a few moments but showed no displeasure. He then proceeded to ask "a great variety of questions" on religion, geography and astronomy. Judson's answers seemed so satisfactory to the members of court who were present that they verbalized a general expression of approval. Afterwards Judson expressed heartfelt gratitude in his journal: "Thanks be to God for the encouragement of this day! The monarch of the empire has distinctly understood that some of his subjects have embraced the Christian religion, and his wrath has been restrained."[2]

Two days later Judson and Price moved into the temporary residence that the king had ordered to be erected for them. It was

2   Ann Judson, *An Account*, p. 304.

"a mere temporary shed" that was hardly adequate to shield them from the rain or the gaze of curious people outside the house. It was located near the palace and next to the wall that surrounded the residence of "Prince M., eldest half brother of the king". This prince, who was "greatly disfigured by a paralytic affection of the arms and legs", promptly conferred with Price about medical matters. He also summoned Judson to converse on science and religion.

Beginning on October 5, Judson was confined for ten days with fever and ague. After his recovery, which would prove to be short-lived, he paid visits to Prince M. as well as to various Atwinwuns and palace officials.[3] Judson sought to engage them in conversation about "the being of God and other topics of the Christian religion" and was greatly encouraged by the openness with which some discussed those matters.

On October 22 the missionaries received a large parcel of letters, magazines and newspapers that had been forwarded to them from Rangoon. Most interesting to Judson was the eight-sheet letter he received from Ann, his first correspondence from her in several months. The last date in the letter was April 24, at which time she was aboard a ship in the Atlantic headed toward England. Another missive from Bengal informed Judson that James Colman had died in Chittagong. While that letter contained no particulars about his colleague's passing, Judson would later learn that Colman had died of fever on July 4, 1822.

Judson had the opportunity to visit repeatedly with Prince M. and his wife, "the Princess of S.", who was one of the king's sisters. "Do not return to Rangoon," the prince and princess encouraged Judson, "but when your wife arrives, call her to Ava. The king will give you a piece of ground on which to build a *kyoung*." (A *kyoung* was a residence for individuals who were considered sacred.) On one occasion Judson ventured to warn the prince of his spiritual and eternal peril, and urged him to make Christianity his "immediate personal concern". For a moment Prince M. appeared to feel the force of Judson's warning. But presently he responded,

3   Concerning *Atwinwuns* and *Wungyis*, see p. 145.

"I am yet young, only twenty-eight. I am desirous of studying all the foreign arts and sciences. My mind will then be enlarged, and I shall be capable of judging whether the Christian religion be true or not."

"But suppose your highness changes worlds in the meantime," the missionary pressed.

The prince's face fell and he replied, "It is true, I know not when I shall die."

"It would be well to pray to God for light," Judson encouraged, "which, if obtained, will enable you at once to distinguish between truth and falsehood."

Judson paid visits to other royal family members as well. Prince T., second brother of the emperor, received the missionary cordially. But after two visits Judson described him simply as "a hopeless case", perhaps referring to his spiritual condition and receptiveness. The Princess of T. was the king's oldest sister and, as such, was consigned by Burmese law to perpetual celibacy. She requested a visit from Judson in order to discuss science and religion, and treated him with "uncommon affability and respect".

Judson also had frequent opportunity to observe and visit with King Bagyidaw himself. A few years later Judson provided a fascinating description of those opportunities and of the emperor:

> During my second residence in Ava, of five or six months, I saw his majesty almost every day. I sometimes saw him at his public levees, but at all times had free access to the palace, and have frequently conversed with the king on subjects of geography, religion, and history, for ten minutes or a quarter of an hour together. His majesty was incapable of giving his attention to any subject for a longer time.
>
> He is a man about forty years of age, of rather a dark complexion, and in person small and slender. His manners are graceful, and in public dignified. In private he is affable, and playful to boyishness. His disposition is obliging and liberal, and he is anxious to see every one around him happy. His mind is indolent, and he is incapable of any continued

application. His time is passed in sensual enjoyments, in listening to music, or seeing dancing or theatrical entertainments; but, above all, in the company of his principal queen, to whom he is devoted even to infatuation. His personal activity is remarkable for an eastern prince, and scarcely a day passes that he does not go on the river in boats, or ride on horseback, or an elephant. He is partial to Europeans. No person of this description comes before him without receiving some marks of kindness. ... His majesty is not bigoted to his own religion. ... [I]n truth, he is indifferent to all religions.[4]

Judson's perspectives of the queen and her brother, on the other hand, were entirely different. On the one occasion that King Bagyidaw sought to introduce the queen to Judson, she looked away, would pay the foreigner no heed and pulled her husband away after her. She was reported to be avaricious, vindictive, intriguing and bigoted. Her influence over the king was so great that other members of the royal family were convinced she was a sorceress. The queen's only brother had a reputation for being cruel, rapacious and scheming. Haughty and reserved, he usually treated Judson "rather uncourteously". He bore the title "Great Prince", reflective of his eminence, and had the rank of chief Atwinwun. Years later Judson would conclude of him: "He is in the entire confidence of his sister, and through her rules the kingdom."[5]

Beginning in November, between recurring bouts of fever, Judson spent much time and effort trying to locate a suitable property where he could build a *kyoung*. Available properties were scarce due to the large numbers of people who were then moving to the new capital. Once while Judson and Price were at the palace on that line of business, King Bagyidaw again asked the senior missionary about the Burmese individuals in Rangoon who had embraced the Christian religion. "Are they real Burmans?" the emperor inquired. "Do they dress like other Burmans?"

4   Wayland, *Memoir*, vol. 2, pp. 441–2.

5   ibid., pp. 443–4.

In answering the king's questions, Judson happened to mention that he preached every Sunday. "What! in Burman?" asked Bagyidaw in surprise. When the missionary responded in the affirmative, the monarch directed, "Let us hear how you preach."

When Judson hesitated, an Atwinwun repeated the king's order. So Judson began to recite a liturgy he had used in the past that first ascribed glory to God then declared "the commands of the law of the gospel". As he did, "the whole court was profoundly silent". When he stopped another Atwinwun instructed, "Go on." Judson proceeded with several more sentences declaring the perfections of God.

His curiosity satisfied, the monarch interrupted Judson. In the course of the conversation to follow, King Bagyidaw asked, "What do you have to say of Gautama?"

"We all know he was the son of King Thog-dau-dah-nah," Judson responded. "We regard him as a wise man and a great teacher, but do not call him God."

At that juncture Judson was more than a little surprised when an Atwinwun who previously had been none too friendly toward him, suddenly declared, "That is right." The Atwinwun went on to summarize clearly and accurately extensive teaching about God and Christ that Judson had recently shared with him.

Apparently emboldened by this unexpected direction the conversation had taken, Atwinwun Maung Zah added, "Nearly all the world, your majesty, believe in an eternal God – all except Burma and Siam, these little spots!"

King Bagyidaw remained silent for a time. Then after making a few more "desultory inquiries", he stood abruptly and retired from the room.

Not until the first week of January 1823, did Judson succeed in purchasing a modest parcel of ground on which to construct a house. Compared to their mission property in Rangoon, this one was small, being forty yards long and twenty-five yards wide. But it was pleasantly situated on the bank of the river, just outside the city walls, about a mile from the palace. When Judson went to pay the chief Wungyi who had agreed to sell him the property, the official gently declined the generous amount the missionary offered.

> "Understand, teacher," the Wungyi explained, "that we do not give you the entire owning of this ground. We take no recompense, lest it become American territory. We give it to you for your present residence only, and when you go away, we shall take it again."

> "When I go away, my lord," Judson responded, "those at whose expense the house is to be built will desire to place another teacher in my stead."

> "Very well, let him also occupy the place. But when he dies, or when there is no teacher, we will take it."

> "In that case, my lord, take it."

Judson oversaw the construction of a small house on the newly-acquired property. He stationed one of the Christians who had accompanied him from Rangoon to live there and watch over the property in his absence. By then Judson had decided to return to Rangoon to await Ann's arrival. After she came, they would settle in Ava as their new center of operation. There they could continue to bear a Gospel witness to various high-ranking rulers and hope to gain greater toleration for Christianity.

Judson went to the palace on January 24 to inform the king of his imminent departure. There he visited with the current port collector at Rangoon, a Spaniard named Lanciego, who had arrived in Ava the previous evening. Coming up to them, King Bagyidaw asked his royal collector, "What are you talking about?"

> "He is speaking of his return to Rangoon," Lanciego replied.

> "What does he return for? Let him not return. Let them both [Judson and Price] stay together. If one goes away, the other must remain alone, and will be unhappy."

> "He wishes to go for a short time only," explained Lanciego, "to bring his wife, the female teacher, and his goods, not having brought any thing with him this time. And he will return soon."

Bagyidaw then looked at Judson and asked, "Will you, then, return soon?"

"Yes, your Majesty."

"When you come again, is it your intention to remain permanently, or will you go back and forth, as foreigners commonly do?"

"When I come again, it is my intention to remain permanently."

"Very well," concluded the monarch.

21

SUSPECTED AS SPIES
(1823-1824)

Judson left Ava the next day, January 25. By journeying day and night on a small boat, he was able to reach Rangoon in just eight days. Upon arriving, he learned that only three or four Burmese Christians were still in Rangoon. Most of the believers had been forced to flee across the river to escape "the heavy taxations and the illegal harassments of every kind" that Rangoon's new Viceroy was permitting. At the instigation of neighbors, the disciples in the village of Nan-dau-gong, not far from Rangoon, had their houses demolished and their property seized by the government.

Judson received a letter from Ann that she had written while in England, informing him of her intention to continue on to America. Consequently, she could not be expected back in Rangoon for several more months. Given the more threatening circumstances that then prevailed in Rangoon, Judson decided to devote his attention to quietly finishing the translation of the New Testament into Burmese. He completed that work on July 12, one day short of exactly ten years after he and Ann first landed in Burma. In the weeks that followed that monumental accomplishment, he composed a twelve-section summary of the Old Testament and "an abstract of the most important prophecies of the Messiah and his kingdom" from Psalms, Isaiah and other prophets.

Ann finally arrived back in Rangoon on December 5. She was accompanied by a new missionary couple, Jonathan and Deborah Wade of Edinburgh, New York. Two days later Judson wrote to Thomas Baldwin in Boston: "I had the inexpressible happiness of welcoming Mrs. Judson once more to the shores of Burma, on the 5th [of this month]. ... Mr. and Mrs. Wade appear in fine health and spirits, and I am heartily rejoiced at their arrival, just at the present time."[1] In a letter to another acquaintance Judson was delighted to report of his wife with her restored health, "It is the Ann Hasseltine of other days!"[2]

What Judson did not divulge in his correspondence was the deep despondency and even hopelessness of ever seeing his wife again that he had descended into just before her arrival. The couple had been apart twenty-seven and a half months. Due to some letters being lost at sea, there had been no news from America or about Ann for many months. The last correspondence he had received from her had been written nearly fourteen months earlier. Ann wrote of their initial reunion:

> I dare not attempt to describe my feelings as the ship advanced towards the Burman coast. It was late in the evening when the vessel anchored; but the first object which caught my eye, as the boat rowed toward the shore, was Mr. Judson. From long expectation and disappointment, he had acquired such an habitual sadness and dejection of spirit, that it required all my exertion to disperse it, and make him Mr. J. again. He had not heard a word from me for thirteen months (owing to the failure of my letters) and the very day I arrived, he had in despair yielded all hope of my existence![3]

Judson had already made arrangements for a boat to transport them to Ava, so most of Ann's belongings were taken directly to the vessel for loading. The reunited couple made their way to the mission house where they began to catch up on the events of each other's lives for the past two and a quarter years.[4] After Ann arrived in Calcutta on September 22, 1821, it was determined she

1   Ann Judson, *An Account*, p. 269.

2   Warburton, *Eastward!*, p. 87.

3   Ann Judson, *An Account*, p. 272.

4   A more detailed account of Ann's journeys and activities during that time is provided in Knowles, *Memoir of Mrs. Ann H. Judson*, pp. 181–99, 216–17.

would need to return for a time to a colder climate if she hoped to recover from her liver ailment. Due to prohibitive expense she was not able to book passage direct to America but a "pious captain" agreed to transport her to England at a reasonable rate. When she agreed to share a cabin with three children who were also making the voyage, their grateful father insisted on paying her fare.

As it turned out, her seeming detour to England the summer of 1822 was providentially orchestrated. There she was hosted in the London home of Joseph Butterworth, a Methodist and a Member of Parliament, who took a marked interest in the Judsons' mission to Burma. Since the story of their missionary venture was not well known in Britain and since there was considerable interest in it, Butterworth encouraged Ann to compose an account of their work for publication. The same suggestion had been urged upon Ann by acquaintances in Calcutta during her recent stay there.

She sailed from England on August 16, 1822, and arrived in New York September 25. Shortly thereafter she returned to her girlhood home in Bradford, Massachusetts. But the colder climate and excessive number of visitors who constantly came to see her overtaxed and weakened her. Adoniram Judson's brother, Elnathan, now a government surgeon in Baltimore, invited her to spend the winter in that warmer clime with him. She accepted gratefully and arrived at his home on December 3. There she rested in near total seclusion and underwent a further course of salivation.

By March 1823, she finished composing *An Account of the American Baptist Mission to the Burman Empire, In a Series of Letters Addressed to a Gentleman in London*.[5] After seeing the book through the press in "Washington City" (Washington, D.C.), she remained to attend

---

5   The anonymous gentleman was Joseph Butterworth. This first edition of the book contained fourteen letters that Ann had written while sailing from England to America and while staying in the United States. The first edition related the Judsons' missionary ventures up through August 21, 1822, the day the eighteenth Burmese Christian was baptized, shortly before Judson and Price departed for Ava. That edition sold out completely before Ann left America to return to Burma. Butterworth published an expanded second edition of the book in February, 1827. It contained additional materials supplied by Ann detailing the Judsons' experiences in Burma from September, 1822, to March, 1826.

the Baptist Triennial Convention. Ann's health was not yet fully restored, so some encouraged her to spend another year in America or England. But she was determined to return to Burma regardless of the outcome for herself. She embarked from Boston with the Wades on June 22.

After reaching Calcutta on October 19, Ann and the Wades were advised not to proceed to Rangoon because the outbreak of war between Britain and Burma seemed imminent. But they considered it their duty, if opportunity presented itself, to continue on to Burma while trusting God to protect them. Within two weeks Ann spotted a newspaper advertisement of a vessel preparing to leave for Rangoon. The missionary trio immediately booked passage on it and embarked November 15.

On December 12, one week after Ann arrived back in Rangoon, the Judsons left for Ava. They were accompanied on the journey by faithful Maung Ing and by Koo-chill, a Bengali cook Ann had brought from Calcutta. The current and headwinds were strong that time of year, so their progress upriver was slow. The boatmen advanced the vessel, which was fifty feet long and seven feet wide, either by pulling it with ropes while walking along the riverbanks or by pushing it forward with long poles. But the weather was pleasantly cool and dry. Nearly every day the Judsons were able to take a walk along the bank and often through one or more of the villages they were passing. Most of the villagers had never seen a foreign woman before, so they commonly came running from their houses to get a good look at Ann.

The Judsons were not accosted by robbers during their journey. But once while passing through one of the river's many strong rapids, the boat's rudder struck the bottom, which immediately turned the vessel across the current and rolled the craft on its side. For several minutes the Judsons were trapped inside their small cabin that was built on the boat's deck.

Another development that caused the missionary couple far greater alarm and concern was the large number of Burmese troops they began to see moving along the river. At Tsen-pyoo-kywon, one hundred miles below Ava, they passed a massive military encampment, part of the thirty-thousand-member force under the command of Burma's premier general, Maha Bandula. The troops were gathering there for an intended excursion into the western region of Arakan. A Burmese offensive in Arakan would bring Burma into conflict with British interests and military forces in that region.

A bit further upriver the Judsons spotted the golden barge of Bandula himself, surrounded by a fleet of golden war boats. One of those vessels sped across the river and intercepted the missionaries' craft. After explaining that they were Americans rather than English and that they were going to Ava in obedience to the king's command, they were permitted to proceed.

The Judsons anticipated receiving a favorable reception from the emperor and his wife. The last letter Judson had received from Price related that King Bagyidaw had inquired "many times" about Judson's delay in returning to the capital. And the queen had expressed "a strong desire" to see Ann in her foreign clothes. But when the missionary couple reached Ava the last week of January 1824, they discovered that Price had fallen out of favor with the Burmese court and a cloud of suspicion hung over most of the foreigners in the capital. Judson visited the palace two or three times but found the king's manner toward him very different than what it had been before. The queen made no inquiries about Ann and did not intimate a wish to see her.

Two or three weeks after the Judsons' arrival, the entire royal family and most of the government officials returned to Amarapura to prepare for the grand occasion of the king and queen taking up residence in the newly-completed palace at Ava. The Judsons were "a little alarmed" when, soon after settling in the new palace, King Bagyidaw issued an order that no foreigner was to be allowed to enter it except Lanciego, Rangoon's port collector.

The missionary couple continued to live on their boat for two weeks after reaching Ava while an initial home was built for them on the piece of riverfront property Judson had acquired earlier. The dwelling had three small rooms and a veranda. Constructed of boards, it soon proved almost unbearably hot. During the hot season (April through June) in Ava, the temperature frequently climbed to around 110 degrees in the shade, causing the little home to become "heated like an oven".

Each evening Judson led a time of worship for a small number of Burmans who assembled at their home. Every Sunday he preached to a gathering of fifteen or twenty people at Price's new brick house at Sagaing on the other side of the river. Ann immediately opened a school for a few small girls, teaching them reading and sewing. Two of the girls were daughters of the Burmese Christian Maung Shway-bay. He had entrusted his daughters to Ann's care after their mother became "deranged". Ann named the girls Mary and Abby after two of her sisters back home.

As brick homes were the only ones to provide some relief from the excessive heat, Judson procured the necessary materials and hired masons. The workmen progressed rapidly in constructing the home, which was built nearby the existing wooden house. The Judsons intended to move into the brick home after its completion and to use the wooden structure for Ann's school.

On May 23, following a worship service at Price's home, a messenger arrived with the stunning news that British military forces had attacked and captured Rangoon. An army of some 12,000 Burmese soldiers was immediately dispatched from Ava to repel the invasion. The Burmans had no doubt they would defeat the British. They viewed Britain as a small, distant island and the British army, due to its frequent reliance on diplomacy, as weak and cowardly. The Burmans' only fear was that the foreigners, upon hearing of the advance of the Burmese army, would board their ships and flee before they could be taken as slaves. The Judsons watched as countless Burmese war boats, filled with soldiers who sang and danced jubilantly, whisked past their house.

All foreigners in Ava were immediately suspected as potential spies. There must have been spies in Burma, some suggested, who tipped off the British to Bandula's intended offensive in Arakan and who guided them in making a pre-emptive strike at Rangoon. There were three British in Ava at the time: Rodgers, the former Rangoon port collector who was already out of favor with the Burmese court; Henry Gouger, a young merchant in his mid-twenties who had made an immense fortune since arriving in Burma more than a year earlier; and Captain Laird, a Scotsman who served as agent for one of the king's brothers in selling teakwood in Rangoon. It was now discovered that these three had been aware of reports in a Calcutta newspaper, which Laird had recently brought with him to Ava, that the British might move against Rangoon. For failing to report this intelligence to the emperor, all three were "put in confinement" though not imprisoned.

Judson and Price were also "summoned to a court of examination" where they were interrogated concerning all they knew about the British offensive. They were also closely questioned about their communications to foreigners concerning Burmese affairs. The missionaries responded that they had always written to their friends in America but had no correspondence with British military officers or Bengal government officials.

At first they were allowed to return to their homes. But when Burmese officials combed through Gouger's financial records they found that he had transferred substantial sums of money to both Judson and Price. The missionaries had befriended and spent considerable time with Gouger in recent months. On occasion he had acted as banker for Judson and Price by fulfilling money orders (in effect cashing checks) they had received from Bengal. Those funds were then reimbursed to Gouger's bank account in Calcutta. But to the suspicious Burmese this made it look like Judson and Price were in the employ of the British, most likely as spies. When the situation was represented that way to King Bagyidaw he angrily ordered that the "two teachers" were to be arrested immediately.

22

THE DEATH PRISON
(1824-1825)

On Tuesday, June 8, as the Judsons were preparing for dinner, the door of their home suddenly burst open and a government official, accompanied by a dozen Burmese, rushed into the house. "Where is the teacher?" the official demanded. When Judson presented himself, the official declared, "You are called by the king." That was the common pronouncement made when a criminal was placed under arrest.

One of the men accompanying the official had a round circle tattooed on each cheek. Judson and Ann realized immediately that he was a "spotted face" – a branded criminal who served as a prison keeper and executioner. Spotted faces had been treated cruelly and inhumanely for their crimes. Some had the name of their crime branded on their forehead or chest while others had their ears or nose cut off or an eye gouged out. Spotted faces relished the opportunity to similarly inflict cruel suffering on those subjected to their charge.

The spotted face instantly seized Judson and threw him to the ground. Pulling Judson's arms behind his back, he slipped a small hard cord around them above the elbow. "The instrument of torture", as Ann described the cord, was sometimes known to be jerked back so forcefully that blood would spurt from a prisoner's nose or his arms would be dislocated. Ann immediately grabbed the spotted face's arm and cried out, "Stop! I will give you money."

"Take her too," the official commanded. "She also is a foreigner." Judson implored the official to let Ann remain at the house until specific orders had been received concerning her. Somewhat surprisingly, the officer granted his request. Ann later related:

> The scene was now shocking beyond description. The whole neighborhood had collected; the masons at work on the brick house threw down their tools and ran; the little Burman children were screaming and crying; the ... servants stood in amazement at the indignities offered their master; and the hardened executioner, with a kind of hellish joy, drew tight the cords, bound Mr. Judson fast, and dragged him off I knew not whither.[1]

Ann repeatedly begged the spotted face to take the silver and loosen the cord but he spurned her offer and promptly left. She then gave the money to Maung Ing, instructing him to follow the arresting party and to make a further attempt at having Judson's "torture" lessened. A short distance from the house, however, "the unfeeling wretches" again threw Judson to the ground and drew the cord so tight that it nearly prevented him from breathing. Maung Ing followed and watched as Judson was hustled off to the court house where an official read the king's order to place Judson in Ava's dreaded death prison. After Judson was taken there and thrust through the outer gates of the prison complex, Maung Ing returned to tell Ann what he had witnessed.

Upon entering the stockade, Judson found himself in a prison yard. There he was confronted by the spotted face who superintended the prison. The word Loo-that, "Murderer", was branded on his chest. The head spotted face mockingly referred to all the prisoners as his beloved children and demanded that they address him as *Aphe*, "Father". An iron maul was used to rivet three pairs of fetters around Judson's ankles. He was then shoved into the prison building itself. As his eyes tried to adjust to the darkness, he was immediately assailed with an overwhelming stench. He was met by a young, fierce-looking spotted face carrying a club. Though still fettered himself, this apprentice guard supervised the inner prison. He led Judson to a far corner

1   Wayland, *Memoir*, vol. 1, pp. 338–9.

of the prison where he commanded him to lie down and remain silent.

Judson discovered that he had been placed with the three British – Rodgers, Gouger and Laird. All of them were fettered as he was. A short while later Price was thrust into the prison with them. A day or two later they were joined by two other foreigners whom Judson had not previously met – Arakeel, a young Armenian merchant, and Constantine, an older Greek who had leprosy.

The prison consisted of one large room about thirty feet wide by forty feet long. It had only one small bamboo door and no windows but a little light and air filtered in through cracks in the walls. Around fifty prisoners, many of them nearly naked, lay fettered on the teakwood floor. Most of the inmates were men but a few women were interspersed among them. About a dozen men lay with their ankles in a sizeable set of stocks made up of one heavy log lying on another. Various types of refuse were scattered around, decaying and stinking in the oppressive heat. Sweating bodies and lack of proper sanitation further fueled the appalling odor. The prison teemed with vermin.

In the center of the room stood a tripod on which was set a large earthen cup filled with crude petroleum. That simple lamp was trimmed and lit at dusk to provide a feeble, albeit smoky, source of light. As night fell, a long, horizontal bamboo pole suspended from the ceiling was lowered by pulleys. After being passed through the prisoners' fettered legs the pole was again hoisted into the air. The prisoners' feet were raised by the pole until only their shoulders and heads rested on the floor. The young prison guard lighted the pipes of any prisoners who wished to smoke, which virtually everyone did, partly in an attempt to mask the terrible smell.

After dawn the next morning the long bamboo pole was lowered to within a foot of the floor, allowing the blood to circulate again through the prisoners' numbed feet and legs. Around eight o'clock the inmates were led, several at a time, into the prison yard for a brief five minutes to relieve themselves. That was the only time throughout the day they were allowed outside the inner prison.

An hour later the prisoners were fed. Ann had sent Maung Ing (armed with a piece of silver to assure his admittance) to the prison with food for Judson if he were still alive. The other foreigners similarly had food provided for them by their servants. As to the Burmese prisoners:

> Most of the natives had food delivered to them by friends and relatives. The others had to depend on the charity of good-hearted Burmese who, mostly women, considered it an act of virtue to supply food for the prisoners. Especially during festival time huge baskets of rice and *ngapi*, wrapped in large ... plantain leaves, were sent in. But since a week might go by with nothing, the friendless recipients rolled what was left over in the plantain leaves, pinned the rolls together with bamboo slivers, and saved them. In time both food and leaves – the latter accumulating inside the prison in heaps – decayed and added to the stench.[2]

During the daytime prisoners were permitted to converse. But as three in the afternoon neared on Judson's first day in the prison a tense hush fell over the inmates. When a large gong was struck, a pair of spotted faces entered the prison. Each went straight to a prisoner and led him away, without a word, to be executed. All prisoners quickly came to realize that if anyone was to be put to death on any given day it would take place at that hour of the afternoon.

Meanwhile, Ann remained confined under guard in her own home. She begged the local magistrate who supervised her house arrest to allow her to go and appeal to a government official in behalf of the imprisoned missionaries. He refused for fear she would try to escape. On Thursday she sent a message to the governor of the city, who oversaw all prison affairs, asking permission to visit him with a present. He granted her request and received her pleasantly. He explained that he could not have the Americans released from prison or their irons but he could

---

2   Anderson, *To the Golden Shore*, pp. 308–9. Warburton, *Eastward!*, p. 99, describes "ngapi" as "a rather unpalatable preparation of fish".

make their situation more comfortable. He then introduced her to his head officer who oversaw the workings of the prison.

This officer's countenance was so thoroughly forbidding and positively evil that it made Ann shudder. He took her aside and demanded secret payment of 200 ticals (equaling about 130 dollars) and two pieces of fine cloth. In exchange he would have Judson and Price placed in a different prison building where she would be able to provide them with pillows and mats. Ann had brought a generous sum of money from her house but did not have the cloth with her. She readily offered the cash payment but begged the official not to insist on the cloth. After considerable hesitation he agreed, not wanting to let so much money out of his sight.

Having obtained permission from the city governor to enter the prison, Ann next went there. The guards allowed her to meet Judson at the wicket door of the inner prison building but did not permit her to enter it. When her husband, who was habitually fastidious about his personal appearance, hobbled out of the darkness Ann was overwhelmed at his "wretched situation" and "ghastly appearance". For a moment she hid her face in her hands before, through supreme effort, regaining control of her emotions. After only five minutes, the "iron-hearted jailers" ordered Ann to leave. When she protested that the governor himself had given his permission for her to be admitted, the guards retorted harshly, "Depart or we will pull you out!" She returned the two miles to her home with an anguished heart.

Her efforts, however, did have the desired effect. That evening the missionaries and other foreigners, each of whom was required to pay the same amount Ann had, were removed from the common prison and confined in an open shed in the prison yard. Though Ann was not permitted to enter the prison compound again for several days, she was allowed to supply the missionaries and other foreigners with food, pillows and mats on which to sleep.

Not long after Judson was placed in the death prison, Henry Gouger's property, valued at 50,000 rupees (then equaling 25,000 American dollars or 5,000 British pounds), was seized and taken to the palace. The three officers who carried out that action then stopped to politely inform Ann they would return the following day to search the Judsons' house. Grateful for the advance notice, she hid "as many little articles as possible together with considerable silver". She knew they would be needed to avoid starvation should the war be protracted. Some of those items, along with the sole copy of Judson's Burmese translation of the New Testament, she carefully wrapped in a bundle and buried somewhere outside the house.[3] The next morning the three officials returned, accompanied by forty or fifty attendants. They took some silver Ann had left in a trunk along with whatever seemed valuable to them, including "every thing new or curious". The officials merely recorded a list of the Judsons' clothes, books, medicines and furnishings to report to the king.

For the next ten days Ann sought admission to the prison but was daily refused. One of the first things Judson asked about when she was finally able to visit him concerned the New Testament manuscript. He was relieved to learn that she had hidden it but they both realized it might soon perish if left in the ground. Where could it be kept safe? They settled on a daring plan. Ann sewed the precious manuscript into another pillow that she brought to Judson. She was careful to make the pillow so hard, lumpy and unattractive that even an avaricious jailer would not be tempted to confiscate it. Thus each night in that Burman death prison Judson rested his head on the only copy of the Burmese New Testament in the entire world.

Nearly every day for the next seven months Ann visited various government officials and royal family members to appeal for their help. Some haughtily and callously spurned her. But several others privately assisted her with articles of food and used their influence at the palace to alleviate the impression that the Judsons were in some way involved in the present war. Ann's exertions throughout that period were even more remarkable in light of the fact that she was again carrying a child. She had become pregnant several weeks before Judson was imprisoned.

3   The exact location was not recorded. Anderson, *To the Golden Shore*, p. 315, states it was in the garden while Warburton, *Eastward!*, p. 102, has it under the house.

By July of 1824, within the first two months after British forces captured Rangoon, the Burmese army, led by a pair of generals, twice suffered crushing defeats while trying to regain control of the port city. Meanwhile General Bandula had enjoyed a degree of success in Arakan. He captured 300 sepoys and had them sent to Ava. In addition, he seized a cache of two or three thousand British rifles. King Bagyidaw became convinced that Bandula was the only general who understood how to fight foreigners, so recalled him to Ava prior to sending him to Rangoon.

According to Ann, Bandula was "in fact, while at Ava, the acting king". Sometime in September she determined to appeal to the general for the release of the missionaries. Judson secretly wrote a petition in which he set forth every factor that might lead the commander to grant him and Price their liberty. "With fear and trembling" Ann approached Bandula, who was surrounded by "a crowd of flatterers", with the petition. He indicated he would think about the matter and invited her to return in a day or two for his decision. But when she did she was informed that the general was very busy with preparations for his campaign at Rangoon. After he had expelled the British from Burma he would release the foreign prisoners in Ava. After that disappointment the Judsons relinquished all hope that the missionaries would be released before the war ended. But Ann continued to visit various officials, especially the city governor, in an effort to make Judson and Price's situation in prison more tolerable.

Each day in the death prison involved enduring nearly insupportable living conditions as well as degrading and oftentimes harsh treatment. Not infrequently prisoners witnessed one or another of their fellow inmates being subject to horrifying forms of torture and even death. Once a prisoner was dragged into the prison yard at midnight and put to death by having his back broken. On another occasion, a young slave who was being starved to death was judged to be making too much noise. An infuriated guard wearing heavy boots stomped and clubbed him to death. Several British soldiers were imprisoned and all but one died of starvation or related digestive complications.

Under such trying circumstances, nerves sometimes frayed and tempers occasionally flared. Judson normally slept next to

Price. The doctor habitually slept on his side with his knees pulled up by his chest. He frequently had nightmares, during which he would forcefully thrust out his legs. After Price's fettered legs had slammed into Judson's back two or three times in the same night, the latter finally erupted, "Brother Price, you are a public nuisance! I insist on your sleeping as other people do." Price took offense, protesting that his thrashing was involuntary, and a heated argument ensued. Gouger quickly stepped in and offered to sleep between them. After that, whenever Price's legs banged into Gouger, the merchant awoke the missionary and smoked a pipe with him. Then he had Price roll over on his other side so the next blow would be directed at Rodgers!

Once Ann sought to provide her husband with a pleasant surprise by preparing him a mincemeat pie like those they had enjoyed back home in America. With the help of Maung Ing and Moo-chil the cook, buffalo meat, plantains and other ingredients were purchased and used in the making of the pie. But when Maung Ing carried the special meal to Judson, the sight of the mince pie immediately flooded his mind with memories of family, friends and former happy times back home. Those recollections compared to their present bitter circumstances proved too much to bear. Judson rested his head on his knees and wept. Then handing the pie to the startled Gouger, who had been observing all this, Judson went off to be by himself.

Some months after Judson and his fellow foreigners were imprisoned, Ann's continued intercessions with various officials resulted in their being permitted to spend the daytime hours in a group of tiny huts along the prison yard's outer stockade. Each hut was about six feet long by five feet wide and barely high enough for a man to stand upright under the peaked center of the roof. But the small bamboo shelters were a welcome relief from the inner prison, where the foreign prisoners were still detained each night. Ann was sometimes allowed to spend two or three hours with Judson in his hut.

General Bandula left Ava in October 1824, and by the following month was encamped outside Rangoon with an army of 60,000 soldiers.[4] The total British force at Rangoon amounted to less

4   The summary of this conflict is taken from Anderson, *To the Golden Shore*, pp. 329–30.

than 4,000, including 1,300 Europeans and 2,500 sepoys. The British had transformed the Shwe Dagon Pagoda into a fortress, complete with twenty mounted guns. On December 1 Bandula launched his main attack on the British army's strongest position at the pagoda but was decisively repulsed. A few days later British forces stormed the Burmese position. Bandula's army scattered and fled. He and his remaining force of only 7,000 men retreated upriver to Danubyu.

Ann gave birth to a daughter, whom she named Maria Elizabeth Butterworth, on January 26, 1825. Twenty days later Ann brought Maria to the prison for the first time. Judson was relieved and delighted to see his wife and baby doing well. Even the ruthless spotted faces crowded around, amazed at the first white child they had ever seen. In his mind Judson composed some verses in honor of his newborn daughter, though it would still be a long time before he could write them down:

Sleep, darling infant, sleep,
   Hushed on thy mother's breast;
Let no rude sound of clanking chains
   Disturb thy balmy rest.

Sleep, darling infant, sleep;
   Blest that thou canst not know
The pangs that rend thy parents' hearts,
   The keenness of their woe.

Sleep, darling infant, sleep;
   May heaven its blessings shed,
In rich profusion, soft and sweet,
   On thine unconscious head![5]

5   The entire poem, consisting of twenty-four stanzas, is recorded in Wayland, *Memoir*, vol. 1, pp. 380–3.

23

FURTHER CONFINEMENT AND FREEDOM
(1825-1826)

On Tuesday, March 1, Judson and the other foreign prisoners were, without warning, led one at a time from their huts along the stockade to the granite block in the middle of the prison yard. Two additional sets of fetters were fastened around their legs and they were placed back in the inner prison building without either pillow or mat.

Judson overheard some of the Burmese prisoners say the foreigners were to be killed. He could hear the spotted faces sharpening their knives out in the prison yard and felt relieved that at least he would not be strangled to death. Three o'clock in the morning was named as the time they were to be executed. As that hour drew near, first Judson then each of the foreigners quietly prayed aloud, some of them for the very first time. But the appointed hour came and went without incident. When dawn came they had renewed hope they would be permitted to go on living.

Ann learned of this concerning development on Wednesday morning but was not able to gain an audience with the city governor until that evening. Through the months he had done as much as he dared to assist her and the foreign prisoners. Now, seeing Ann's distress, the old governor actually broke down and wept himself. He revealed that three times he had refused to carry out the order of the queen's powerful brother to assassinate all the foreign prisoners privately. The governor had got them out of sight in the hope that they might be forgotten about and their lives spared. But with the hot season approaching and over one hundred prisoners presently crowded into the prison, the foreigners were in a distressing situation. In an effort to provide them with a little relief, the governor had the foreign prisoners placed just inside the inner prison's wicket door and allowed them to eat their rice in the prison yard.

On April 1 Bandula was killed at Danubyu by an exploding British shell. Two months earlier a high-ranking official, called a Pakan Wun, was placed in Ava's death prison under suspicion of treason. He had been next in command under Bandula during one of Burma's earlier military conquests. Now the Pakan Wun sent word to King Bagyidaw from prison, offering himself as the commander of a new army which he would personally enlist. Apparently concluding he had no better options, the monarch accepted the Pakan Wun's proposal, released him from prison and set him over the military. The Pakan Wun, who despised and hated all foreigners, immediately had Lanciego, the Spaniard, arrested and thrown in the death prison.

Around the time of Bandula's death, Judson came down with a fever. Ann saw him weakening and feared for his life. She besieged the governor with requests that Judson be released from the inner prison. The official finally gave that order as well as his permission for Ann to enter the prison yard at any time to care for her husband. She again provided Judson with a small bamboo enclosure, a mat and a pillow. Judson was able to exchange this newer pillow for the old, hard one that a spotted face had seized weeks earlier. The jailer had no idea of the old pillow's precious contents and was amazed that the American wanted it back.

On May 2 Ann brought Judson his breakfast but discovered he did not feel well enough to eat it. As they were conversing, she suddenly received an urgent summons from the city governor, asking her to come at once. The Judsons were alarmed, but when Ann arrived at the governor's residence she was relieved to learn he merely wanted to consult with her about his watch. He was very pleasant and detained her quite some time. When at last she was able to excuse herself, she started back to the prison. She had gone only a short distance when a servant came running, his face registering evident concern. "All the white prisoners are carried away!" he blurted out.

Ann hastened back to the governor who, now with grave demeanor, admitted, "Yes, Lady Teacher, I heard of it, but I did not want to tell you." He had learned of the intended removal of the foreign prisoners only a short time before it was to happen and had summoned her to his residence in an effort to shield her from witnessing the distressing events as they unfolded.

Ann had no sooner left the prison yard to respond to the governor's summons, when a spotted face rushed over and hurried Judson to the granite block. There the jailer stripped off all Judson's clothes except his shirt and trousers and struck off his fetters. A rope was tied around his waist and, along with the other foreign prisoners who had been similarly bound, he was led off to the court house. The prisoners were tied in pairs and each twosome was guarded by a spotted face who carried a spear and held the rope that bound them. The group of prisoners and guards, all on foot, was under the charge of a commander on horseback. At first, upon leaving the court house, the prisoners thought they were being led out to the execution ground. But soon they were directed, instead, onto the road leading to Amarapura, the former capital, six miles from Ava.

It was nearing noon and the scorching sun beat down on them mercilessly. The soles of their bare feet quickly began to blister from walking on the searing sand and stones. As those blisters burst, each step on the sharp gravel and burning sand became excruciating. Legs that had been fettered and lacked adequate exercise from the eleven months they had been in the death prison now strained to support them on the rigorous trek. Constantine collapsed after they had gone less than a mile. After being beaten and prodded by a spear, he managed to get up and continue on a little further. When he again fell, this time totally helpless, the guards put him in a cart. Tragically, he died before they reached Amarapura.

As they crossed a bridge over the Mootangai, a tributary to the Irrawaddy, Judson, overcome with hopelessness and anguish, "ardently longed" to end his suffering by throwing himself thirty feet down into the river below. But "the sin attached to such an act"[1] along with the fact that he was tethered to Laird led him to resist the temptation. Judson was weak from fever and from having eaten nothing that day. For a time Laird allowed Judson to lean on his shoulder for support, until the Scotchman's own strength began to give out under the extra strain. Presently Gouger's Bengali servant overtook them. Tearing his turban in two, the servant gave half to Gouger and half to Judson so they could wrap their raw, bleeding feet. He then helped to support Judson and in that way they made it through to Amarapura.

The prisoners were supposed to be taken four miles further that day, to a rural prison at Oung-pen-la (alternatively spelled Aungbinle), but they simply could not manage it. All of them collapsed to the ground, some in a shed, others under a cart. The commander's wife took pity on them and provided them with fruit. After a breakfast of rice the next morning they were all loaded onto carts for the final miles to their destination.

Their new prison was a dilapidated wooden structure with no door and part of the roof fallen in. It was located about a quarter mile from the village of Oung-pen-la and was surrounded by a grassy plain that had once been a rice field. The space underneath the prison's elevated floor was completely filled with kindling, which was stacked there to prevent the prisoners from escaping through the rotted floor. Each prisoner was placed in one pair of ankle fetters.

Ann arrived at the run-down prison at dusk. That morning she had set out from Ava with baby Maria, the two Burmese children, Mary and Abby, and Koo-chil the cook. Maung Ing and a Bengalese servant had stayed behind to watch over the house at Ava. Ann's small company rented a boat to transport them to Amarapura and from there hired a cart to take them on to Oung-pen-la. Ann was refused permission to build a small shelter near the prison where she and her charges could stay. Seeing her desperate plight, one of the jailers took pity on her. His own two-room dwelling was nearby. He and his small family lived in one

---

1   Knowles, *Memoir of Mrs. Ann H. Judson*, p. 246.

room while the other was half full of grain. Ann's group could stay in the latter. That cheerless, crowded room would be their home for the next six months.

At the jail the prisoners had been placed in stocks. After nightfall their feet were hoisted into the air, leaving the inmates in the same upside-down position they had experienced each night in the death prison. Only here at Oung-pen-la mosquitoes swarmed in off nearby fields and settled on the prisoners' raw, unprotected feet. After a time, mercifully, the guards lowered the stocks enough for the captives to fan away the insects with their hands.

The next day Mary came down with a fever and broke out with smallpox. Ann inoculated her own children and those of the jailer whose small house they shared. Maria, like Mary, developed a serious case of the disease but the other children were largely spared. Just as Mary and Maria were recovering, Ann fell ill, likely with dysentery. Leaving Koo-chil to care for the children, she went back to Ava for medicine and better food. Upon her return to Oung-pen-la, she collapsed at the jailer's hut. When Koo-chil saw how emaciated she had become he burst into tears. For the next few days he cared for Ann and provided Judson's food. Without his help, it's likely they would have perished.

Ann was too weak to breastfeed Maria. Koh-bai, the head jailer, permitted Judson, under guard, to take Maria into the village each day so she could be nursed by various Burmese women. Occasionally Judson was allowed to spend an hour or two with his family at their tiny abode.

Once in the middle of the night the prisoners heard strange loud roars approaching the stockade. The next morning they discovered a huge lioness confined in a cage mounted on wheels. At first the prisoners feared one or more of them might be fed to the beast. But the lioness was allowed to slowly starve. After it had died and was buried, Judson considered the large, airy cage with its good floor and roof. He requested and was granted permission to occupy the cage as his private dwelling. From then on he was locked inside the cage each night rather than in the prison's stocks.

Through Koh-bai the prisoners learned that the Pakan Wun who now commanded Burma's military had been born in Oung-pen-la. The village's name could be roughly translated "Field of Victory". A rumor reached the prison:

> When the Pakan Wun was ready to proceed against the British, he planned to assemble his headquarters staff at Oung-pen-la, where the white prisoners were to be offered up to propitiate the spirits of war by being buried alive at the head of the army. Planting their bodies in the Field of Victory could result only in a harvest of victory.[2]

A few days before the sacrifice was reportedly to take place, Gouger's servant arrived from Ava with the news that the Pakan Wun was dead. The commander had overstepped his bounds with King Bagyidaw, leading the monarch to believe the general was plotting to seize his throne. The Pakan Wun was beaten, dragged through Ava to the place of execution where he was trampled to death by elephants.

One day in August a group of Burmese officials arrived at the prison to have the foreigners transported by cart to Amarapura. There at the house of the city governor they were each placed in a separate room and told to translate a document offering terms of peace from Sir Archibald Campbell, commander of the British forces. By that time the British army had relocated further upriver to Prome, about halfway between Rangoon and Ava. This translation incident pointed out the need both Burmese and British officials (who could not speak, read or write each other's language) would have for capable interpreters when it came time to negotiate an end to the war. The prisoners were taken back to Oung-pen-la, Burmese officials rejected Campbell's offer of peace and the conflict dragged on.

Finally on the evening of November 4 an order came from the palace in Ava that Judson was to be released. The next morning his fetters were removed. The jailers at first said they would not allow Ann to leave as the government orders did not include her

2 Anderson, *To the Golden Shore*, pp. 349–50.

name. But after the Judsons agreed to leave behind a large load of food that had just arrived for Ann from Ava, they were allowed to depart with their children and Koo-chil.

From Amarapura Judson was taken to the hall of justice in Ava while his family and Koo-chil hired a boat to transport them to the Judsons' home on the river. The morning of November 7 Judson and Ann were permitted a brief visit together at their home. Judson was being taken immediately on a boat three days downriver to the Burmese military camp at Maloun. There he was to translate documents and otherwise assist in dealing with the British.

During that brief visit Judson received thrilling intelligence from Maung Ing. The day Judson was taken to Oung-pen-la, Maung Ing visited Ava's death prison to see if any of the missionary's possessions might be salvaged. He discovered that Judson's old, hard pillow had been cast aside and was able to retrieve it. Providentially the translation of the Burmese New Testament had been preserved and was safely in the possession of the faithful Maung Ing.

By the time Judson reached Maloun, where he was placed under guard in a bamboo hut, he had developed a fever. Documents were brought to him for translation but his fever worsened and for a day or two he became delirious. But when the fever broke and he regained consciousness, he found his mind clearer and more active than it had been since his initial imprisonment near the beginning of the war.

Judson remained at Maloun until the latter half of December when he was transported back to Ava. There he was placed in a shed at the courthouse to await his anticipated transfer back to the Oung-pen-la prison. Maung Ing located him there a day later. He informed Judson that Ann had sent him to appeal to the governor of the North Gate, who had been friendly toward them in the past, that Judson not be sent back to Oung-pen-la. Maung Ing also reported that Little Maria was well. Not until after Maung Ing left did Judson fully realize that when he had asked about Ann's welfare the Burman had been somewhat evasive. That realization left Judson ill at ease.

The governor of the North Gate promptly presented a petition to the highest court for Judson's release and even offered himself as security. Judson was freed on the final day of 1825 and hurried to his home. When he entered it he saw a corpulent Burmese woman squatting beside a pan of coals and holding a dirty, scrawny baby on her knees. He failed to realize that the pathetic looking child was his own daughter, Maria. Hurrying into the bedroom, he found Ann:

> Across the foot of the bed, as though she had fallen there, lay a human object that, at the first glance, was scarcely more recognizable than his child. The face was of a ghastly paleness, the features sharp, and the whole form shrunken almost to the last degree of emaciation. The glossy black curls had all been shorn from the finely-shaped head, which was now covered by a close-fitting cotton cap, of the coarsest and ... not the cleanest kind.[3]

Two weeks after Judson had left for Maloun, Ann was attacked by the dreaded spotted fever, cerebral spinal meningitis. Fortunately, that same day a Burmese wet nurse offered to care for Maria. Ann soon lost consciousness and fell into a raging fever for at least two weeks. Just at that time Price was released from the Oung-men-la prison to assist with another translation project, and succeeded in obtaining permission to visit Ann at the mission house. He thought it likely she would live only a few more hours but as a last resort ordered her hair shaved and blisters applied to her head and feet. Nearly a week later she began to regain consciousness and slowly she improved. When Judson returned, she was not yet able to sit up.

A few days later Judson and Ann moved into the house of the governor of the North Gate, where they had been invited to reside. They stayed there the remainder of their time in Ava. They would not have been able to continue living in their home beside the Irrawady because the Burmese military soon seized riverfront properties to prepare for the anticipated arrival of British forces that were again moving upriver toward the capital.

3   Wayland, *Memoir*, vol. 1, p. 394.

The Burmese government had rejected a proposed treaty that had been forged while Judson was at Maloun. The treaty stipulated that Burma must pay an indemnity of a crore of rupees, worth one million British pounds. After receipt of this, British forces would withdraw from all but four coastal provinces of Burma, thus leaving most of the country to be governed by the Burmese. But Burman officials simply could not believe that the British would keep their promise. As Gouger reported: "Such an unheard-of thing as conquering a country and then restoring it was incredible! Measuring British faith and honor by their own standard, they concluded the intention was first to impoverish them, and then to march on the Capital."[4] When this treaty proposal was spurned, British forces advanced up the Irrawaddy and routed the Burmese army at Maloun.

Price and a recently captured British officer were sent late in January to see if the British would offer easier peace terms. The only alteration Sir Archibald Campbell and his commissioners offered was that the indemnity could be paid in four installments, with the first quarter needing to be paid within twelve days. In addition, all foreign prisoners in the hands of the Burmese were to be released immediately to the British. Adoniram, Ann and Maria Judson were specifically named among those to be freed. Upon hearing this, King Bagyidaw objected of the Judsons, "They are not English, they are my people. They shall not go."

Burma mounted one final attempt at repelling the foreign army. A hastily-assembled force of 15,000 Burmese soldiers were put to flight by 900 British troops at Pagan, one of the country's ancient capitals downriver from Ava. At last the queen asserted her dominance by insisting that the first instalment of the indemnity must be paid immediately. Even gold and silver vases, pitchers and dishes from the palace were melted down to help raise the necessary funds. Enough silver bars to meet the initial installment were loaded onto boats, ready to be taken downriver.

On Tuesday, February 21, 1826, the first installment, along with all the foreigners who desired to depart, headed down

4   Anderson, *To the Golden Shore*, pp. 357–8.

the river in six or eight boats. Aboard one of those vessels were Adoniram, Ann and Maria Judson, Maria's wet nurse, Mary and Abby, Maung Ing and Koo-chil. As they floated quietly along the river that cool, moonlit night, Maria slept contentedly in Judson's arms and Ann rested against his side. Judson and Ann were thrilled and unspeakably relieved to be free again after twenty-one months of imprisonment and misery.

The Judsons spent two weeks at General Campbell's headquarters at Yandabo, about forty miles south of Ava. The commander and his men treated them with great respect and exceptional kindness. Ann afterward wrote to Elnathan Judson, "I presume to say, that no persons on earth were ever happier, than we were during the fortnight we passed at the English camp."[5]

5   Knowles, *Memoir of Mrs. Ann H. Judson*, pp. 259–60.

24

BEREAVEMENTS
(1826-1827)

On March 6 the Judsons left Yandabo aboard the gunboat *Irrawaddy*. They arrived in Rangoon fifteen days later, having been away from it for two and a quarter years. The Burmese Christians at Rangoon had been scattered during the war. Maung Shway-bay was still at the mission house, which was standing but in quite a ruined condition. Maung Ing returned with the Judsons from Ava. At Prome, midway between Ava and Rangoon, they met Mah Men-lay and her sister-in-law Mah Doke, both of whom had been among their earlier converts. Those women immediately returned with the Judsons to Rangoon. Besides those four, no other Burmese Christians were still in the area.

At the outset of the recent war, as the British fleet approached Rangoon, George Hough and Jonathan Wade were imprisoned and nearly executed. But when the foreign vessels began bombarding the town, their captors fled in terror and the missionaries were rescued by British soldiers. The Houghs and Wades went to Calcutta for the duration of the war, intending to return to Burma when hostilities ceased.

Jonathan Price had decided to remain in King Bagyidaw's service in Ava. His medical skill gave him favor with the Burmese court and he was frequently able to discuss Christianity with high-ranking officials. A number of boys, sons of prominent government officials, came under his tutelage. But in less than two years he died of tuberculosis.

Burmese officials had begged Judson to remain in royal service in Ava and promised him rich compensation if he would. The

British likewise offered him a salary equivalent to 3,000 dollars (nearly three times his annual salary as a missionary) to continue in government service as a translator. He declined both those offers.

According to the provisions of the treaty made at Yandabo, Rangoon was left under Burmese rule. The coastal provinces of Arakan in the west and Tenasserim in the southeast came under British control. John Crawfurd, a distinguished orientalist, was appointed civil commissioner under the British Governor General, Lord Amherst. Crawfurd was given the responsibilities of determining a suitable site for a new British capital for Tenasserim and of negotiating a commercial treaty between the East India Company and the Burmese government.

The Judsons supposed (rightly so, as it turned out) that no more religious toleration would be experienced in Rangoon than had been the case before the war. Knowing a more stable base of missionary operation would be beneficial, Judson enthusiastically accepted Crawfurd's invitation to be part of the exploratory journey to determine the location of the new British capital. The peninsula at the mouth of the Salween River, at the upper end of Tenasserim, was selected. There, on April 6, the British flag was hoisted, a salute of guns fired and the place was named Amherst in honor of the Governor General. Judson concluded the ceremony by reading Isaiah 60 and offering prayer.

Back in Rangoon, Judson had the mission's old zayat dismantled and the boards shipped to Amherst for use in building a new residence there. The four faithful Burmese Christians – Maung Shway-bay, Maung Ing, Mah Men-lay and Mah Doke – went ahead of the Judsons to establish dwellings in Amherst. The last two days of June and the first two days of July Judson accompanied Ann and Maria on their short journey aboard the *Phoenix* from Rangoon to Amherst, where he helped to get them settled. Captain Fenwick, the civil superintendent of Amherst, vacated his own new house in order to provide Ann with it as a temporary residence. By that time the infant settlement consisted of about fifty houses, most of them Burmese, as well as the British military post.

Just three days after their arrival, Judson departed on the *Phoenix* to return to Rangoon. He had reluctantly agreed to accompany Crawfurd in traveling to Ava to forge a commercial agreement. At first Judson had declined the civil commissioner's request for assistance in that matter. But when Crawfurd promised to attempt to have a provision guaranteeing religious liberty for all Burmans included in the treaty, Judson considered it his duty to help promote that prospect and acquiesced. Ann steadfastly affirmed him in that decision. Judson further related of their optimistic outlook at that time:

> I left ... my beloved wife, at Amherst, the 5th of July last, in good health, comfortably situated, happy in being out of the reach of our savage oppressors, and animated in prospect of a field of missionary labor opening under the auspices of British protection. ... Our parting was much less painful than many others had been. We had been preserved through so many trials and vicissitudes, that a separation of three or four months, attended with no hazards to either party, seemed a light thing. We parted, therefore, with cheerful hearts, confident of a speedy reunion, and indulging fond anticipations of future years of domestic happiness.[1]

The compensation Judson was to receive from the British government for his service at the Treaty of Yandabo and as part of Crawfurd's embassy to Ava would be considerable. Judson was well aware that the entire situation raised perplexing questions, fraught with potential perils, concerning what type of employment missionaries should be involved in and what they were to do with the income they received from opportunities other than their regular missionary work. Over twenty-five years later Francis Wayland summarized Judson's convictions and recommendations in this situation:

> He conceived that the whole time of the missionary was to be consecrated to the work of propagating the gospel; that the board at home became responsible for his whole support,

1   Wayland, *Memoir*, vol. 1, p. 417.

and therefore that he could not, with propriety, enter into any other engagements without their consent, or, in special emergencies, the consent of his associates [on the field]; and that whatever remuneration should accrue from his services was to be considered not his own property, but the property of the board. He saw also that a decision on this subject would become more universally binding, if it were proposed by him on the eve of entering upon an engagement which would be both honorable and lucrative. With these views he wrote immediately to the board, and suggested the rules on this subject by which this and all future cases should be decided. They were adopted in this country without alteration, and remain unchanged to the present moment.[2]

As it turned out, for his services to the British government Judson received payment of 5,200 rupees. He received an additional 2,000 rupees in gifts given to him while in Ava. He turned over that entire amount, equaling some 3,600 American dollars, to the mission.

Crawfurd's sizeable delegation did not leave Rangoon for Ava until September 1. After arriving there at the end of the month, they encountered one delay after another in seeking to negotiate an agreement with the Burmese government. They did not succeed in gaining an audience with King Bagyidaw until October 20. The Burmese officials appeared to have little interest in making a commercial treaty. To Judson's deep disappointment, from the outset it became apparent that there was no hope of having a religious toleration clause included as part of any agreement that might be reached.

At the end of October Judson received a letter Ann had written on September 14:

> I have this day moved into the new house, and for the first time since we were broken up at Ava, feel myself at home.

2   ibid. p. 406. Judson wrote the mission board on June 10, 1826, while in Rangoon, before the Crawfurd embassy left for Ava. A complete copy of Judson's letter and proposed "Regulations of the Managing Committee of the Board of Missions of the American Baptist Convention" is recorded, ibid., pp. 407–10.

The house is large and convenient, and if you were here, I should feel quite happy. The native population is increasing fast, and things wear a rather favorable aspect. Maung Ing's school has commenced with ten scholars, and more are expected. Poor little Maria is still feeble. Sometimes I hope she is getting better; then again she declines to her former weakness. When I ask her where Papa is, she always starts up and points toward the sea. ... Pray take care of yourself, particularly as it regards the intermittent fever at Ava. May God preserve and bless you, and restore you in safety to your new and old home, is the prayer of your affectionate Ann.[3]

A correspondence from Captain Fenwick, dated October 18, arrived the middle of November and related:

I can hardly think it right to tell you, that Mrs. Judson has had an attack of fever, as before this reaches you, she will, I sincerely trust, be quite well, as it has not been so severe as to reduce her. This was occasioned by too close attendance on the child. However, her cares have been rewarded in a most extraordinary manner, as the poor baby, at one time, was so reduced, that no rational hope could be entertained of its recovery; but at present a most favorable change has taken place, and she has improved wonderfully. Mrs. Judson had no fever last night, so that the intermission is now complete.[4]

Another letter from Amherst reached Judson on November 24. This one had been penned by Captain Fenwick's assistant on October 26. The envelope bore a black seal and the man who delivered it to Judson stated as he handed it to him, "I am sorry to inform you of the death of your child." Opening the letter, Judson was stunned and overwhelmed by the even more grievous news it brought him:

---

3 ibid., p. 418. The "new house" of which Ann spoke was their own home, the construction of which she oversaw after arriving at Amherst.

4 ibid.

My Dear Sir: To one who has suffered so much and with such exemplary fortitude, there needs but little preface to tell a tale of distress. It were cruel indeed to torture you with doubt and suspense. To sum up the unhappy tidings in a few words – *Mrs. Judson is no more.*

Early in the month she was attacked with a most violent fever. From the first she felt a strong presentiment that she would not recover, and on the 24th about eight in the evening, she expired. Dr R[ichardson] was quite assiduous in his attentions, both as friend and physician. Captain F. procured her the services of a European woman from the 45th regiment, and be assured all was done, that could be done, to comfort her in her sufferings, and to smooth the passage to the grave. We all feel deeply the loss of this excellent lady, whose shortness of residence among us was yet sufficiently long, to impress us with a deep sense of her worth and virtues. It was not until about the 20th that Dr R. began seriously to suspect danger. Before that period, the fever had abated at intervals; but its last approach baffled all medical skill. On the morning of the 23rd, Mrs. Judson spoke for the last time. The disease had then completed its conquest, and from that time up to the moment of dissolution, she lay nearly motionless, and apparently quite insensible. Yesterday morning, I assisted in the last melancholy office of putting her mortal remains in the coffin; and in the evening her funeral was attended by all the European officers now resident here. We have buried her near the spot where she first landed; and I have put up a small rude fence around the grave to protect it from incautious intrusions.[5]

When Judson wrote Ann's mother on December 7 to share the news of her daughter's passing he spoke briefly of the mixture of wrenching grief and Christian consolation he had been experiencing:

5   ibid., p. 419. Of the condolence that the bearer of this letter expressed to the missionary as he handed it to him, Judson afterward remarked, "I know not whether this was a mistake on his part, or kindly intended to prepare my mind for the real intelligence" (ibid., p. 418).

I will not trouble you, my dear mother, with an account of my own private feelings – the bitter, heart-rending anguish, which for some days would admit of no mitigation, and the comfort which the gospel subsequently afforded – the gospel of Jesus Christ, which brings life and immortality to light [2 Tim. 1:10].[6]

In ending the letter that he wrote to his sister, Amelia, that same day, Judson similarly stated:

We will not, then, mourn as those who have no hope; "for if we believe that Jesus died and rose again, even so them also which sleep in Jesus will God bring with him" [1 Thess. 4:14].

Yet, notwithstanding the consolations of the gospel, grief claims its right, and tears their course; and I must subscribe myself

Your brother, in the deepest sorrow,

A. Judson, Jr.[7]

After settling for a lackluster commercial agreement, Crawfurd's embassy left Ava on December 13. When the delegation arrived at Rangoon they found it besieged by Peguan rebels from the district some fifty miles west of Rangoon. Climbing atop a high roof inside Rangoon's stockade, Judson could see that the old mission house, outside the city wall, had been all but destroyed. Only its posts and part of the roof remained.

At last, on January 24, 1827, Judson arrived back at Amherst. There he was welcomed by Jonathan and Deborah Wade who had returned from Calcutta and settled in Amherst about a month after Ann's death. The Wades had at once assumed care of Maria and moved into the mission house built under Ann's supervision. Judson returned to Amherst just two days before Maria's second birthday. Due to her recurring illnesses, she was a puny, feeble child. When Judson, weeping, at first went to take her in his arms she did not recognize him and drew back in fear. Wade then

6   ibid., p. 420.
7   ibid., pp. 415–16.

showed him to the site where Ann's body had been buried under the shade of a large hopia (hope) tree. The tree was nearby the mission house and garden and overlooked the sea.

From the Burmese Christians living in Amherst, Judson learned a few more details about the closing days of Ann's life. She had sometimes stated to the indigenous believers, "The teacher is long in coming and the new missionaries are long in coming. I must die alone and leave my little one. But as it is the will of God, I acquiesce in his will. I am not afraid of death but I am afraid I shall not be able to bear these pains. Tell the teacher that the disease was most violent and I could not write. Tell him how I suffered and died. Tell him all that you see. And take care of the house and things until he returns."[8]

Even after Ann had stopped taking notice of other things, she continued to call Maria to herself and to charge the nurse to be kind to the child until her father returned. Throughout Ann's last two days she lay "almost senseless and motionless" on one side with her head resting on her arm and her eyes closed. Mercifully, she was free from pain that final pair of days. When her attention was roused by repeated queries about how she was doing, she responded, "I feel quite well, only very weak." At the end, after uttering a single exclamation of distress in Burmese, she quietly stopped breathing. She was only thirty-six years of age.

Upon returning to Amherst, Judson discovered that the new settlement, not yet one year old, had fallen into decline. That was due to the fact that General Campbell had chosen to establish his headquarters about twenty-five miles up the Salween River at Maulmain (modern Moulmein). Though Maulmain lacked Amherst's harbor for large vessels, it was determined to be a more strategic military location. Most of the Burmese emigrants had settled there.

The first week of February Judson traveled to Maulmain "to pay my respects to Sir Archibald Campbell, and also to obtain an interview with Dr R[ichardson]". Of the latter visit Judson reported:

8   ibid., pp. 421–2.

He has the character of a kind, attentive, and skillful practitioner; and his communications to me have been rather consoling. I am now convinced that every thing possible was done, and that, had I been present myself, I could not have essentially contributed to avert the fatal termination of the disease. The doctor was with her twice a day, and frequently spent the greater part of the night by her side. ... The doctor is decidedly of opinion that the fatal termination of the fever is not to be ascribed to the localities of the new settlement, but chiefly to the weakness of her constitution, occasioned by the severe privations and long-protracted sufferings she endured at Ava.[9]

On Sunday, January 28, four days after returning to Amherst, Judson led a worship service in Burmese for the first time in two and a half years. About twenty people were present. In the weeks that followed a number of "hopeful inquirers" began attending the Lord's Day services. Judson and his missionary colleagues met each evening for worship. The Burmese believers joined them for this Tuesday and Friday evenings.

The missionaries were pleased when Maung Ing, on his own initiative, expressed his desire to undertake "a missionary excursion" to Tavoy, 150 miles down the Tenasserim coast. After being officially appointed as "a preacher of the gospel and teacher of the Christian religion", he set out at the end of February. In the months that followed he ministered both at Tavoy and his former residence of Mergui, 130 miles further down the coast.

For years Judson had sought to govern his personal spiritual life and ministry with a high degree of discipline. Nearly eight years earlier – on April 4, 1819, the Sunday that Judson first began ministering publicly at the missionary zayat in Rangoon – he adopted a set of personal "rules" by which to live:

1.   Be diligent in secret prayer, every morning and evening.

2.   Never spend a moment in mere idleness.

9   ibid., p. 422.

3. Restrain natural appetites within the bounds of temperance and purity. "Keep thyself pure."

4. Suppress every emotion of anger and ill will.

5. Undertake nothing from motives of ambition, or love of fame.

6. Never do that which, at the moment, appears to be displeasing to God.

7. Seek opportunities of making some sacrifice for the good of others, especially of believers, provided the sacrifice is not inconsistent with some duty.

8. Endeavor to rejoice in every loss and suffering incurred for Christ's sake and the gospel's, remembering that though, like death, they are not to be willfully incurred, yet, like death, they are great gain.

While in Ava as part of Crawfurd's embassy, Judson had, on Sunday, October 29, 1826, "re-adopted" those rules and drafted an additional set of "minor rules" to further regulate his behavior:

1. Rise with the sun.

2. Read a certain portion of Burman every day, Sundays excepted.

3. Have the Scriptures and some devotional book in constant reading.

4. Read no book in English that has not a devotional tendency.

5. Suppress every unclean *thought* and *look*.

Now at Amherst, Judson rededicated himself to continue to live, with God's help, by both those sets of high standards:

Revised and re-adopted all the above rules, particularly the second of the first class ["Never spend a moment in mere idleness"], on Sunday, March 11, 1827.

> God grant me grace to keep the above rules, and ever live to
> his glory, for Jesus Christ's sake.[10]

During March and April the Amherst missionaries were kept busy clearing trees and brush from the mission premises. They also completed construction of a mat house for the girls' school which Ann had begun and Deborah Wade was continuing. When Maria developed a serious bowel complaint that April, Judson and Mrs. Wade took her to Dr Richardson in Maulmain. Unfortunately, the physician could do little for the child and her condition was still precarious when she was brought back to Amherst on April 20.

A new missionary family, George and Sarah Boardman and their six-month-old daughter Sarah Ann, had arrived at Amherst while Judson was away at Maulmain. The joy over their arrival was overshadowed by Maria's continued rapid decline. She died in the middle of the afternoon on Tuesday, April 24. She was two years and three months old. George Boardman built her small coffin. The following morning her body was buried beside her mother's grave beneath the hopia tree.

Early the next month the Boardmans went up to Maulmain so that Sarah could consult Dr Richardson about health concerns. Judson visited them there May 7. Sir Archibald Campbell offered them ground for a mission station and they selected a site about a mile south of the British military post and beside the large native town that had sprung up there. After returning briefly to Amherst, the Boardmans settled in Maulmain later that month.

Judson, still in Amherst, invested most of his time during the month of June in revising his translation of the Burmese New Testament. He also prepared an astronomical and a geographical catechism for use in their Burman schools. On July 5 he started a Burmese translation of the book of Psalms.

That same month Judson received word that his father had died the previous November. The senior Judson was seventy-four years of age at the time of his death. The missionary son had doubtless been gratified when, ten years earlier, his father had come to share his baptismal convictions and his denominational

---

10   ibid., pp. 322–3. Bracketed words are the present author's clarifications.

affiliation. But now his sense of grief and desolation were likely deepened by this awareness of the loss of a third close family member to death within just a few months' time.

25

A NEW BEGINNING
(1827-1828)

In its first year as a settlement Amherst had grown into a town of 1,200 inhabitants. Maulmain, meanwhile, had mushroomed into a city of 20,000. On Saturday, August 11, 1827, Judson returned to visit the Boardmans in Maulmain. Impressed with the potential he saw there, he soon decided to remain more permanently.

Maulmain stretched out for two miles along the eastern bank of the Salween. On the other side of that broad, swift river was the Burman province of Martaban. A long range of hills, dotted here and there with pagodas, lay behind Maulmain while far off to the seaward side the high hills of Ballou Island (modern Bilugyun) were visible.

The Boardmans had erected a house in the center of the mission property. That parcel of ground was approximately 400 yards long and 250 yards deep. Sir Archibald Campbell had offered them a site on the British military post but they chose to settle next to the Burmese community. They were the only Europeans living outside the British cantonments. In that isolated location they were exposed to the danger of tigers roaming the surrounding woods and bands of robbers from across the river in Martaban. Shortly after the Boardmans arrived in Maulmain in fact, thieves had entered their home and rifled through their belongings while the missionary family slept soundly, oblivious to the danger they were in. Nearly all their possessions of any significant value were stolen on that occasion. After that Sir Archibald posted a guard of sepoys at the mission house each night. Subsequently one of those guards was mauled, thankfully not seriously, by a wild beast on the veranda of their home.

In September the missionaries decided to focus their entire missionary effort in Maulmain rather than trying to maintain the struggling ministry in declining Amherst. A home was built for Judson and the Wades to share. Maung Ing came from Mergui in October. The Wades arrived from Amherst in the middle of November. They brought with them Maung Shway-bay, eleven students from Deborah Wade's girls' school and two orphan boys. A few other Burmese families connected with the mission in Amherst made their way to Maulmain in the days that followed. Two Sundays later, on November 25, Judson reported:

> We have arranged a large room in the front of the house, in the manner of a zayat, and today set up worship, in the old Rangoon fashion; and a busy day it has been. About seventy persons, great and small, attended worship in the forenoon; after which twenty or thirty women followed Mrs. Wade into another room, and listened to her instructions. In the evening we had about thirty; and after worship some animated conversation ensued, in which Mah Doke's husband, Maung Dwah, came out very decidedly on the side of Christianity. Maung Ing has a good degree of missionary spirit, and affords much assistance in the work.[1]

The second Sunday in December a man named Maung Noo attended evening worship at the mission house and "paid uncommon attention" to the truths that were shared. Two days later he came in both the morning and evening to inquire further about spiritual matters. After the evening worship service, he asked with earnestness, "What shall I do to be saved?"

"Believe on the Lord Jesus Christ."

"I do believe. I do believe. This religion is right. I have been all wrong. What shall I now do?"

"If you have begun to believe, let your faith increase. Attend worship. Keep the Lord's Day. Become the Savior's servant. Do all His will. Give yourself, soul and body, into His hands.

1   Wayland, *Memoir*, vol. 1, p. 439.

Will you do so?"

"I will, I will. But I do not know all His will."

"Read the Scriptures."

"I can read Talaing only, not Burman."

"Come then, and we will read to you. Come every day to worship, and at all times of day, and we will instruct you."

Judson had become aware that "a large majority of the population of these parts", like Maung Noo, could not read themselves but understood the Scriptures in Burmese when they heard them read. He recruited Maung Shway-bay to open a "reading zayat" at which he would read and explain the scriptures to anyone who cared to stop and listen. A "shed" was erected for that purpose not far from the mission house and Maung Shway-bay began dividing his time daily between that ministry and teaching at the girls' school. At the reading zayat he sometimes had opportunity to proclaim the Gospel to "a great many".

Around that same time Jonathan Wade opened a preaching zayat about half a mile south of the mission house on the main road leading from Maulmain. He went there regularly after breakfast to spend the day in ministry. Maung Ing devoted himself to full-time evangelistic work, assisting Wade at the preaching zayat as well as proclaiming the Gospel at various locations around the city. As 1827 drew to a close, George Boardman started a school for boys.

On Friday, January 11, 1828, Judson opened and commenced daily ministry at another preaching zayat, this one in a heavily populated part of town two and a half miles north of the mission residence. He later described this zayat in its setting as "a little shed, projecting into one of the dirtiest, noisiest public streets of the place".[2] Judson was soon able to record the names of several individuals who seemed to be seriously inquiring about the Christian faith. In the opening quarter of the year, six Burmese were baptized after publicly professing faith in Christ.

Encouraging reports began arriving from Rangoon. On March 20 Judson reported, "We hear that our old friend Maung

2   ibid., p. 466.

Thah-a [one of the early Burmese converts] is now in Rangoon, and that there are several of the old inquirers who listen to his instructions." One month later Judson related: "Received a letter from Maung Thah-a, of Rangoon, stating the names of thirteen men and three women who are disciples of Jesus, 'but secretly, for fear of the Jews' [John 19:38]."[3]

"With the cordial approbation of all the members of the mission", George and Sarah Boardman left Maulmain for Tavoy on March 29. They took with them four schoolboys and a fifty-year-old Karen named Ko Tha Byu.[4] The Karens were a peaceful, migratory tribe primarily from the mountainous jungles of lower Burma. They lived largely in isolation and were considered uncivilized and "as untamable as the wild cow of the mountains". As a young man Tha Byu became a robber and murderer who, by his own estimate, was involved in at least thirty murders. During the recent war he went to Rangoon where he ended up in debt and was put up for sale as a slave. Maung Shway-bay learned of his plight and paid off his debt, thus becoming his temporary master. When Maung Shway-bay moved to Amherst, he took Ko Tha Byu with him. There he came under the Christian teaching of the missionaries and was converted. In Tavoy he proved an invaluable assistant to the Boardmans in reaching his fellow Karens.

At some point in 1828 (the exact time has not been preserved) Judson took a decisive step intended to strengthen his missionary endeavors. Francis Wayland explains:

> From the close of the war to his removal to Maulmain, Dr Judson had been intimately associated with many of the civil and military officers of the British government. When the seat of the chief commissioner was established at that place [Maulmain], this intimacy for some time continued; and he was frequently the honored and cherished guest of the gentlemen to whom the care of the ceded provinces was

3   ibid., pp. 451–2.

4   " 'Ko' is a title applied to mature men, just as 'Maung' is applied to younger men" (Anderson, *To the Golden Shore*, p. 386).

committed. He, however, soon perceived that engagements of this kind, from being mere relaxation, began to engross too much of that time the whole of which he had devoted exclusively to the Burmans. In a matter of duty, he was incapable of doing a thing by halves. He immediately resolved to cut off every thing like fashionable intercourse with his English friends – a resolution to which he steadfastly adhered to the close of his life. The first person to whom he communicated his intention of never again dining out of the mission was Sir Archibald Campbell himself. The announcement created of course a variety of impressions in the small society of Maulmain. Some regretted that so agreeable a man should become a mere devotee; others believed that sorrow for the loss of his wife had made him mad; while others, who understood him better, honored what they considered his self-immolation in a good cause; and, on the whole, he was regarded with a sort of reverential sympathy. ... No one enjoyed intelligent and cultivated society more keenly than he; and he surrendered it only in obedience to those principles by which he designed to govern his life. He was, however, always punctilious in the performance of those simpler civilities which required no sacrifice of precious time; and he was on intimate terms with nearly all the civil commissioners stationed on that coast, standing to most of them in the relation of a confidential adviser.[5]

Edward Judson further observes of this decision by his father:

It was not because he was unendowed with social sensibility that he so cut himself off from the State or conventional dinner and from a fashionable intercourse with Sir Archibald Campbell, and other cultivated Englishmen, as to incur the stigma of being called "odd." ... On the contrary, one who knew him most intimately says that "Perhaps his most remarkable characteristic to a superficial observer was the extent and thoroughly genial nature of his sociableness."

5   Wayland, *Memoir*, vol. 1, pp. 446–7.

"His ready humor," Mrs. [Emily] Judson writes, "his aptness at illustration, his free flow of generous, gentlemanly feeling made his conversation peculiarly brilliant and attractive, and such interchanges of thought and feeling were his delight."[6]

Judson made another decision, this one in May 1828, that doubtless struck many as unusual. Five years earlier, Brown University, his alma mater, had conferred on him a Doctor of Divinity degree. Now he wrote the editor of the *American Baptist Magazine*:

> I beg to be allowed the privilege of requesting my correspondents and friends, through the medium of your magazine, no longer to apply to my name the title which was conferred on me in the year 1823 by the corporation of Brown University, and which, with all deference and respect for that honorable body, I hereby resign.

> Nearly three years elapsed before I was informed of the honor done me, and two years more have been suffered to pass, partly from the groundless idea that it was too late to decline the honor, and partly through fear of doing what might seem to reflect on those who have taken a different course, or be liable to the charge of affected singularity, or superstitious preciseness. But I am now convinced that the commands of Christ and the general spirit of the Gospel are paramount to all prudential considerations, and I only regret that I have so long delayed to make this communication.[7]

That same month and again three months later, Judson reached and initiated two significant financial decisions that reflected his willingness to make marked material sacrifices in order to help promote the cause of missions. On May 31 he wrote the corresponding secretary of his mission board:

6   Edward Judson, *The Life of Adoniram Judson*, p. 322.

7   ibid., p. 320. "The commands of Christ" referenced by Judson likely included passages such as Matthew 23:8–12. "Later he gave up his objection to the use of this degree [and title], as is evident from the fact that his wife Emily often used it, not only in referring to him in letters to others, but even in correspondence with Judson himself" (Warburton, *Eastward!*, p. 117).

When I left America, I brought with me a considerable sum of money, the avails of my own earnings, and the gifts of my relatives and personal friends. This money has been accumulating, at interest for many years, under the management of a kind friend of the mission, and occasionally receiving accessions from other quarters, particularly at the close of the late war, until it amounts to twelve thousand rupees [some six thousand dollars]. I now beg leave to present it to the board, or rather to Him "who loved us, and washed us from our sins in his own blood" [Rev. 1:5]. I am taking measures to have the money paid to the agent of the board, and the payment will, I trust, be effected by the end of this year.[8]

On September 1 Judson and Wade issued a bold motivational challenge to their mission board and the Baptist pastors of their homeland. They had been told that the Baptist churches in America were sending out so few missionaries due to lack of financial support rather than a shortage of willing missionary candidates. Judson and Wade proposed to have one twentieth of their annual salary designated to help meet that need. They "respectfully suggest[ed]" that Baptist pastors in the United States do the same and indicated that when one hundred ministers had agreed to do so they would "relinquish a second twentieth of our allowance, that is, one tenth of the whole".

Several weeks earlier, on Monday, July 28, Judson had related in his ministry journal that five individuals had been baptized the previous day. One of those was a twenty-eight-year-old former Hindu named "McDonald". A number of years earlier he had renounced that religion and been christened by an English clergyman on the Madras coast. Subsequently, however, he encountered contrary spiritual teaching that "unsettled his mind, and reduced him to a state of darkness and perplexity for several years." Recently he appeared at the zayat where he heard and immediately embraced the clear Gospel truths. "He brought with him, yesterday," Judson reported, "a large bundle, which,

8   Wayland, *Memoir*, vol. 1, pp. 453–4.

he informed us, contained the tracts and publications which had given him so much trouble; and when he was baptized, he buried them, with his former character, in the watery grave."[9]

On that same occasion Judson commented on Ko Myat-kyau who had been baptized the previous March. Nearly fifty years old, Ko Myat-kyau was a brother of the foremost native chief in the region and was of the "most respectable rank in society". He possessed a sharp mind and was eloquent and energetic. For years he had diligently sought the truth in Buddhism, Hinduism and Islam. When he became a Christian his wife filed for divorce and his brother "publicly declared that, if he had the power of life and death, he would instantly wipe out with his blood the disgrace brought upon the family." Ko Myat-kyau responded with exemplary Christian meekness, forbearance and love, with the result that, "His wife has relinquished her suit, and begins to listen to the word; his brother has become silent; and some few of the relatives begin to speak in our favor."[10]

Mah-ree, Maung Shway-bay's twelve-year-old daughter (whom Ann had renamed Mary in Ava), and another pupil from the girls' school, Mee Aa, were among those baptized the last Sunday of July.[11] "These two girls," remarked Judson, "are the first fruits of an incipient revival in the school, similar to those glorious revivals which distinguish our beloved native land."[12] Three more girls – Mee Tan-goung, Mee Nen-mah and Mee Nen-yay – were baptized the following Sunday, August 3.

Early the next morning, before any of the missionaries or students were awake, Mee Tan-goung's mother came to the school zayat and ordered her oldest daughter, who was also a student, to let her in. Upon gaining entrance, she started beating Mee Tan-goung, then fled. Returning a short while later and finding Mee Tan-goung outside, the mother struck her on the head with an umbrella and threatened to sell her as a slave. The furious mother

9 ibid., pp. 454–5.

10 ibid., p. 456.

11 "Mee" was a title designating a girl, "Mah" a young woman and "May" an old woman.

12 Wayland, *Memoir*, vol. 1, pp. 455–6.

then went to the town marketplace where she raged that her daughter "had entered a religion which prevented her lying and cheating, so that she was quite lost to all purposes of trade"![13]

Later that same morning, Mee Nen-mah's mother arrived at the school and verbally accosted Deborah Wade with "as bad language as she dared". She then ran into the schoolroom, grabbed her daughter by the hair and dragged her outside toward a woodpile. When Deborah intervened, the seething mother went off, threatening vengeance. That evening the three newly-baptized girls were taken into the mission house lest their infuriated relatives should try to assault them during the night.

Mee Aa, who had been baptized with Mah-ree on July 27, greatly feared the imminent arrival of her mother from Amherst. Judson had "no doubt" the mother would immediately take the daughter away and use every means within her power to make her renounce Christianity. A few days later Mee Aa came trembling to Deborah Wade with the news that her mother had just arrived at the landing-place. When the girl asked what she should do she was told to go meet her mother and to pray as she went.

Mee Aa had already been praying incessantly for her mother and it soon became apparent that God had heard her prayers and softened her mother's heart. When the mother heard that her daughter had actually been baptized, she merely made a strange face, as if she were choking, and asked, "It was *so*, was it not? I hear that some quite die under the operation." Mah Kai, the mother, "soon settled down among us [the Christians], drank in the truth from her daughter's lips and then followed her example."[14] Having professed faith in Christ, Mah Kai was later baptized on October 6. That same day Mah Lan, wife of the faithful evangelist Maung Ing, was also baptized.

For the first nine months of 1828 Judson had laid aside Bible translation work in order to give himself full-time to evangelistic ministry. Early in October, however, assisted by Wade, he began

13   ibid., p. 458.
14   ibid., pp. 458, 461.

devoting considerable time to revising his earlier translation of the Burmese New Testament.

On the second anniversary of Ann's passing, October 24, Judson moved into a cottage he had built back in the woods, behind the house he had been sharing with the Wades. Dubbed by Judson as "the Hermitage", the cottage provided him with increased privacy and solitude for study and devotional exercises. Judson often ate by himself in his cottage while at other times he shared meals with the Wades at their home. That first night in the Hermitage, Judson wrote a letter to Ann's sisters, Mary and Abigail Hasseltine, in Bradford:

> You see from the date that it is the second anniversary of the triumph of death over all my hopes of earthly bliss. I have this day moved into a small cottage, which I have built in the woods, away from the haunts of men. It proves a stormy evening, and the desolation around me accords with the desolate state of my own mind, where grief for the dear departed combines with sorrow for present sin, and my tears flow at the same time over the forsaken grave of my love and over the loathsome sepulchre of my own heart.[15]

Perhaps Judson desired or even needed to be alone with his thoughts and grief that evening. But doubtless the isolated, cheerless circumstances surrounding him that night contributed to the deepening of his despondent thoughts and feelings on that occasion.

One of three converts baptized in Maulmain the final Sunday of November was a former Hindu named Ram Sammy, meaning "god Ram". Of his being christened as Matthew, Judson explained: "We have not been in the habit of changing Burman names, as they are generally destitute of any bad signification; but the names of the Hindus are sometimes (as in the present case) utterly abominable, and require to be cast off, with all their other abominations."[16] Two Sundays later, December 14, another former

15   ibid., pp. 482–3.
16   ibid., p. 462.

Hindu was baptized and christened Thomas. He proved to be the thirtieth and final baptized convert in Maulmain that year.

26

An Excessive Tendency
(1829)

Early in November 1828, Ko Thah-a, the Rangoon evangelist, arrived at Maulmain to confer with the missionaries about how to proceed with the Christians in his area who desired to be baptized. He was fifty-seven years old, possessed "steadiness and weight of character", and exhibited both humility and devotedness in his ministry endeavors. He also had considerable knowledge of Burmese literature which Judson noted he could use to advantage in "taking up arms against the religion of his country". On the first Lord's Day of 1829 Judson reported with evident delight:

> We commence this year with an auspicious event – the ordination of Ko Thah-a as pastor of the church in Rangoon ... He has been so evidently called of God to the ministry that we have not felt at liberty to hesitate or deliberate about the matter. But, if it had been left to us to select one of all the converts to be the first Christian pastor among his countrymen, Ko Thah-a is the man we should have chosen.[1]

Ko Thah-a returned to Rangoon one week later.

In a letter that Judson penned to his mission board at the end of January, he revealed significant perspectives and desires he had concerning his ongoing Bible translation work:

> My ideas of translating are very different from those of some missionaries,[2] better men than myself, but mistaken,

1 Wayland, *Memoir*, vol. 1, p. 463.

2 Doubtless Judson was referring, among others, to Carey and his Serampore associates.

I think, in this particular. I consider it the work of a man's whole life to procure a *really good* translation of even the New Testament in an untried language. ... I would only say that, in many instances, missionary labor has been dreadfully misdirected, and hundreds of thousands [of pounds or dollars] most foolishly thrown away. As to us, we wish to proceed, *slow* and *sure*, and to see to it that whatever we do, in regard to the inspired word, is *well done*. About four months ago, being convinced that the New Testament, notwithstanding all my labor upon it, was still in a very imperfect state, brother Wade and myself undertook a thorough revision. We have now done one quarter of it; and I have some hope that by the time the printer and press arrive,[3] we shall be able to warrant the whole. After that, we propose to work and rework at the precious book of Psalms, until we can venture to warrant that also. And so, God willing, and giving us life and strength, we hope to go on. But we beg still to be allowed to feel, that our great work is to preach the gospel *viva voce*,[4] and build up the glorious kingdom of Christ among this people. To this end, we consider a good translation of the New Testament, the Psalms, and some other portions of the Old Testament, essentially necessary – the whole very desirable.[5]

In the months that followed, even as Judson continued on with his translation ministry, a number of things that he wrote and did manifested a definite tendency toward quietism[6] at this juncture in his Christian life. The influence of both Roman Catholic and

---

3   As it turned out, the anticipated printer did not arrive till nearly a year later.

4   A Latin phrase meaning literally "with living voice" but most often translated "by word of mouth".

5   Wayland, *Memoir*, vol. 1, p. 467.

6   Webster defines quietism as "a system of religious mysticism teaching that perfection and spiritual peace are attained by annihilation of the will and passive absorption in contemplation of God and divine things": *Webster's New Collegiate Dictionary* (Springfield, MA: Merriam, 1976), pp. 947–8.

Protestant writers stood behind that inclination.[7] Several other factors, such as Judson's increased isolation and his ongoing efforts at processing deepest personal grief, likely contributed to this becoming a pronounced emphasis in his life at this time.[8] The excessive tendency proved to be only temporary and moderated in the months and years that followed.

In February Judson wrote a pamphlet entitled "The Threefold Cord". It was written in English and was apparently intended for an English-speaking rather than a Burmese audience.[9] The Threefold Cord was Judson's attempt to provide professing Christians with a system of spiritual disciplines by which they could "grow in grace, and attain the perfect love and enjoyment of God". The three strands in Judson's cord were "Secret Prayer", "Self-denial" and "Doing good". Of the first, Judson encouraged believers:

7   Wayland notes Judson's allusions in several of his letters to "the works of Lady Guyon and some other distinguished quietists of the Catholic church" (Wayland, *Memoir*, vol. 1, p. 534). Edward Judson writes: "Before proceeding directly to consider Mr. Judson's life in Maulmain, it may be well to describe a peculiar phase of his mental and spiritual experience, which has been termed Guyonism. He seemed at one time to be inclined to embrace the mystical tenets of Thomas à Kempis, Fenelon, and Madame Guyon, and it was feared that he was leaning toward those monkish austerities which belong peculiarly to the spirit of the Roman Church" (*The Life of Adoniram Judson*, p. 303). Edward Judson also stated that his father "trod the perilous pathway leading toward monastic asceticism", albeit with "cautious and stealthy steps" (ibid.). The son further described his father's life during this period as manifesting "traces of a morbid inclination toward the monastic quietism of the Romish Church" (ibid. p. 305). Protestant works that influenced Judson at this time included Robert Leighton's *Rules and Instructions for a Holy Life* and William Law's *A Practical Treatise upon Christian Perfection* and *A Serious Call to a Devout and Holy Life*.

8   Wayland, *Memoir*, vol. 1, pp. 534–41, provides a helpful analysis of this uncharacteristic period in Judson's life.

9   "The Threefold Cord" is reproduced in full in Wayland, *Memoir*, vol. 2, pp. 459–66, and Edward Judson, *The Life of Adoniram Judson*, pp. 571–7. Anderson wrongly asserts that Judson composed the work "primarily for the guidance of repentant Burmans" (Anderson, *To the Golden Shore*, p. 389). There is no record that "The Threefold Cord" was ever used among the Burmese. In his Autobiographical Record of Dates and Events, Adoniram Judson himself recorded that he wrote the pamphlet in English in February, 1829 (Edward Judson, *The Life of Adoniram Judson*, p. 565). A letter that Judson wrote in December, 1829, to a former acquaintance of Ann's in London, reveals that "The Threefold Cord" had been printed in Bengal; Judson enclosed a copy of the pamphlet with his letter to the Englishwoman (Wayland, *Memoir*, vol. 1, pp. 481–2).

Arrange thy affairs, if possible, so that thou canst leisurely devote two or three hours every day, not merely to devotional exercises [including Bible reading], but to the very act of secret prayer and communion with God. Endeavor, seven times a day, to withdraw from business and company, and lift up thy soul to God in private retirement.[10]

Concerning self-denial, Judson urged: "be content with the plainest diet ... fast often ... dress in coarse and poor apparel; discard all finery ... Occupy a poor habitation ... Allow no amusements ... Get rid of the encumbrance of worldly property; sell what thou hast, and give to the poor." [11] Of the third cord, Judson expanded with the commendable outlook of a broadminded evangelical missionary:

Do good – all the good in thy power – of every sort – and to every person. Regard every human being as thine own brother; look with eyes of love on every one thou meetest, and hope that he will be thy loving and beloved companion in the bright world above. Rejoice in every opportunity of doing him any good, either of a temporal or spiritual kind. Comfort him in trouble; relieve his wants; instruct his ignorance; enlighten his darkness; warn him of his danger; show him the way of salvation; persuade and constrain him to become thy fellow-traveler in that blessed way. ...

... As a true follower of Christ, seek not thine own profit, but the profit of many, that they may be saved. Since Christ has suffered, that whosoever believeth on him should not perish, but have eternal life [John 3:16], extend thy good wishes to earth's remotest bounds; and wherever a human being exists, let thy prayers and thine efforts combine to bring down eternal blessings on his beloved soul. But let the members of the household of faith, whatever be their language, country, or religious denomination, share in thy warmest love. ...[12]

10 Wayland, *Memoir*, vol. 2, p. 459.

11 ibid., p. 461.

12 ibid., pp. 464–5.

On Sunday, February 22, Maung Ing was ordained as pastor of the tiny Christian congregation that existed in Amherst. He and his wife, Mah Lan, soon joined three other believers living there. One month later three British soldiers in Maulmain who had come to faith in Christ were baptized. Of them Judson revealed:

> They have been in the habit of attending certain evening meetings, in which we have lately indulged ourselves a little, though averse to every interruption to native work. These soldiers we have not received into the Maulmain church, but have recognized them to be the Baptist church in his majesty's 45th regiment.[13]

That same month of March Judson composed a new Burmese tract entitled "The Golden Balance". It contrasted Buddhism and Christianity, pointing out the incomparable superiority of the latter. Judson had no way of foreseeing that the tract would have a significant influence in Burma for over a century.[14]

The middle of that month Judson received a letter from his sister, Abigail, concerning the settling of the family inheritance from their father. Her letter had crossed in the mail with one he had written more than a year earlier. In that earlier correspondence he had provided a quitclaim to the family inheritance, so his portion could be used to support his mother and sister. Along with the quitclaim, he had sent Abigail twenty dollars, perhaps to help cover legal costs relative to settling the estate. She offered to return the money but Judson instructed her to keep it with an interesting stipulation:

> In regard to the twenty dollars, I have no occasion for the money, and present it to you, my sister, in remembrance of

13 Wayland, *Memoir*, vol. 1, p. 470.
14 An English translation of "The Golden Balance" is recorded in Wayland, *Memoir*, vol. 2, pp. 448–57. More than one hundred years after it was originally written, the tract was still in use in revised form. Twentieth-century missionary A.C. Hanna testified of "The Golden Balance": "It has probably more powerfully influenced the thinking of the Burmese people, and caused them to see the insufficiency of Buddhism, than anything else ever written by a foreigner" (Warburton, *Eastward!*, p. 158).

that handful of money which you gave me when we parted in Boston for the last time. But I give it on the express condition that you appropriate part of it to purchase for yourself the *Life of Lady Guyon* ... And I hope you will read it diligently, and endeavor to imitate that most excellent saint, so far as she was right. Two other books that I would particularly recommend to you are Law's *Serious Call*, and his *Treatise on Christian Perfection*.[15]

Though Judson obviously esteemed Madame Guyon highly, his qualified encouragement to imitate her "so far as she was right" shows he did not indiscriminately accept everything she taught by word or example. Guyon and Law's influence is discernible in a set of resolutions that Judson put to paper less than two months later, on May 14:

1. Observe the seven seasons of secret prayer every day.

2. "Set a watch ... before my mouth, and keep the door of my lips." [Ps. 141:3]

3. See the hand of God in all events, and thereby become reconciled to his dispensations.

4. Embrace every opportunity of exercising kind feelings, and doing good to others, especially to the household of faith. [Gal. 6:10]

5. Consult the internal monitor on every occasion, and instantly comply with its dictates.

6. Believe in the doctrine of perfect sanctification attainable in this life.[16]

It would appear from the last resolution that at this time Judson believed sinless perfection could be attained on earth. But such a perspective was only temporary and, of course, never fulfilled this side of heaven. Francis Wayland testifies of Judson: "The

15 Wayland, *Memoir*, vol. 1, p. 473.
16 ibid., p. 474.

more he examined his own heart, and tested his own motives, the farther did he seem removed from that perfect holiness to which he aspired. He did not, I believe, ever conceive himself to have arrived at the perfection which he sought ..."[17]

Before that month of May ended Judson received another letter from Abigail, this one indicating that his original quitclaim had not proved legally acceptable. Judson reiterated his ready willingness to provide the necessary legal document but this time attached a stringent condition to his doing so:

> I am rather glad, however, that the first did not answer, because I have now a request to make which I doubt whether you would comply with, if I did not make your compliance a condition of my returning you the said instrument. My request is, that you will entirely destroy all my old letters which are in your and mother's hands, unless it be three or four of the later ones, which you may wish to keep as mementoes.[18]

Wayland offers the following explanation of what led Judson to take such a drastic step:

> In youth, he had cherished an intense desire for reputation; and even his father had cultivated, rather than repressed, this infirmity. The severe dispensations which had been meted out to him had, in a great measure, corrected this propensity; but there yet lingered within him a desire for posthumous reputation. To mortify this weakness, he caused all his correspondence, so far as it was in his power, to be destroyed ...[19]

That same motivation also led Judson to commit to the flames an official letter of thanks for his services that Sir Archibald Campbell had written to him along with "several other documents of a similar character."

17   ibid., p. 538.
18   ibid., p. 475.
19   ibid., p. 536.

Though the dates have not been preserved, on two other occasions during this general period of Judson's life he exhibited highly unusual behavior. The first instance, in fact, qualifies as bizarre. Sometime after moving into The Hermitage he sought to conquer a long-standing fear through a morbid means. Wayland explains:

> He had suffered much from a peculiar form of dread of death – not the separation of the soul from the body, or any doubt of ultimate acceptance with God, but a nervous shrinking from decay and corruption – the mildewing and moldering in dark, damp, silent ghastliness. He believed this to be the result of pride and self-love; and, in order to mortify and subdue it, he had a grave dug, and would sit by the verge of it, and look into it, imagining how each feature and limb would appear days, months, and years after he had lain there.[20]

At another time, having become worn out through his diligent translation work, Judson trekked over the nearby hills and far back into the jungle to seek out a secluded spot where he could find spiritual refreshment. He discovered a deserted, moss-covered pagoda where not even the most devout Buddhists went any longer for fear of the tigers that roamed the remote area. Sitting down under the jungle trees, Judson spent the day reading his Bible, meditating and praying. Late in the day he returned to The Hermitage.

When he made his way back to the same secluded spot the next morning he was surprised to find a rude bamboo seat placed there for him as well as some of the tree branches woven into a canopy for his head. Though Judson never learned the identity of his benefactor, Ko Dwah, a devoted deacon in the Maulmain church, had set aside his own fear of tigers, secretly followed the missionary to the jungle retreat and provided these rustic comforts for him. Judson returned to the spot daily for forty days, taking nothing but his Bible and a little rice for his food. The Maulmain Christians considered that isolated region of the

20 ibid., pp. 536–7.

jungle so dangerous that they regarded Judson's preservation through the forty days he spent there as a miracle on a par with Daniel's life being spared in the lions' den!

Due to his self-imposed austerities, Judson found himself able to recommend to his mission board a further reduction in his salary, beyond what he had proposed the previous year. On June 19, 1829, he wrote the corresponding secretary:

> I propose, from this date, to lessen my usual allowance by one quarter, finding, from experience, that my present mode of living will admit the retrenchment; this arrangement not to interfere with the proposals made under date of September last, concerning the one twentieth and one tenth.[21]

Throughout the first five months of that year Judson was "chiefly engaged in going forward with the revision of the New Testament" while the Wades carried out evangelistic ministry in Maulmain. Two former Hindus and ten Burmans professed faith and were baptized during that time. At the end of May Judson reported:

> Truth is spreading slowly on every side; prejudices are weakening; opposition is growing more violent in some parts, and in other parts it seems subsiding. The husband of Mah Kyan [she had been baptized January 25], who tore his infant from the mother's breast, and pursued his poor wife through the street with a great knife, has become a lamb. He has made a comfortable place in his house for Mrs. Wade to sit and receive company, to the great annoyance of other opposers in that quarter.[22]

Also among the recently-baptized believers were Ko Man-poke and his wife, Mah Tee. Of them Judson testified:

> Ko Man-poke ..., a steady, excellent old man, [is] a considerable scholar in the Talaing language. He has translated all our Burmese tracts into the Talaing, and will

21 ibid., p. 475.
22 ibid., p. 470.

perhaps be encouraged to go on with some parts of the New Testament. We consider him as one of the most valuable accessions to the cause that we have ever received; and his wife stands almost unrivalled among the female converts. She always accompanies Mrs. Wade, and is of inestimable use in explaining things in the Talaing to those who cannot well understand the Burmese; and that is the case with a great part of the population of British Pegu.[23]

Not everyone who professed faith and requested baptism was affirmed and accepted into the church. Judson revealed on the first Sunday in June, "Several applications for baptism have lately been refused, the applicants being relatives of professors of religion, and influenced, we fear, by the example and persuasion of others, rather than by the impulse of [God's saving] grace."[24]

That same day, however, an interview took place with an elderly woman who gave every evidence of being a genuine believer. She was the mother-in-law of a "petty chief" who had proven to be one of the mission's bitterest opponents. She fairly trembled at the likely negative family and social consequences of changing her religion. But when interviewed before the church she answered the leaders'questions with such promptness and conviction that people were moved to tears:

"How old are you, mother?"

"Eighty years."

"Can you, at such an age, renounce the religion that you have followed all your life long?"

"I see that it is false, and I renounce it all."

"Why do you wish to be baptized into the religion of Jesus Christ?"

"I have very, very many sins; and I love the Lord, who saves from sin."

23 ibid., pp. 470–71.
24 ibid., p. 471.

"Perhaps your son-in-law, on hearing that you have been baptized, will abuse you, and turn you out of doors."

"I have another son-in-law, to whom I will flee."

"But he also is an opposer. Suppose that you should meet with the same treatment there."

"You will, I think, let me come and live near you."

We made no reply, willing that she should prove her sincerity by bearing the brunt alone. Her name is May Hlah. Behold the venerable woman, severing, at her time of life, all the ties which bind her to a large circle of connections and friends, hazarding the loss of a comfortable, respectable situation, the loss of character, the loss of a shelter for her grey head, throwing herself on the charity of certain foreigners, and all for the sake of "the Lord who saves from sin". O, blessed efficacy of the love of Christ![25]

A little over two months later, on August 12, Judson reported that, following her baptism, May Hlah left her son-in-law's house and "took refuge" with her oldest daughter. Through May Hlah's influence that daughter "begins now to give some evidence of [possessing saving] grace" and "even her husband has become rather favorably disposed."

Once again on the anniversary of Ann's death, October 24, Judson penned a transparent, melancholy letter to her sisters, Mary and Abigail Hasseltine:

And now the third anniversary returns, and finds me in the same cottage, except it has been removed nearer the mission house, to make way for a government building. I live alone. When I wish to be quite so, Mrs. W. sends me my food; at other times I am within the sound of a bell that calls me to meals.

"Blest who, far from all mankind,
This world's shadows left behind,
Hears from heaven a gentle strain,

25   ibid., p. 472.

Whispering love, and loves again."

But O, that strain I have hitherto listened in vain to hear, or rather have not listened aright, and therefore cannot hear.

Have either of you learned the art of real communion with God, and can you teach me the first principles? God is to me the Great Unknown. I believe in him, but I find him not.[26]

In the midst of his lingering grief, Judson still experienced seasons, like this one, when he felt at a distance from God and His love.

Throughout most of that year Judson had continued to diligently pursue various translation projects. By the end of November he was able to report:

... we have finished revising the New Testament and the Epitome of the Old – a work in which we have been closely engaged for above a year. We have also prepared for the press several smaller works, viz.:

1. "The Catechism of Religion." This has already passed through two editions in Burmese. It has also been translated and printed into Siamese, and translated into Talaing or Peguan.

2. "The View of the Christian Religion", thoroughly revised for a fourth edition in Burmese. It has also been translated into Talaing and Siamese.

3. "The Liturgy of the Burman Church".

4. "The Baptismal Service".

5. "The Marriage Service".

6. "The Funeral Service"; the three last consisting chiefly of extracts from Scripture.

26   ibid., p. 483.

7. "The Teacher's Guide"; or, a Digest of those parts of the New Testament which relate to the Duty of Teachers of Religion, designed particularly for Native Pastors.

8. "A Catechism of Astronomy".

9. "A Catechism of Geography".

10. "A Table of Chronological History", or a Register of principal Events from the Creation to the present Time.

11. "The Memoir of Mee Shway-ee".[27]

12. *The Golden Balance*; or, the Christian and Buddhist Systems contrasted. This has been translated into Talaing.

The Gospel of St Matthew was also translated into Siamese by Mrs. Judson, and is now being translated into Talaing by Ko Man-poke, our assistant in that department.[28]

In mid-December Judson received letters informing him of the death of his brother Elnathan on May 8 of that year. He had died in Washington, D.C., at age thirty-five. One of those letters contained the following account from one who had attended Elnathan at his passing:

A few hours before his death, and when he was so low as to be unable to converse or to move, he suddenly raised himself up, and clasping his hands, with an expression of joy in his countenance, cried, "*Peace, peace!*" and then he sunk down,

27 Mee Shway-ee was a five-year-old slave girl who had suffered horrific physical abuse at the hands of her master before being rescued by Judson and the Wades while they were still ministering in Amherst. Seven months after being brought to Maulmain, Mee-Shway-ee died following a lingering illness of six weeks. About a month before her death, however, she came to saving faith in Christ and joyously anticipated going to live with her newfound Savior in heaven. Her moving tragedy-to-triumph story is related in some detail in Knowles, *Memoir of Mrs. Ann H. Judson*, pp. 305–8, and Edward Judson, *The Life of Adoniram Judson*, pp. 335–6.

28 Wayland, *Memoir*, vol. 1, pp. 477–8.

without the power of utterance. About ten minutes before he expired, it was said to him, "If you feel the peace of God in your soul, open your eyes." He opened his eyes, and soon after expired, and, as we believe, in the triumphs of faith.

Judson shared his response to this intelligence in a letter to his sister:

When I read this account, I went into my little room, and could only shed tears of joy, my heart full of gratitude, and my tongue of praise. I have felt most anxious about him for a long time; to hear at last that there is some good reason to conclude that he has gone to heaven is enough.[29]

Another special blessing that came to Judson around that same time was the receipt of a dozen copies of James Knowles's biography on Ann's life that had been published earlier that year in Boston. Knowles served as pastor of Boston's Second Baptist Church. In writing to thank Knowles for these complimentary copies, Judson commented: "In regard to the Memoir, it becomes me not to expatiate. I would only say that I am extremely gratified, perhaps too much so, with the execution of the work in all its parts."[30]

On the last day of December Judson reported that twenty-eight individuals had been baptized as professing Christians in Maulmain that year. That number included ten British soldiers from the forty-fifth regiment. In addition, seventeen Burmans at Rangoon and eight individuals at Tavoy, most of them Karens, had been baptized, bringing to fifty-three the total number of converts to have been baptized in Burma that year.

At Amherst, unfortunately, the prospect had become "quite dark". Despite his diligence and faithfulness, Maung Ing had met with no success. He eventually returned to Rangoon to assist

29 ibid., p. 480.

30 ibid., p. 481. The biography went on to enjoy a wide circulation: "Within two years three editions had been issued in America, totaling 12,500 copies, besides three or four editions in England. In 1831 a fourth edition was printed in a smaller size, to secure a still wider reading" (Warburton, Eastward!, p. 115).

Ko Thah-a in the work there. Sadly, Maung Ing's wife, Mah Lan, refused to relocate with him. Judson related: "Her conduct has been very exceptionable since her baptism, and soon after her husband's departure, she became openly vicious. She is now suspended from communion – the first case of church discipline that has occurred amongst the native members."[31]

---

31   Wayland, *Memoir*, vol. 1, p. 479.

27

EVANGELISTIC MINISTRY IN PROME
(1830)

For nearly a year Judson and his ministry associates had been eagerly anticipating the arrival of a new printer. That longed-for addition to the mission staff was realized in mid January 1830, with the arrival of Mr. and Mrs. Cephas Bennett and their two young children. One week after the Bennetts arrived in Maulmain, Jonathan and Deborah Wade left for Rangoon to help advance the mission's work there.

The following month Sarah Boardman came to Maulmain to recuperate her health. The two years the Boardmans had been in Tavoy had proved extremely difficult. Sarah had given birth to a son, named George after his father, in August 1828. Both the Boardmans' children fell gravely ill the following July. Daughter Sarah died three months short of her third birthday but son George survived. One month later the Boardmans narrowly escaped death when Tavoyan rebels laid siege to Tavoy. For some thirty-six hours, the Boardmans, along with hundreds of women and children as well as a few Europeans and a small contingent of sepoy soldiers, were trapped in a wooden warehouse on the wharf. There they came under intermittent fire from the rebels until a platoon of British soldiers arrived to rescue them and put down the uprising.[1]

Sarah Boardman gave birth to her second son five months later, in January 1830. The boy was named Judson Wade

---

1 An expanded account of the rebellion is recorded in Emily C. Judson, *Memoir of Sarah B. Judson, Member of the American Mission to Burmah* (New York: Lewis Colby, 1849), pp. 96–113.

Boardman, after the veteran missionaries in Burma at that time. As it would turn out, the infant lived only nine and a half months. Following the birth of this child, Sarah became deathly ill. After a partial recovery, she came to Maulmain to continue her recuperation. Her husband, whose health had also been declining with manifestations of tuberculosis, intended to join her there soon.

For several weeks the Wades had been encouraging Judson to join them in Rangoon with a view to ministering there and in other towns in that region. After receiving a letter from Boardman in the latter half of April stating that he would soon be coming to Maulmain, Judson, knowing that there would be two missionary couples to carry on the work there, began making plans to leave for Rangoon. After arriving there on May 2, he temporarily moved into the home the Wades were renting "in the midst of the town, where we have a great deal of company".

But toward the end of that month, Judson stated in his journal:

> ... every day deepens the conviction in my mind that I am not in the place where God would have me to be. It was to the interior, and not to Rangoon, that my mind was turned long before I left Maulmain; and while I feel that brother and sister Wade are in the right place, I feel that I am called elsewhere.[2]

"Under these impressions" he set out on May 29 with five Burmese Christians, Maung Ing among them, for Prome. At several towns and villages along the way, Judson engaged groups of people in conversation about spiritual matters and distributed tracts and catechisms, sometimes scores at a time. At a sizeable village named Yay-gen, Judson bore a Gospel witness to a large crowd and then distributed about thirty pieces of literature. Several individuals followed Judson and Maung Ing back to their boat and "begged very hard" for a tract. Small parties continued to row out to their boat to receive literature. When, late in the evening, the captain of Judson's boat wearied of this "annoyance", he

2 Wayland, *Memoir*, vol. 1, p. 487.

pushed his craft further out into the river. Still people continued to come to the shore and called out across the water, "Teacher, are you asleep? We want a writing to get by heart." After being promised a pamphlet if they would come and get it, the eager seekers used a canoe to approach Judson's boat. A long pole with a tract fastened to its end was extended to them. A steady stream of visitors continued to come for literature in this way till nine o'clock. The captain, having gone ashore, returned to the boat to report that in nearly every house someone was at a lamp reading aloud one of the tracts. After leaving another location, a small boat pursued them, offering rice and beans in exchange for a pamphlet.

Upon arrival at Prome around the middle of June, Judson was invited by a Mr. M., the only European living in the city at the time, to stay with him until he could find accommodations of his own. But the kindly host's dwelling left something to be desired, for Judson described it as a "shattered house ... with the rain beating in on every side". When Judson went searching for quarters to rent, he quickly discovered that people were afraid to have any dealings with a foreigner and suspected him as a spy for the British.

"In the heart of the town" he discovered an old, abandoned zayat standing in front of a pagoda and surrounded by a small parcel of vacant ground. After appealing to the deputy governor and the local magistrates, Judson obtained permission to repair and use the old zayat as his residence. The structure was forty-five feet long by twenty wide. Judson and his companions partitioned part of the building into rooms to be used as living quarters while the other part they "left open for the reception of company".

At first a number of local residents came to visit and seemed favorably disposed toward the evangelists' message. But as soon as the favor of government people cooled toward Judson, as a result of the rumor persisting that he was a spy for the British, inquirers at the zayat fell off almost entirely. "To-day I have had no company at all," Judson reported on July 2. The next day Maung Ing returned from a visit to an outlying village and related that the same suspicion was spreading throughout the region. Judson recorded further:

Pastor Ing says that the country is full of villages, and there is some disposition to listen to religion, but that in the present state of the public mind, if I should make the tour of those parts, as I had some intention of doing, there is not a house where the owner would dare to ask me to sit down at the entrance of the door.

Feel extremely dejected this evening. Never so heartily willing to enter into my rest, yet willing to offer, and I do, with some peculiar feelings, offer, my poor life to the Lord Jesus Christ, to do and to suffer whatever he shall appoint, during my few remaining days.

July 4, Lord's day. Another Burman day of worship, and a great day, being the first day of Lent, a season which continues three months. After usual worship [with the Burmese Christians], took a stroll through the place. All smiles and looks of welcome are passed away; people view me with an evil eye, and suffer their dogs to bark at me unchecked.[3]

Despite those discouraging circumstances, that same day Judson visited Prome's premier Buddhist temple, the Shway San Daw Pagoda. The zayats surrounding the esteemed pagoda were "crowded with devout-faced worshippers". Finding a vacant spot under a shed that had been built over a large brick idol, Judson sat down there and conversed with small groups of people that passed by. The Christians also had some company at their home that morning and evening.

After that, in addition to witnessing to those who visited their residence, the evangelists determined to divide up and go out every day to share the Gospel in various public places. Maung Ing, Maung Dway and Maung En were the three Burmans who played an active role with Judson in those outreach efforts. In mid-July Maung Dway and one of the other Burmese believers left Prome to return to Rangoon and Maulmain, leaving only two indigenous evangelists to work with Judson. On August 23 Judson summarized developments of the previous weeks:

3   Wayland, *Memoir*, vol. 1, p. 495.

At one period the whole town seemed to be roused to listen to the news of an eternal God, the mission of his Son, the Lord Jesus Christ, and the way of salvation through his atonement. A considerable proportion of the hearers became favorably disposed. At length the enemy assumed a threatening aspect; the poor people became frightened; many sent back the tracts they had received; and there was a general falling off at the zayats. I was summoned to undergo a long examination at the court house, not, however, on the subject of religion, but concerning all my past life since I have been in Burma. The result was forwarded to Ava. The magistrates still preserve a perfect neutrality, in consequence of the absence of the governor. ... I have some company at the zayats every day, and crowds on [Burman] days of worship. Most of the hearers are opposers; but I observe in distant corners those who listen with eagerness. There are five persons who have, I trust, obtained a little grace; but in the present dark time, they give no satisfactory evidence.[4]

In September the rise of the river prevented Judson and his associates from going to the zayats in distant parts of the town where they were accustomed to ministering. After three months of ministry in Prome, they left the city on Saturday, September 18, to return to Rangoon. In addition to preaching the Gospel nearly every day while in Prome, Judson and his fellow evangelists had distributed some 500 tracts and catechisms. Another 500 tracts were distributed in towns and villages all along the way during the one-week journey from Prome to Rangoon.

While Judson was away at Prome the Wades had returned to Maulmain when George Boardman became gravely ill and his death was thought to be imminent. Thankfully, Boardman had recovered somewhat. But in the absence of a missionary, opponents of Christianity in Rangoon were emboldened. Men were stationed a short distance from the mission house to threaten those who visited there and to confiscate the Christian literature

4   ibid., pp. 498–9. Prome's governor was away in Ava throughout Judson's stay in Prome.

they received. Reports were circulated that government officials were about to make a public example of heretics. People stopped visiting the mission house and even Pastor Thah-a left it to retreat to his own "obscure dwelling". But after Judson returned, he and Ko Thah-a again took up the ministry there. Christian disciples were strengthened and spiritual inquirers once more began to surface.

On October 8 Judson learned that more than a month earlier King Bagyidaw had issued a peremptory order for his removal from Prome. A British officer, Major H. Burney, was carrying out a diplomatic mission in Ava at the time. Burney's personal journal on September 1 revealed:

> The [government] ministers requested my advice as to the measures which they ought to pursue with respect to Dr Judson, who, they said, is come up to Prome, and is there distributing tracts among the inhabitants, and abusing the Burmese religion, much to the annoyance of the king. I told them that Dr Judson is now exclusively devoted to missionary pursuits; that I possess no power or authority over him, but that I know him to be a very pious and good man, and one not likely to injure the Burmese king or government in any manner. The minister replied that the king is much vexed with Dr Judson for the zeal with which he is distributing among the people writings in which the Burmese faith is held forth to contempt, and that his majesty is anxious to remove him from Prome. I said that the Burmese king and government have always enjoyed a high reputation among civilized nations for the toleration which they have shown to all religious faiths; that there are thousands, in Europe and America, who would be much hurt and disappointed to hear of any change in the liberal policy hitherto observed by the King of Ava, and that I hoped the ministers would not think of molesting or injuring Dr Judson, as such a proceeding would offend and displease good men of all nations. They replied that it was for this reason, to avoid hurting Dr Judson, that they had consulted me; and they

proposed that I should write and advise Dr Judson of the king's sentiments towards him. ... I begged the ministers to leave him alone, which, however, they said they could not, as his majesty has expressed himself much displeased with his conduct. I consented at last to write to Dr Judson, but I told the ministers to recollect that I had no right to interfere with him, who would, notwithstanding any letter he might receive from me, act in whatever manner his own judgment and conscience might dictate. The ministers begged of me only to recommend Dr Judson to return to Rangoon, and confine his missionary labors within that city.[5]

5   ibid., pp. 500–1.

28

A LITERATURE BLITZ
(1830-1831)

After returning to Rangoon, Judson again sought to give much of his time to Bible translation work, first picking up his unfinished translation of the Psalms. He "confined" himself to the garret of the mission house while some of his Burmese associates occupied the front rooms on the main floor of the home, visiting with spiritual seekers and distributing Christian literature there. More serious inquirers were shown upstairs to confer with Judson. Even with this arrangement, more than half his time was spent counseling inquirers, some of whom came "from all parts of the country".

Sometime that autumn Judson received an unexpected visit from a trio of English travelers – Miss Emma Roberts, who went on to become the authoress of the book *Scenes and Characteristics of Hindoostan*, and the sea captain and his wife with whom she was traveling. Miss Roberts afterwards described Judson's upstairs quarters and summarized their visit with him:

> It was a Burman habitation, to which we had to ascend by a ladder; and we entered a large, low room through a space like a trap door. The beams of the roof were uncovered, and the window frames were open, after the fashion of Burman houses. The furniture consisted of a table in the centre of the room, a few stools, and a desk, with writings and books neatly arranged on one side. We were soon seated, and were most anxious to hear all that the good man had to say, who, in a resigned tone, spoke of his departed wife in a manner which plainly showed he had set his affections "where alone

true joy can be found". He dwelt with much pleasure on the translation of the Bible into the Burman language. He had completed the New Testament, and was then as far as the Psalms in the Old Testament, which having finished, he said he trusted it would be the will of his heavenly Father to call him to his everlasting home.

Of the conversions going on amongst the Burmese he spoke with certainty, not doubting that when the flame of Christianity did burst forth, it would surprise even him by its extent and brilliancy. As we were thus conversing, the bats, which frequent the houses at Rangoon, began to take their evening round, and whirled closer and closer, till they came in almost disagreeable contact with our heads; and the flap of their heavy wings so near us interrupting the conversation, we at length reluctantly took our leave and departed. And this, thought I, as I descended the dark ladder, is the solitary abode of Judson, whom after ages shall designate, most justly, the great and the good. ...[1]

From the time Judson first returned to Rangoon from Prome he repeatedly wrote his fellow missionaries in Maulmain, especially Cephas Bennett the printer, urging them to send him a steady and sizeable supply of Christian literature. His requests for hundreds of copies of various tracts soon turned to pleas for thousands. Near the end of September he wrote:

Dear Brother Bennett: I write a line to beg most earnestly that you will not, after receiving this, suffer a single vessel to leave the port of Maulmain without having on board 500 of the *View*, and two hundred and fifty of the *Balance*, also a few hundred of the "Catechism of Religion". ... I wrote to Maulmain last night, but did not mention the want of tracts, thinking on my first arrival here there was some stock on hand. But on rummaging the boxes to-day, I find only about fifty of the new tracts, and a couple of bundles of the old, and

1   Wayland, *Memoir*, vol. 1, pp. 505–6.

about twenty of the *Balance*; so that we shall be completely exhausted, however fast you run after receiving this.[2]

Judson sounds positively provoked in his correspondence of November 13:

> Dear Brethren: ... We continue to distribute about forty tracts a day, and should gladly double the number if we could depend on a supply from Maulmain. By tracts I mean not the single sheets or handbills [two-page tracts of Scripture Extracts], containing merely a scrap of Scripture, which, being wholly inadequate to give any full idea of the Christian religion, it is impossible to mock any poor soul with, when he holds out his hand for such spiritual food as his case requires. ... But by tracts I mean the *View*, the *Catechism*, the *Balance*, and the *Investigator*.[3] I earnestly beg the brethren to wake up to the importance of sending a regular supply of all these articles. How long we shall be allowed a footing in Rangoon is very uncertain. ... Rangoon is the key of the country. From this place tracts go into every quarter. ... Six weeks have elapsed since I wrote for the *Balance*, and for a few only, as I did not wish to distress any one, and though it was then out of print, it is not yet put to press. And why? Because the *Epitome* has been in the way. I am glad the *Epitome* is printed; but after all, we shall not give away one a week of that article. The state of things does not immediately require it. But of the *Balance* I shall give away one hundred a week. There are daily calls for it. During the last six weeks I should have given away one thousand of the *Balance*, and they would now be circulating all over the country. I found twenty in the house on my arrival, and have been dealing them out like drops of heart's blood. There are few left. I did expect some by Maung En; but alas! Out popped two bundles of *scrippets* [the two-page tracts mentioned above]. ... I do not write this with any disposition to find fault. I am sure you have done

---

2   ibid., p. 507.

3   "The Investigator" was an evangelistic tract written that year by Jonathan Wade.

all for the best; and I feel for brother Bennett in his labors at the press. I only blame myself that I have not been more explicit, and written more urgently on the subject.[4]

Just three days later he wrote again to further explain the pressing need:

Dear Brethren: We were obliged to give away ninety-five tracts and Scriptures yesterday, besides refusing several. This morning [during his daily exercise walk at dawn] I took twenty in my hand, as usual, and though I avoided streets, and kept to the jungle, and walked as fast as possible, yet, notwithstanding every precaution, they fleeced me of fifteen by sunrise. We shall not be able to stand it longer than fifteen or twenty days at this rate. They come from all parts of the country, and the thing is spreading and increasing every day. I hope you will not fail me in the hour of need. We want thousands of the *Catechism*, the *View*, the *Balance*, and the *Investigator*. Next to these we shall want a thousand or two of the Gospel of Luke, that is, after the "Scripture Extracts" are done, which will be shortly, if you will only send them along. I am more and more convinced that Burma is to be evangelized by tracts and portions of Scripture. They are a reading people beyond any other in India. The press is the grand engine for Burma. Every pull of brother Bennett at the press sends another ray of light through the darkness of the empire. ...[5]

Despite the many inquirers, few Burmese had the courage to become committed followers of Christ. Occasionally, however, Judson was able to relate testimonies of definite conversions and dramatic transformations. In a November 21 letter to the Corresponding Secretary of his mission, Judson told of:

... an old woman of seventy-four, who has met with violent opposition from a host of children and grandchildren, who for

4   Wayland, *Memoir*, vol. 1, pp. 508–9. The two bracketed explanations are supplied as footnotes in Wayland's citation of this letter.

5   ibid., p. 510.

a time confined her, lest she should be baptized; and at last she was baptized by stealth. On her return from the water, in wet clothes, she suddenly met three of her sons, grown men, who, it seems, were suspecting some mischief. At first she thought of avoiding them; but feeling very happy that she was now a full disciple, life and death, praise and abuse, became, at the moment, indifferent to her; she met them courageously, and to their rude questions, "What have you been about, mother?" she mildly and promptly replied, "I have been baptized into the religion of the Lord Jesus Christ, to the entire renunciation of the religion of our ancestors." The young men appeared to be astonished, and, contrary to her fears, refrained from all abusive treatment, and suffered her to proceed home quietly, as if nothing had happened.[6]

In that same letter Judson testified of the transformed life and demeanor of one of his Burmese ministry assistants:

Maung En has returned from Maulmain ...; and of all the disciples I have yet employed, he seems to be the best qualified to receive promiscuous company. He was, when I first knew him, extremely irritable. He was frequently betrayed into a passion, at the Goung-zay-gyoon zayat. But now he bears with imperturbable composure, and a smiling countenance, the floods of contradiction and abuse which sometimes pour upon him. Nor is he ever so much in his element, as when surrounded by a large company, some contradicting and some approving.[7]

On February 1, 1831, with Burma's premier annual religious festival at Rangoon's Shwe Dagon Pagoda less than a month away, Judson submitted his largest request by far to date for additional Christian literature:

Dear Brethren: The great festival falls this year on the 25th. Alas! alas! what shall I do? I beg and entreat that you will not

6   ibid., p. 511.
7   ibid., p. 512.

give any tracts in the vicinity of Maulmain until after the 1st of March; but let everything that can possibly be got ready be sent with all possible expedition to this place. I do beg you will all make one effort, and, if possible, send me fifteen or twenty thousand tracts between this and the 25th or 28th. The festival will last several days. I have lost all hope of hoarding up my present stock. We have been obliged to give away above one thousand within the last three days. It is not here as at Maulmain, where a great many are destroyed. Here, I am persuaded, after a great deal of inquiry, not one in a hundred is destroyed. The people are eager to get tracts. We don't give to every one we meet, as you do, but to those only who ask earnestly. Don't think the tracts you print, and stitch, and trim, with a great deal of labor, and send here, are lost. I trust that the most of them will come to light at the day of judgment.[8]

Early that same month of February, Judson reported to his mission board that, since returning from Prome, he had finished translating Psalms, Song of Solomon and Daniel, "all of which were begun some time ago". He also indicated that during 1830 a total of forty-seven Christians had been baptized in Burma. That number included seven at Rangoon, twelve at Maulmain (five of those being Europeans) and twenty-eight at Tavoy. Judson further observed:

The most prominent feature in the mission at present is the surprising spirit of inquiry that is spreading everywhere, through the whole length and breadth of the land. I sometimes feel alarmed, like a person who sees a mighty engine beginning to move, over which he knows he has no control.[9]

Though still extremely weak from his tuberculosis, George Boardman had returned with his wife to Tavoy the previous

8   ibid., p. 516.
9   ibid., p. 523.

November. A fortnight after their return, Ko Ing[10] baptized nineteen Karen believers, Boardman being too weak to do so. A new missionary, Francis Mason, arrived at Tavoy on January 23, 1831. Early in February he joined the Boardmans in journeying three days into the jungle where they met with nearly one hundred Karens who had gathered from a number of scattered settlements to that central location. There Boardman, who by then was clearly approaching death, joyfully watched as Mason baptized thirty-four Karens. Early the next morning the missionaries set out to return to Tavoy but Boardman died before reaching it.[11] Judson learned of Boardman's death later that month.

Through the tireless efforts of Bennett and his Maulmain colleagues, Judson was supplied with 10,000 tracts and catechisms for Rangoon's religious festival. Though Judson and his native associates sought to distribute the literature judiciously, there were so many requests for it – several hundred per day – that their stock was exhausted. Judson afterward reported that they could have given away twice as many tracts if they had possessed a sufficient supply. In a letter that he penned on March 4, he further related of those who had requested literature at the festival:

> Some come two or three months' journey, from the borders of Siam and China – "Sir, we hear that there is an eternal hell. We are afraid of it. Do give us a writing that will tell us how to escape it." Others come from the frontiers of Kathay, a hundred miles north of Ava – "Sir, we have seen a writing that tells about an eternal God. Are you the man that gives away such writings? If so, pray give us one, for we want to know the truth before we die." Others come from the interior of the country, where the name of Jesus Christ is a little known – "Are you Jesus Christ's man? Give us a writing that tells about Jesus Christ."[12]

---

10 Formerly Maung Ing but now bearing the designation Ko, indicating an older man. Ko Ing had intended to return to his hometown of Mergui but stopped to assist the Boardmans at Tavoy (Emily Judson, *Memoir of Sarah B. Judson*, p. 118).

11 A moving account of Boardman's final itineration and death is recorded in Emily Judson, *Memoir of Sarah B. Judson*, pp. 124–41.

12 Wayland, *Memoir*, vol. 1, p. 528.

That same day Judson wrote an earnest letter to Sarah Boardman concerning the death of her husband and her future plans:

> My Dear Sister: You are now drinking the bitter cup whose dregs I am somewhat acquainted with. And though, for some time, you have been aware of its approach, I venture to say that it is far bitterer than you expected. It is common for persons in your situation to refuse all consolations, to cling to the dead, and to fear that they shall too soon forget the dear object of their affections. But don't be concerned. I can assure you that months and months of heart-rending anguish are before you, whether you will or not. I can only advise you to take the cup with both hands, and sit down quietly to the bitter repast which God has appointed for your sanctification. As to your beloved, you *know* that all his tears are wiped away, and that the diadem which encircles his brow outshines the sun. Little Sarah and the other [Judson Wade] have again found their father, not the frail, sinful mortal that they left on earth, but an immortal saint, a magnificent, majestic king. What more can you desire for them? While, therefore, your tears flow, let a due proportion be tears of joy. Yet take the bitter cup with both hands, and sit down to your repast. You will soon learn a secret, that there is sweetness at the bottom. ...
>
> I think, from what I know of your mind, that you will not desert the post, but remain to carry on the work which he gloriously began. The Karens of Tavoy regard you as their spiritual mother; and the dying prayers of your beloved are waiting to be answered in blessings on your instructions.
>
> As to little Georgie, who has now no earthly father to care for him, you cannot, of course, part with him at present. But if you should wish to send him home, I pledge myself to use what little influence I have in procuring for him all those advantages of education which your fondest wishes can desire. Or if you should be prematurely taken away, and should condescend, on your dying bed, to commit him to me, by the briefest line or verbal message, I hereby pledge my

fidelity to receive and treat him as my own son, to send him
home in the best time and way, to provide for his education,
and to watch over him as long as I live. More than this
I cannot do, and less would be unworthy of the merits of his
parents.[13]

After the festival, Judson turned his attention again almost
exclusively to Bible translation. By the middle of May he had
finished translating the books of Genesis and Isaiah. He continued
to distribute tracts, by then around seventy per day, to those who
asked for them during his daily early morning walk. Judson also
supervised his Burmese assistants who actively witnessed to
people and distributed Christian literature in Rangoon and other
communities upriver.

Encouraging reports were received from Maulmain. Besides
Francis Mason and his wife in Tavoy, two other new missionary
couples – Mr. and Mrs. John Jones and the Kincaids – had settled
in Maulmain. In addition to making good progress in learning the
language, Kincaid and Jones were preaching to "large and attentive
assemblies" in their ministry to British soldiers. Jonathan Wade
had formed a congregation of fourteen Karens in the Maulmain
region.

The first week of June, however, word arrived that Deborah
Wade, whose health had been poor for months, was "rapidly
sinking" and a long voyage would be necessary to try to save her
life. Since Jonathan's health had also been declining, the other
Maulmain missionaries urged the Wades to return immediately
to America together. Judson's fellow missionaries also asked him
to return to Maulmain to resume ministry there. He consented
once the Joneses agreed to take his place in overseeing the work in
Rangoon. By the time they arrived on July 23, Judson had finished
translating the first twenty chapters of Exodus.

13   ibid., pp. 526–7.

29

EVANGELIZING THE KARENS
(1831-1834)

Following "a very tedious passage" of seventeen days, Judson reached the Maulmain mission premises on August 11. He had been away nearly sixteen months. Two weeks later the missionaries opened a school for teaching adults to read, with five students in attendance initially.

Mid-September found Judson about eighty miles northeast of Maulmain, at the location on the Dah-gyne River[1] where Wade had baptized the first Karen converts in that region. That settlement had no name, so Judson called it Wadesville. A trio of indigenous evangelists had been ministering in the area in recent months. Now twenty-two Karens from Wadesville and two other locations that Judson visited were examined concerning their profession of faith, then baptized.

After a week of such ministry Judson developed a serious fever and was forced to return to Maulmain. Three Karens whom Judson had selected from among those recently baptized soon followed him to Maulmain, bringing their wives and children with them. "It is our intention to place the men in the adult school," Judson explained, "and qualify them to read and interpret the scriptures to their countrymen."[2]

The ship on which the Wades had left Maulmain three months earlier, destined for Bengal on the first leg of their intended return to America, had not been heard of since and was feared lost.

1   The Dah-gyne (today the Dagyaing) flowed into the Salween from the east.
2   Wayland, *Memoir*, vol. 2, p. 12.

The Maulmain missionaries were "astonished" and overjoyed, therefore, when the Wades suddenly appeared at their station on October 8. Having encountered severe weather in the Bay of Bengal, their vessel, battered and sinking, managed to limp to the Arakan coast. Deborah's health improved so much during their two-month stay there that they decided to return to southern Burma rather than continue to America. After a brief visit at Maulmain, they settled at Mergui, where it was hoped Deborah could recover further. Ko Ing was summoned from Tavoy to assist the Wades in establishing a church in his hometown.

Kincaid's ministry among the British troops at Maulmain had continued to blossom. On November 6 the hundredth member was added to the European church there. All of those except the first fifteen had been baptized by Kincaid since his arrival less than a year earlier. By contrast, the work among the indigenous population was far from encouraging, as Judson related:

> The opposition in this place was never more steady and strong. The [Buddhist] priests have all taken a more decided stand; and the people seem to have resolved to stand or fall with their priests. When any person is known to be considering the new religion, all his relations and acquaintance rise *en masse*; so that to get a new convert is like pulling out the eye tooth of a live tiger.[3]

Still, the statistics Judson reported to his mission board at the end of 1831 provided a basis for significant praise and thanksgiving. That year 217 believers had been baptized in Burma, including 136 in and around Maulmain, seventy-six in the region of Tavoy and five at Rangoon. That number consisted of 109 Karens, nineteen Burmans or Talings (Peguans), and eighty-nine foreigners. The Judsons had ministered in Burma for six years before seeing a single convert, and only eighteen Burmans professed faith in Christ and were baptized in their first thirteen years of ministry. By contrast, in the four years from 1828 to 1831, 351 converts had been baptized. Of the 373 believers to have been baptized

3   ibid., p. 13.

throughout Judson's ministry in Burma, 260 were Burmese while 113 were foreigners.

At the end of December Judson left Maulmain to undertake another evangelistic itineration among the Karens in the area to the north and east. He arrived at Wadesville the first day of 1832. For a week his several indigenous assistants scattered out to minister at various locations in the region. The Christian disciples of that area desired to move to a different location, so Judson accompanied them a few miles down the Dah-gyne. There a settlement was established under the quaint name of Newville.

For the next few weeks Judson and his assistants traveled along the Dah-gyne and Salween Rivers as well as a number of their tributaries. They ministered a day or two at a time in villages all along the way and encountered a variety of situations and responses. At Kwan-bee they had to investigate the case of a professing Christian disciple named Loo-boo who had backslidden by following the indigenous custom of presenting an offering to a nat (demon) when his child became extremely ill. The Karens thought demons ruled over disease and presented them with offerings in an effort to appease them. Loo-boo readily confessed his transgression and promised not to repeat it, so he was pronounced forgiven rather than brought under discipline.

Judson, in an effort to promote the directives of 1 Timothy 2:9 and 1 Peter 3:3, generally discouraged Christian women from wearing jewelry and ornate clothing. This issue surfaced when Loo-boo's wife applied for baptism:

> [She] ... presented herself for baptism, with twelve strings of all manner of beads around her neck, and a due proportion of ear, arm, and leg ornaments! And, strange to say, she was examined and approved, without one remark on the subject of her dress. The truth is, we quite forgot it, being occupied and delighted with her uncommonly prompt and intelligent replies. ...

But when Loo-boo's wife and others came to be baptized the next day:

> ... Being formerly prevented by illness from animadverting [making observations and passing on one's judgment] on female dress in this district, ... I took an opportunity of "holding forth" on that subject before breakfast; and it was truly amusing and gratifying to see the said lady, and another applicant for baptism, and a Christian woman who accompanied them, divest themselves, on the spot, of every article that could be deemed merely ornamental; and this they did with evident pleasure, and good resolution to persevere in adherence to the plain dress system.[4]

All the candidates, including Loo-boo's wife, were duly baptized that day.

Though most Karens were not Buddhists, an influential individual in one of the Karen villages Judson visited did adhere to Buddhism. Upon learning that Judson was approaching his village, this man sent a message to the missionary to the effect that "when the English government enforced their religion at the point of the sword, and he had seen two or three suffer death for not embracing it, he would begin to consider, and not before." He added, however, that if the teacher desired to visit his village he could not be inhospitable but would let him come. Judson responded gravely: "I sent back word that I would not come, but, as he loved falsehood and darkness, I would leave him to live therein all his days, and finally go the dark way ..."[5]

After nightfall, at their boat, Judson and his companions heard footsteps approaching in the dark, then the voice of the old Buddhist, "My lord, please to come to the village."

> "Don't call me lord," Judson responded. "I am no lord, nor ruler of this world."

---

4   ibid., pp. 20–21. See also ibid., pp. 476–85, for an interesting "letter on ornamental and costly attire" that Judson had written the previous October to Christian women in America. In it he appealed to them to set an example for Christian women in Burma (who looked to their lead) by not wearing jewelry.

5   ibid., p. 26.

"What must I call you? Teacher, I suppose."

"Yes, but not your teacher, for you love to be taught falsehood, not truth."

"Teacher, I have heard a great deal against this religion, and how can I know at once what is right and what is wrong? Please do come and let me listen attentively to your words."

Without making further reply, Judson rose and followed the old man to his house. The host spread a cloth for him to sit on, "manifested great respect" for the missionary and listened carefully to what he had to say. After Judson left he commented to others "that it was a great thing to change one's religion; that he stood quite alone in these parts; but that, if some of his acquaintance would join him, he would not be behind."[6]

Near the spot where the Chummerah rivulet emptied into the Salween, Judson was invited by two area villages to establish a zayat. He agreed, naming the new settlement Chummerah and appointing one of the indigenous evangelists to be in charge of it. At yet another village further south on the Salween, a Karen chief named Rajah came to faith in Christ and requested to be baptized. None of his people, however, attended his baptism, though he had invited them. They chose, instead, to side with the chief's adult son who had become a devout Buddhist.

Judson returned to Maulmain on February 11, having been away for six weeks. During his itineration he had baptized twenty-five believers and had met a similar number of "hopeful inquirers". Upon arriving, he learned that the Joneses had recently returned from Rangoon. Kincaid left on February 23 to take their place there, carrying with him 12,000 tracts to use in Rangoon's great annual festival that was near at hand.

Six days later, Judson, accompanied by half a dozen assistants, set out again for the Karen villages up the Salween. As on their previous itineration, practically each new day found them ministering in a different village or two along the way. At the village immediately downriver from Chief Rajah's settlement,

6   ibid., p. 27.

Judson responded with unexpected reserve to the mistreatment of one of his native evangelists:

> Maung Zuthee unfortunately encountered a very respectable Burman priest, with a train of novices, who, not relishing his doctrine, fell upon him, and gave him a sound beating. The poor man fled to me in great dismay, and, I am sorry to say, some wrath, begging leave to assemble our forces, and seize the aggressor, for the purpose of delivering him up to justice. I did assemble them; and, all kneeling down, I praised God that he had counted one of our number worthy to suffer a little for his Son's sake; and prayed that he would give us a spirit of forgiveness, and our persecutors every blessing, temporal and spiritual; after which we left the field of battle with cool and happy minds.[7]

Rajah was found to be standing firm in his Christian faith, though none had joined him in following Christ except his wife.

At Chummerah a zayat had been built by the area believers and more than twenty disciples gathered for a worship service. Afterward five more Christians gave their testimonies and were baptized. Further up the Salween Judson was forced to "pronounce the sentence of suspension" on a married couple. Shortly after their baptism during the previous itineration, the couple had made an offering to the demon of diseases when their youngest child suddenly fell seriously ill. They had since been unrepentant and remained so despite the exhortation of Judson and his ministry companions. Six other hopeful inquirers during the earlier visit to that village had all "fallen off" as well, so that, according to Judson, "we are obliged to retire with the dispirited feelings of beaten troops." Interestingly, the missionary made the following appeal to his mission agency in reporting this disappointment:

> I respectfully request, and sincerely hope, that this article may be neither suppressed nor polished. The principle of "double selection", as it is termed, that is, one selection by

7   ibid., p. 41.

the missionary and another by the publishing committee, has done great mischief, and contributed more to impair the credit of missionary accounts than anything else. We in the East, knowing how extensively this principle is acted on, do scarcely give any credit to the statements which appear in some periodicals, and the public at large are beginning to open their eyes to the same thing. It is strange to me that missionaries and publishing committees do not see the excellency and efficacy of the system pursued by the inspired writers – that of exhibiting the good and the bad alike. Nothing contributes more to establish the authenticity of the writing. A temporary advantage gained by suppressing truth is a real defeat in the end, and therefore "We must sacrifice only to truth".[8]

Returning to Chummerah, Judson administered the Lord's Supper to thirty-six communicants. From there he and some of his ministry associates journeyed overland on foot to the Dah-gyne. They reached Newville, some forty miles from Chummerah, in four days. Only two families had settled there but others were planning to join them soon and a couple was baptized during this visit.

Judson arrived back in Maulmain on March 27, after an absence of nearly a month. He had baptized nineteen believers during the evangelistic venture and brought with him a number of Karens to attend the "adult" school in Maulmain. The school soon had an average attendance of twenty students – adults and children, mostly Karens. As soon as the students learned to read they were sent back to their home areas, armed with Christian literature to use in evangelizing their fellow countrymen. New students regularly arrived at Maulmain to take the place of those who had returned home. In time the school grew to around fifty.

A "complete fount of types" had recently arrived from Calcutta and Cephas Bennett was ready to start printing the Burmese New Testament. Three days after Judson's return, he corrected

8   ibid., p. 46. "We must sacrifice only to truth" is Wayland's translation in a footnote of a short Greek phrase that ended Judson's original quotation.

the first proof sheet so Bennett could get underway. Early in April the Wades made their way to Rangoon, having left the little church in Mergui under the care of Ko Ing. A few weeks later Jonathan Wade experienced "a violent attack of disease" and the couple hastened to Maulmain for medical assistance. Judson prevailed upon them to stay and take over supervision of the Burmese congregation in Maulmain, so he could turn his full attention to printing and translation concerns. In addition to overseeing Bennett's printing of the New Testament, Judson had determined to take up his translation of the Old Testament again. He had already translated one-third of the Old Testament and calculated that by translating twenty-five to thirty verses a day he could complete the work in an additional two years' time. He shut himself up in a room at the end of the native chapel in order to pursue that work.

Around that same time Judson and his fellow missionaries sent out an impassioned appeal to their mission board for additional missionary recruits to spread the Gospel not only throughout Burma but also to neighboring countries.[9] In addition, Judson, his missionary colleagues and a Mr. J. Nisbet – a pious, high-ranking officer in the East India Company – made generous pledges toward the establishment of a mission to the Jews in Palestine. They pledged 2,400 dollars toward a proposed total of 10,000 dollars for such a mission, then appealed to missionary-minded leaders in America to raise the remainder of the funds and launch the new enterprise. While the appeal for fresh missionary recruits for Burma met with some success in the months and years to follow, the proposal of a Jewish mission apparently fell on deaf ears. No response was ever received from the leaders to whom the latter proposal was made.[10]

Aided by a new missionary printer named Oliver Cutter and a second printing press, Cephas Bennett produced an astounding

9   ibid., pp. 51–4, records that appeal.

10   ibid., pp. 32–7, relates Judson's promotion of this proposal as well as a significant encouragement he received near the end of his life indicating that God had honored and blessed his concern for the Jewish people. Providentially, a tract detailing part of his personal testimony played a part in the conversion of a number of Jews.

volume of printed materials by the end of the year. Bennett and Cutter printed a three-thousand-copy edition of the Burmese New Testament, 33,000 copies of tracts and catechisms (in Burmese as well as some in Karen and Talaing), and a Karen spelling book. All told, some two and a half million printed pages came out of their presses in 1832. That year 143 believers had been baptized and added to the church in Burma, including 126 indigenous people, most of them Karens, along with seventeen foreigners.

On January 12 of the following year, Judson penned a fervent, even pointed letter to the Corresponding Secretary of his mission board, expressing deep concern over a matter that had just come to light:

> Rev. and Dear Sir: It is with regret and consternation that we have just learned that a new missionary has come out for a limited term of years. I much fear that this will occasion a breach in our mission. How can we, who are devoted for life, cordially take to our hearts and councils one who is a mere hireling? On this subject all my brethren and sisters are united in sentiment. We should perhaps address a joint letter to the board; but such a measure might not appear sufficiently respectful. May I earnestly and humbly entreat the board to reconsider this matter, and not follow implicitly in the wake of other societies (I beg pardon), whether right or wrong.
>
> I have seen the beginning, middle, and end of several limited term missionaries. They are all good for nothing. Though brilliant in an English pulpit, they are incompetent to any real missionary work. They come out for a few years, with the view of acquiring a stock of credit on which they may vegetate the rest of their days, in the congenial climate of their native land. ... As to lessening the trials of the candidate for missions, and making the way smooth before him, it is just what ought not to be done. *Missionaries need more trials on their first setting out, instead of less.*
>
> The motto of every missionary, whether preacher, printer, or schoolmaster, ought to be, "*Devoted for life*". A few

days ago, brother Kincaid was asked by a Burmese officer of government how long he intended to stay. *"Until all Burma worships the eternal God,"* was the prompt reply. If the limited term system, which begins to be fashionable in some quarters, gain the ascendancy, it will be the death blow of missions, and retard the conversion of the world a hundred years.[11]

The previous November the Wades had finally been forced to sail for America in an effort to preserve Jonathan's life. Their departure required Judson to once again assume more oversight of the indigenous work at Maulmain and its outstations. Consequently, he was away from Maulmain the better part of three months, from January 18 to April 9, spending that time in Chummerah. There he supervised the native evangelists in their regional outreach ministries, led a worship service each evening and every Sunday morning with the assistance of Karen interpreters, and continued translating twenty-five or more Old Testament verses per day. Eight believers were baptized during that stay at Chummerah. In addition, a new missionary, Miss Sarah Cummings, arrived to supervise the school that had been established there.

A short while after Judson returned to Maulmain, the Bennetts departed for Rangoon to fill a vacancy created by Kincaid's removal to Ava. Five months later, on September 24, the Cutters left for Rangoon, from which they intended to proceed to Ava. They took with them one of the printing presses and several thousand tracts for distribution along the way.

By the end of June, Judson still needed to translate the Minor Prophets and the historical books from 1 Kings to Esther. At that point he held out hope of finishing the Old Testament by year's end but had to relinquish that expectation after losing a month through "a complication of ailments". However, on January 31, 1834, Judson, full of humble gratitude, informed his mission board of the completion of his translation of the Old Testament into Burmese:

11 ibid., pp. 62–3.

Thanks be to God, I can *now* say I have attained. I have knelt down before him, with the last leaf in my hand, and imploring his forgiveness for all the sins which have polluted my labors in this department, and his aid in future efforts to remove the errors and imperfections which necessarily cleave to the work, I have commended it to his mercy and grace; I have dedicated it to his glory. May he make his own inspired word, now complete in the Burman tongue, the grand instrument of filling all Burma with songs of praise to our great God and Savior Jesus Christ. Amen.[12]

At that same time he reported that seventy-six believers had been baptized in Burma the previous year, including nineteen Burmans, thirty-five Karens and twenty-two foreigners. Especially noteworthy was the fact that Kincaid had baptized the first two Christian converts, both Burmans, in Ava.

Judson immediately set to work revising his Old Testament translation so that the printing of it could begin. The first two weeks of March he took a brief break from his revision work in order to visit Newville, where nine believers were baptized. In the opening days of the following month he ventured to Tavoy for a special, though heretofore undisclosed purpose.

12   ibid., pp. 75–6.

30

A NEW FAMILY
(1834-1835)

Judson's journal entry datelined "Tavoy, April 10" [1834], having been preceded by not a single word of foreshadowing, records matter-of-factly:

> I arrived here on the evening of the 6th. Am delighted with this station, and every thing about it. The few native Christians whom I have seen, and the schools, appear excellently well. But the glory of this station, the two hundred Karen converts, and their village of Ma-tah-myu, I found myself not at leisure to visit. Indeed, I have hardly found time to step out of the mission enclosure since my arrival; and to-day, having received the benediction of the Rev. Mr. Mason, I embark for Maulmain, accompanied by Mrs. Judson, and the only surviving child of the beloved founder of the Tavoy station.

Judson did add an eloquent, if brief, statement placing his and Sarah's new marital union in the context of remembering their honored, deceased spouses:

> Once more, farewell to thee, Boardman, and thy long-cherished grave. May the memory be ever fresh and fragrant, as the memory of the other beloved, whose beautiful, death-marred form reposes at the foot of the hopia tree. May we, the survivors, so live as to deserve and receive the smiles of those sainted ones who have gone before us. And at last may we all four be reunited before the throne of glory, and form

a peculiarly happy family, our mutual loves all purified and consummated in the bright world of love.[1]

Nearly seven and a half years had passed since Ann's death and Boardman had been dead for just over three years. Judson was forty-six years old and Sarah thirty-one at the time of their wedding. No record of how and when they decided to marry has been preserved. A good degree of personal warmth seems discernible in a letter of commendation that Sarah had written to Judson several weeks earlier, on February 17, shortly after he completed his initial translation of the Old Testament into Burmese:

My Dear Brother,

The translation of the Bible into Burmese is an event, to which thousands have looked forward with joyful anticipation, and for which, thousands now perishing in their sins, should fall on their knees in thanksgiving to God, and through which, thousands yet unborn will praise him for ever and ever.

My dear brother, I dare not pass encomiums upon a fellow-mortal in speaking of the Word of God; and if you think me guilty of this impiety in what I may say, bear with me yourself, and pray God to forgive me. I have, for the last four years, been in the daily practice of reading attentively the New Testament in Burmese; and the more I study it, the better I am pleased and satisfied with the translation. I am delighted with the graphic style of the narrative part; and think many of the doctrinal passages are expressed with a force and perspicuity entirely wanting in our [English] version. How much of this is due to your vivid manner of expression, and how much to the nature of the language, I do not know. I sometimes tell the Masons, that I should be willing to learn Burmese for the sake of being able to read the Scriptures in that language.

Last Lord's day, while reading a portion of Scripture, I was affected to tears, and could scarcely proceed, as is

1   Wayland, *Memoir*, vol. 2, pp. 82-3.

often the case, in reading striking passages; and the effect was also observable on the old Tavoyan, for he managed to bring a great part of it into his prayer, which immediately followed. My scholars are now reading the Gospel of Luke; and I am reading St John's Gospel and Revelation alternately, at evening worship.

Yours affectionately,

Sarah H. Boardman[2]

It is not hard to see how Judson was attracted to Sarah. Following her husband's death she had courageously determined to carry on in the Tavoy ministry, despite the strong encouragements of friends and relatives in America to return to her homeland with her young son. In addition to supervising a number of schools in Tavoy and its surrounding villages, she continued to make evangelistic forays to Karen settlements in the jungle. She had demonstrated keen, self-sacrificial loyalty to her husband and children. Her temperament and demeanor were steady and modest. Though no portrait was ever painted of her, a circumstance Judson would later "exceedingly regret", years later he spoke of "her soft blue eye, her mild aspect, her lovely face and elegant form".[3]

Sarah was born on November 4, 1803, in Alstead, New Hampshire. She was the oldest of an eventual thirteen children born to Ralph and Abiah Hall. While Sarah was still a young girl her parents moved from Alstead to Danvers, Massachusetts, and subsequently to Salem. Though helping her mother care for the growing family prevented Sarah from attending school, she exerted herself to pursue her education at home. At age seventeen she became a teacher and a student at a local school. In exchange for teaching a class of young girls in the afternoon she was able to take classes herself in the morning on such subjects as Christian apologetics, rhetoric, logic, geometry and Latin.

Sarah publicly professed her faith in Jesus Christ when she was sixteen years old. Following her conversion, she had a marked

---

2   Emily Judson, *Memoir of Sarah B. Judson*, pp. 165-6.

3   ibid., p. 247.

concern for the salvation of her own siblings as well as other people. She became "assiduously engaged" in tract distribution and established a weekly young women's prayer meeting through which a number of individuals, most of them older than herself, came to faith in Christ. She also manifested definite interest in foreign missionary endeavor. After reading an account of the life of Samuel J. Mills, who died at age thirty-five after devoting his brief career to the tireless promotion of foreign missions, Sarah desired to become a missionary herself. Due to her humility and self-doubts concerning her fitness for such a ministry, however, she sought to put down the desire. But when it persisted she contemplated and even made inquiries concerning the possibility of serving as a missionary to American Indians.

Not long thereafter Sarah met George Dana Boardman, a graduate of Waterville College (originally The Maine Literary and Theological Institute, present-day Colby College of Waterville, Maine), who was then enrolled at Andover Seminary and preparing for a missionary career. The Boardmans were married in Salem's First Baptist Church on Sunday, July 3, 1825, and a few weeks later departed for India. They studied the Burman language at Chittapore, near Calcutta, while awaiting the end of the Anglo-Burmese War, after which they proceeded to Amherst, Burma.

Now, seven years later, as Sarah returned with Judson as her new husband to Maulmain, she did so in weakened health. Thin and pale and possessing little appetite, she could scarcely walk half a mile. Soon after their arrival in Maulmain she endured a long, severe attack of dysentery, the disease that had plagued her now and again throughout her years in Burma. She sank lower than ever before and was brought "to the brink of the grave". Though he did not tell her so until she had begun to improve, her attending physician lost all hope she would recover. For weeks she lay confined to her bed. Sometimes Judson carried her in his arms from the bed to the couch so she could have a small change of scenery.

Gradually she began to recover, though she remained very weak for a long time. As soon as she was able, at Judson's recommendation, she began taking a ride on horseback every morning before sunrise. After she had been riding four or five months, her "nice little pony" suddenly died. Sarah and Judson then began a new regimen of walking together for exercise early each morning. Every day they were out together, "walking at a rapid pace, far over the hills beyond the town, before the sun was up". Eventually Sarah was able to report, "... during these years, my health has been better than at any time previous, since my arrival in India; and my constitution seems to have undergone an entire renovation."[4]

The house that Judson provided for his new family in Maulmain contained three large and two small rooms. The walls were made of bamboo mats and the roof was thatched. A wide, shaded verandah ran along the entire front of the house and faced on the principal street. The house was located a short distance from the mission chapel, school, printing house and other missionary residences.

Judson continued to dedicate most of his time to revising his Old Testament translation in preparation for its going to press. By the end of June about one quarter of the Testament had been printed. A humorous incident that took place shortly after Judson's marriage to Sarah pointed out the need for further revisions. A faithful old Christian approached Judson very troubled in spirit and with the revelation that he feared his teacher was to be among the lost. "You know," stated the Burman, "the Bible says that God will deliver his children from the snare of the widow. But he has not delivered you; you have been snared by the widow." They turned to Psalm 91:3 and discovered that it read exactly as the old man had indicated. The feminine form of the word "hunter" had been employed, which was the Burmese term for "widow". The mistaken translation was speedily emended.[5]

The first part of December the Wades and several new missionaries arrived in Maulmain from America. A Miss Gardener joined the Wades in proceeding to Tavoy. Mr. and Mrs. Howard

4   ibid., p. 181.

5   Warburton, *Eastward!*, p. 145.

went to Rangoon while Grover Comstock and Mr. Simons ventured to the Arakan coast. Mr. and Mrs. Vinton went to fill the vacancy at Chummerah resulting from "the lamented death of dear sister Cummings" sometime earlier that year. (The exact cause of Sarah Cummings's death after less than two years on the field is no longer known.) Another leadership vacancy, this one in Mergui, had been left unfilled following the death that same year of faithful Ko Ing. One of the new missionary couples, Mr. and Mrs. Osgood, settled in Maulmain to help with the printing ministry there. By year's end Judson had revised nearly half of his Old Testament translation, and 2,000 copies of all the books from 1 Samuel to Job had been printed.

Before her marriage to Judson, Sarah had determined that she would send her son, George, now aged six, to America. In that era missionary couples commonly sent their children to their homeland so they could receive a formal education and to increase the likelihood that they would live to adulthood. Two years earlier the Bennetts had sent their two young daughters, Elsina and Mary, back to America for those reasons. The *Cashmere*, the ship that recently brought the Wades and a number of other missionaries, intended to return directly to Boston after only a brief stop at Singapore. The next opportunity to have George transported so directly to America very well might not present itself for another year or two. Due to George's sensitive spirit and his tender attachment to his mother, the decision to take advantage of the present opportunity was wrenching for Sarah. To an unidentified "sister" she wrote:

> After deliberation, accompanied with tears and agony and prayers, I came to the conviction that it was my duty to send away my only child, my darling George, and yesterday he bade me a long farewell. ... Oh! I shall never forget his looks, as he stood by the door and gazed at me for the last time. His eyes were filling with tears, and his little face red with suppressed emotion. But he subdued his feelings, and it was not till he had turned away, and was going down the steps that he burst into a flood of tears. I hurried to my room; and

on my knees, with my whole heart, gave him up to God; and
my bursting heart was comforted from above. I felt such
a love to poor perishing souls, as made me willing to give up
all, that I might aid in the work of bringing these wretched
heathen to Christ. The love of God, manifested in sending
his only-begotten and well-beloved Son into this world, to
die for ours sins, touched my heart, and I felt satisfaction in
laying upon the altar my only son.[6]

Judson escorted his step-son by boat to Amherst, holding the boy
in his arms the entire way. He saw George's little bed prepared
and everything settled as comfortably as possible for him in
his cabin aboard ship. At first George's trip went well, with
people being attentive to his needs and happiness. But tragedy
threatened when it came time for him to be taken back aboard
the *Cashmere* after it had stopped for a few weeks in Singapore.
Two missionaries, J. T. Jones and William Dean, were escorting
George to the ship in a small boat rowed by a local. Ten miles
from shore and five miles from the *Cashmere*, they were attacked by
harbor pirates in a small sailboat. Jones was thrown into the sea
and Dean was stabbed in the side, then impaled through the wrist
with a three-pronged fishing spear. All this George witnessed
while cowering in terror under a bench. The pirates fled after
seizing a box of letters to various family members back home in
America, wrongly assuming it to contain money. Thankfully, the
oarsman was able to haul Jones back into the boat and the small
party reached the *Cashmere* without further incident.

Maulmain had become the central mission station in Burma.
New missionaries were often sent there first and veteran
missionaries tended to return there to confer with missionary
colleagues and to seek medical assistance. At times a number of
missionaries ended up congregated in Maulmain all at the same
time. On May 6, 1835, Judson wrote a letter of concern to his
mission board, expressing marked concern over this tendency
and suggesting a more profitable plan for missionary placement:

6   Emily Judson, *Memoir of Sarah B. Judson*, pp. 190-1.

Formerly, having spent many years alone, I felt desirous of missionary society, and was disposed to encourage a few to stay together, not doubting but that we should all find enough to do. But I have now learned that one missionary standing by himself, feeling his individual responsibility, and *forced to put forth all his efforts*, is worth half a dozen cooped up in one place, while there are unoccupied stations in all directions, and whole districts, of thousands, and hundreds of thousands, perishing in the darkness of heathenism. ... [W]hen I think of seven families – eight when the _____s are here, which will probably be every rainy season – my spirit groans within me. ...

... I have now five native assistants, who spend an hour with me, every morning, in reporting the labors of the preceding day, in receiving instructions, and in praying together. These men penetrate every lane and corner of this place and the neighboring villages; and since I have adopted this plan – about four months – there are some very encouraging appearances. As soon as I get through with the Old Testament complete, I want to double their number, and devote part of my time to instructing them systematically. Now, ten such persons, half students, half assistants, cost no more than one missionary family; and for actual service they are certainly worth a great deal more. This is the way in which I think missions ought to be conducted. One missionary, or two, at most, ought to be stationed in every important central place, to collect a church and an interest around him; to set the native wheels to work, and to keep them at work. ... An additional missionary would doubtless do good; but nearly all the good he would do would probably be done if he were away, laboring in some other place, which, but for him, would be unoccupied, and where, of course, all that he should effect would be so much net gain to the cause.[7]

Besides meeting daily to guide and pray with his indigenous assistants, Judson remained "closely employed in revising the

---

7   Wayland, *Memoir*, vol. 2, pp. 99-101.

translation of the Old Testament, and reading proof sheets of Scripture and tracts". By mid-year 2,000 copies of Genesis through Ruth had been printed as well as "our standard tracts, in editions of thirty and forty thousand". Sarah had set to work learning Talaing so she could assist in preparing tracts and portions of the New Testament for the numerous Peguan people in that region. Judson finished his Old Testament revision on September 26. As pastor once again, of the local Burmese congregation, he preached every Sunday to a crowded assembly and each weeknight to an average gathering of thirty. A new, larger chapel was built to accommodate the growing numbers. Sarah led women's prayer meetings, held classes for mothers, advised indigenous believers and settled "little difficulties" among them.

On the last day of October Sarah gave birth to a daughter. The infant was named Abigail Ann in honor of Judson's mother, sister and first wife. In the letter Judson wrote the next day to his mother and sister, informing them of Abigail Ann's arrival; he also made a significant personal revelation concerning his missionary career:

> I alluded above to the attainment of the great objects of my missionary undertaking. I used to think, when first contemplating a missionary life, that if I should live to see the Bible translated and printed in some new language, and a church of one hundred members raised up on heathen ground, I should anticipate death with the peaceful feelings of old Simeon. The Bible in Burmese will, I expect, be out of the press by the end of this year; and – not to speak of several hundred Burmans and Karens baptized at different stations – the Burmese church in Maulmain, of which I am pastor, contains ninety-nine native members, and there will doubtless be several more received before the end of the year. Unite with me, my dear mother and sister, in gratitude to God, that he has preserved me so long, and, notwithstanding my entire unworthiness, has made me instrumental to a little good.[8]

8   ibid. p. 105.

In his end of year accounting to the mission board, Judson shared that the number of members in Maulmain's indigenous congregation had reached 102. Especially notable among the believers who were baptized at Maulmain that year was Koo-chil, the Islamic servant who had faithfully assisted the Judsons through their distresses in Ava. Though he had remained in the employ of various mission families since then, he steadfastly resisted Christian instruction and clung to his allegiance to Mohammed. He married a Burmese woman who afterward became a Christian, and largely through her witness he was led to faith in Christ. Judson also reported that the printing of the Old Testament in Burmese had been completed on December 29. Three printing presses were constantly at work and a fourth was used in producing proof sheets. The translation of the New Testament into Talaing had proceeded up through the book of Hebrews.

31

THE BURMESE BIBLE
(1836-1840)

Toward the end of February of the following year, 1836, the ship *Louvre* arrived at Amherst, bringing new missionary reinforcements as well as a member of the missionary board. In an effort to improve both understanding and communication, Reverend Howard Malcom, pastor of Boston's Federal Street Church, had been sent out by the mission board to conduct its first-ever on-site survey of conditions in the field. While in Maulmain, Malcom stayed in Judson and Sarah's home. He took a survey trip up the Salween with Judson and another up the Dagyaing with Sarah.

After Malcom left to visit Rangoon and Ava in May, Judson commenced a second revision of the Burmese New Testament. He also produced a two-hundred-page volume on *The Life of Christ*. The New Testament revision was completed in March of the following year, 1837, and was printed in an edition of 10,000 copies. The initial edition of 15,000 copies of *The Life of Christ* in 1836 was followed by a second printing of 40,000 copies the middle of 1837.

On March 22, 1837, the day the final New Testament proof sheet went to press, Judson recorded the following "Miscellaneous Resolutions":

1. Use no intoxicating liquor as a beverage.

2. Indulge in no foreign – that is, English or American – newspaper reading, except a regular course of some one

religious paper, and sometimes an occasional article from other papers.

3. Observe the seasons of secret prayer every day, morning noon, and night.

4. Embrace every opportunity of preaching the gospel to every soul.

5. Endeavor to keep the "resolution for promoting brotherly love".

6. Read a certain portion of Burmese every day, Sundays excepted.

7. *Go* and *preach* the gospel, every day.[1]

Around that same time Judson paid a visit to an out-station that had been established by a new missionary, Miss Eleanor Macomber, at Dong-yan. Under her ministry among Pwo Karens at the foot of Mount Zwai-ka-ben, a small Christian church had formed. After Judson baptized three individuals during his visit, the congregation consisted of ten confirmed believers. After returning to Maulmain Judson fell very ill from "imprudent exposure to the sun". As a result, he was "hardly able to participate in the joy" occasioned by the arrival of another small group of new missionaries who arrived just at that time on the *Rosabella*. They paid a brief visit to Maulmain before continuing on to other parts of the country.

Sarah gave birth to a son on April 7 and he was named Adoniram Brown. Even with two little ones to care for, Sarah continued her Talaing translation work with the assistance of Ko Man-boke. They translated four of the standard Burmese tracts into Talaing and each of those was printed in an initial edition of 10,000 copies. Sarah was also preparing "a voluminous work" entitled "Bible Questions for use in Bible classes and Sunday schools". A Sabbath school ministry had been started under the super-intendence of Mr. Osgood, the printer, and Sarah was assisting with that. Sadly,

1   Wayland, *Memoir*, vol. 2, p. 114.

after less than three years on the mission field, Osgood's wife died of tuberculosis on October 5.

Throughout the final four months of 1837 Judson worked at compiling an elaborate "Digest of Scripture, consisting of Extracts from the Old and New Testaments". In it he sought to include "the most important passages of Scripture" that pertained to a succession of topics beginning with "The Scripture of Truth" and ending with "The Retribution of Eternity". "I trust this work will be as valuable as *The Life of Christ*," he commented, "and perhaps more useful, as a book of reference."[2] Sarah and her assistant had translated *The Life of Christ* into Talaing and a first edition of 5,000 copies was produced.

A temporary shortage in paper supply curtailed the progress of further printing efforts during the opening months of 1838. For a time Judson was able to hold meetings "all over town" five or six nights a week and to do some daytime zayat preaching as well. As he revealed in a letter to the Corresponding Secretary of his mission board, his ministry efforts were routinely impaired that time of year by compromised health: "As to my health, the annual fever, which I have had for nine years in succession, from November to March – except the year I spent in Burma [Rangoon] – has been gradually growing lighter; but it still hangs on, and deprives me of a good deal of time."[3]

Baby Adoniram, not yet one year old, was inoculated for a mild case of small pox in February or March. "He is one of the prettiest, brightest children you ever saw," Judson wrote his mother and sister shortly after the disease had run its course. His parents nicknamed him Fen and the local residents called him Pwen, both words meaning "flower". Abby, now nearing two and a half years of age, was growing rapidly and spoke Burmese quite fluently. Though an active child, "she attends family and public worship with us, and has learned to sit still and behave herself." Of young Adoniram his father revealed, "But Fen ... when he is brought into the chapel, and sees me in my place, has the impudence to roar out

2   ibid., p. 118.
3   ibid., p. 122.

Bah (as the Burmans call father) with such a stentorian voice, that his nurse is obliged to carry him out again."[4]

Around that same time, Judson began revising parts of the Old Testament in preparation for "a new edition of the whole Bible, to be comprised in one volume quarto". He anticipated that undertaking would require virtually all his time for the year to come. A third child, a son, was born to Judson and Sarah on July 15. He was named Elnathan in memory of his deceased uncle. With Sarah's increased domestic responsibilities, she needed to turn over her Talaing translation work to one of the newer missionaries at Maulmain, James Haswell.

During the latter months of 1838 Judson started to lose his voice, developed soreness in his lungs and throat and came to have a persistent, painful cough. Normal conversation became difficult and public speaking impossible. These symptoms were cause for concern as perhaps being early manifestations of encroaching tuberculosis, which had already carried off so many of the early missionaries. Judson's physician and colleagues urged him to take a long sea voyage in an effort to regain his health. Consequently, on February 20, 1839, he boarded the *Snipe*, bound for Calcutta. During the voyage Judson's cough and soreness largely abated.

Throughout the three weeks that he spent in Calcutta, beginning March 8, Judson made the acquaintance of fellow Baptists as well as missionaries of other denominations. He visited a number of Christian churches and schools. Many evenings were devoted to "missionary company", enjoying fellowship and stimulating conversation with various missionaries. He even took time on two occasions to do some shopping at the city's bazaars. Judson spent one weekend upriver at Serampore where he stayed at "old Mrs. Marshman's". He enjoyed meeting the missionaries who currently served there but with Carey, Marshman and Ward all deceased, Judson could not help but feel that "the glory has departed from Serampore".

While returning to Maulmain, again aboard the *Snipe*, Judson tested the strength of his voice by conducting a worship service

4   ibid., p. 120.

in his cabin with Koon-gyah, the Burmese Christian who had accompanied him on the trip. Though the exertion was only slight, Judson was dismayed when the old soreness and tendency to cough returned that afternoon. By the time he reached Maulmain he had recovered again to the degree that he could use his voice in common conversation without much difficulty. But as soon as the rainy season commenced a couple weeks later, his throat complaint returned "with fresh violence". Some urged him to take another voyage but he thought the benefit would be only temporary. Others encouraged him to return to America for a year or two but he believed he would be of no value to the missionary cause there without a voice.

During Judson's recent absence from Maulmain, the printing of his *Digest of Scripture* was completed. The volume, which he had started composing over a year and a half earlier, was printed in 136 octavo pages. After his return, the printing of the new edition of the Burmese Bible was recommenced, beginning at 1 Samuel 26.

Judson, for the first time in about ten months, attempted to preach the last Sunday of October. His sermon was short and he spoke in a low voice. Afterwards he experienced no ill effects. "How pleased you would have been," Sarah wrote to Judson's mother a few days later, "to see the joy beaming from the countenances of the dear native Christians, as they saw their beloved and revered pastor once more take the desk!"[5] At year's end Judson was still preaching each Sunday morning and was hoping to resume leadership of the nightly worship services in the months to follow. By that time Maulmain's Burmese congregation consisted of 133 baptized members in good standing. Printing of the new edition of the Bible had proceeded up through the book of Isaiah.

One other significant blessing occurred on the final day of 1839 when Sarah gave birth to another son. Judson reported playfully to Mason in Tavoy, "Master Henry came into notice the last day of the year; but there was no earthquake, nor any thing."[6]

5 ibid., p. 149.
6 ibid., p. 154.

Judson spent ten days in Rangoon the following February. He found the condition of the city "considerably improved" and estimated its size to be about twice as large as Maulmain. But official opposition to Christianity remained strong there. One day midway through Judson's visit, he and some of the local Christians distributed around one thousand tracts at the mission house. People were "greedy to get them". But then Ko En, Judson's longtime faithful assistant in evangelism and Bible translation, was summoned to the government house by the city governor and detained. Knowing that Judson was out of favor with local officials, Captain Boothby who had traveled with him from Maulmain and Mr. Staig, an Englishman who then resided in Rangoon, appealed to the governor and succeeded in gaining Ko En's release.

At some point in 1840, Eleanor Macomber, having served four years in Burma, stopped at Maulmain after making an extended evangelistic tour to isolated Karens of the Pwo tribe far up the Houng-ta-ran River. It soon became apparent that she had contracted the so-called "jungle fever", which led to her death a short time later. Judson honored Eleanor by writing a sketch of her brief but fruitful ministry career.[7]

Mr. and Mrs. Edward Stevens had arrived in Burma as missionaries two years earlier and were currently stationed at Maulmain. A letter written by Mrs. Stevens on May 12, 1840, sheds light on declined spiritual conditions that had crept into Maulmain's indigenous church at that time and Judson's determination to rectify the situation:

> We had a pleasant visit last evening from Mr. and Mrs. Judson. Mr. Judson feels sadly about the state of the church; many of the young members falling into open sin, and the older ones cold and negligent of religious duties. He is desirous of doing something for its improvement, and has thought of several plans. He has framed a covenant of eight items, taken from the New Testament, which all must sign. The quarto Bible is now [nearly] complete, a copy of which

7   The sketch is preserved, ibid., pp. 495–7.

Mr. Judson intends to present to each head of a family, in rather a formal manner, carrying it himself to the house, and there solemnly enjoining its daily perusal, and the habit of morning and evening family worship, which has been much neglected by the church. He intends having henceforth three services for the natives on the Sabbath, which will probably supersede the brethren's prayer meeting at Mr. Osgood's.[8]

The revision and printing of the entire Burmese Bible were completed on October 24 – "and a happy day of relief and joy it was to me," Judson commented. The new translation consisted of about 1,200 quarto pages. In making his translation, Judson had adhered carefully to the original Hebrew and Greek texts, seeking "to make every sentence a faithful representation of the original". In addition, "Long and toilsome research among the biblical critics and commentators ... was frequently requisite to satisfy my mind that my first position was the right one. Several fellow missionaries had assisted him in his translation work: "Of [their] several hundred suggestions that have been sent me from different quarters, I have sooner or later adopted by far the greater part, though, in some cases, with some modification." Of another invaluable aid, Judson stated, "Nor ought I to forget my native brother, Maung En, my faithful fellow-laborer for many years, even before the present revision was begun – one of our most judicious and devoted assistants." In summary, Judson said of his new translation:

> I have bestowed more time and labor on the revision than on the first translation of the work, and more, perhaps, than is proportionate to the actual improvement made. ... Considerable improvement, however, has been made, I trust, both in point of style and approximation to the real meaning of the original. But the *beau ideal* of translation, so far as it concerns the poetical and prophetical books of the Old Testament, I profess not to have attained. If I live many more years, of which I have no expectation, I shall have to

8   ibid., pp. 156–7.

bestow much more labor upon those books. With the New Testament I am rather better satisfied, and the testimony of those acquainted with the language is rather encouraging. At least, I hope that I have laid a good foundation for my successors to build upon.[9]

A letter written by a missionary in Burma two years after Judson's death bears glowing testimony to the high quality of his Burmese Bible:

The translation of the Holy Scriptures into the Burman language by the late Dr Judson is admitted to be the best translation in India; that is, the translation has given more satisfaction to his contemporaries and successors than any translation of the Bible into any other Eastern language has done to associate missionaries in any other part of India. It is free from all obscurity to the Burmese mind. It is read and understood perfectly. Its style and diction are as choice and elegant as the language itself, peculiarly honorific, would afford, and conveys, doubtless, the mind of the Spirit as perfectly as can be.[10]

With the completion of the Burmese Bible, operations in the Maulmain printing department ceased for a time. They had an ample supply of Bibles and tracts on hand for use in the British-controlled territories of Arakan and Tenasserim. Due to recent rumors of war between Burma and Britain (unfounded reports that never materialized), all parts of the country under Burmese control were presently "closed against all missionary operations", including the distribution of Christian literature.

Judson resumed his supervision of the indigenous evangelists, which he had set aside while completing his revised translation.

9   All the above quotations concerning Judson's Bible translation are recorded, ibid., pp. 160–2.

10 ibid., p. 168. Other more extensive descriptions and estimations of Judson's Bible translation endeavors are provided: ibid., pp. 163–8; Warburton, *Eastward!*, pp. 143–56. Judson's Bible translation was used for over eighty years in Burma until the Baptist mission issued a revision of his New Testament translation in 1924 and of the Old Testament in 1933 (Warburton, *Eastward!*, p. 155).

Once again, he met with them each morning for prayer and instruction before they went out to evangelize at zayats and throughout the city. The Maulmain church had 145 members at that time, though eight of those were suspended from receiving communion for disciplinary reasons.

32

Family Illness
(1841)

The year 1841 proved to be extremely trying for the Judson family health-wise. All four of the Judson children came down with whooping cough in the opening months of the year. Before they were entirely recovered from that ailment, three of them developed dysentery. Sarah gave birth to a stillborn son, who was named Luther, on March 8.[1] She, too, was struck with dysentery and sunk so low that she was unable to speak. "The dear sisters of the mission" came to say their final farewells. The three ailing children were taken to other homes and Judson devoted all his time to caring for his wife. Sarah recovered somewhat but she and the two oldest children, Abby and Adoniram, remained so weak from recurring bouts of diarrhea that the doctors pronounced them in imminent danger. The physicians, missionary colleagues and Burmese believers "became clamorous" that the Judsons needed to take an extended sea-voyage in an effort to save lives and recoup health.

For weeks Judson had labored all hours day and night seeking to care for his ailing family. Now he had the full responsibility of doing the packing and other preparations for his family to undertake the voyage. He arranged their cabin aboard ship with four small berths for the children on one side, Sarah's bed on the other, and a removable cot for himself in between. They embarked on June 26. It was monsoon season and on the fourth night of the voyage the ship struck on shoals. For about twenty minutes it

1   Anderson, *To the Golden Shore*, p. 429.

was feared the vessel would break apart. But the rising tide lifted the ship from the rocks and it was able to tack away from the peril.

After arriving at Calcutta on July 11, the Judsons continued upriver to the healthier environs of Serampore. Despite the fact that Judson rented "a nice dry house, on the very bank of the river", the fickle weather was unfavorable toward the recovery of his family members: "At one time it was so oppressively hot," Sarah related, "that we could scarcely breathe, and the next hour the cold, bleak winds would come whistling in, at the high windows, completely chilling the poor invalids."[2]

They were encouraged to extend their sea voyage and unsuccessfully made inquiries about ships that might take them to Isle of France. Just then Captain Thomas Hamlin, Jr, a pious Scotsman with whom the Judsons had some acquaintance from Maulmain, paid them a visit, knowing nothing of their present desires. His ship, the *Ramsay*, was scheduled to sail for Isle of France in ten days, and from there he intended to return to Maulmain. He offered to transport them on the longer, circuitous route at no greater expense than it would have cost them to sail directly back to Maulmain. "We should then have the benefit of being at sea two months or more," Judson explained, "and a few weeks' residence at the Isle of France, the most healthy part of the East."[3] At first they hesitated, dreading the rough passage they were almost certain to encounter during that stormiest season of the year. But when "Dear Little Enna" (Elnathan) suffered "an alarming relapse" and the health of the other children and Sarah remained compromised, they accepted Hamlin's offer.

On July 23 Sarah took the two older children and went down to Calcutta to make some necessary preparations and purchases for the upcoming voyage. Judson remained at Serampore to continue caring for the two younger boys. When Sarah left, Elnathan was already recovering nicely and Henry seemed as well as he had for weeks. Four days after her departure, however,

2   Emily Judson, *Memoir of Sarah B. Judson*, p. 218.

3   Wayland, *Memoir*, vol. 2, p. 173.

Henry's condition took a sudden, unfavorable turn. The next day he grew worse and Elnathan came down with a fever. Judson sent word of these developments to Sarah at Calcutta. That evening Judson began to despair of the toddler's life. The following day the attending physician gave the boy up as beyond recovery. They stopped giving him any more medicine because he could not keep it in his stomach even a single minute. "My only prayer was, that he might not die before his mother arrived," Judson later recalled. "O, what heavy hours now passed!"

Upon receiving her husband's message the morning after he sent it, Sarah immediately made arrangements to return upriver after the tide turned early that evening. Though she had no way of knowing how grave Henry's condition had become, she was eager to get back to her little ones. The upriver journey progressed slowly and it was two in the morning before Sarah reached their temporary residence at Serampore. Judson met her at the door, embraced her, and said, "Oh, my love, you have come to the house of death!"

"What! O, what is it?"

"Dear little Henry is dying."

Sarah hastened to the youngster and was shocked at how changed he was. She had left him "a bright little boy, running about the floor". Now he was pale, listless and emaciated. "Can this be Henry?!" she involuntarily exclaimed. She was relieved when Henry cried out coherently, "Drink! Drink!" She gave him a small amount of wine and water and was pleased when his stomach did not reject it, as it had rejected all other food and liquid throughout the past twenty-four hours.

The next morning, however, it was clear to both parents that the youngster was dying. All through the day Judson and Sarah hovered over their toddler, giving him water and picking him up when he stretched out his arms to them. No sooner would they pick him up than he would want to be laid back down again, so relentless was his discomfort and restlessness that day. As all this was going on, Elnathan lay nearby "in a violent fever, with his head shaved and a plaster on his chest". In the afternoon and again in the evening Henry suffered a series of convulsions.

At last Sarah, who had been up all the previous night, laid down on a cot beside Henry's crib and instantly fell asleep. About nine o'clock the dying boy began to breathe very loudly. Judson sat down beside him and spoke quietly to him, "Henry, my dear son Henry." The boy opened his eyes and looked affectionately at his father. But then his eyes drooped shut and he stopped breathing. Judson immediately awoke Sarah. Henry gave out two or three final gasps then slipped into eternity. He died at one year and seven months of age on July 30. The following evening his little body was buried in the Serampore mission cemetery, not far from the earthly remains of Carey, Marshman and Ward.

As it turned out, the *Ramsay* was delayed in leaving for Isle of France until August 16. Elnathan had improved considerably by then and en route to Isle of France both he and Abby recovered completely. Sarah's health and strength also improved. But Adoniram, the oldest son, continued to suffer severe relapses of chronic dysentery, leaving his parents "still trembling" over the possible outcome. Adoniram had been ill so long that Elnathan, though fifteen months younger, was "actually stouter and stronger" than his older brother.

The six-week passage to Isle of France turned out to be one of the stormiest voyages Judson had ever experienced. On September 3 the storm brought down half the vessel's masts and sails with "a tremendous crash", and "the rolling and pitching of the ship were dreadful". Despite the difficult weather, the ship was able to be refitted at sea and was in good condition when it docked at Port Louis on October 1.

In terms of spiritual results, Judson considered the voyage to Isle of France a great success. He led worship every Lord's Day while Captain Hamlin and he took turns leading worship each evening. These services were attended by most members of the European crew. Before they reached Isle of France, three seamen "gave pleasing evidence of being converted to God". Sixteen crew members, along with Judson and Hamlin, solemnly signed a covenant in the ship's great Bible to faithfully live for God.

Judson described Port Louis, with its "very few religious people" among some 30,000 inhabitants, to be "a very wicked place". A few pious individuals had petitioned Isle of France's governor for permission to renovate an old government ship in the harbor into a seamen's chapel. Captain Hamlin took the lead in raising subscriptions for that purpose during his stay at the port. The captain also provided his own ship as a place for Sunday worship services while they were there. Judson was troubled by the port city's moral conditions and stunned by its inflated prices: "A fowl is one dollar, and a common pair of shoes three dollars, and every other article almost in the same proportion."[4]

After spending a month at Port Louis, the *Ramsay* set sail for Maulmain, arriving there on December 10. All the Judsons except young Adoniram returned to their home in restored health. A long time would yet pass before Adoniram would recover fully.

Captain Hamlin refused to accept any compensation for having transported the Judsons on their roundabout voyage from Calcutta to Isle of France then back to Maulmain. Normally the fare for the double passage would have been 2,000 rupees, equaling nearly 1,000 dollars. Judson was deeply gratified the Sunday after they arrived back in Maulmain to baptize Hamlin, his first officer and two crew members. Of the captain's influence on his crew, Judson testified, "Many of them have been converted or had previous impressions deepened, through the faithful dealing of Captain Hamlin. He is, indeed, one of the most consistent, zealous, devoted Christians I have met in this part of the world."[5]

---

4   ibid., p. 178.

5   ibid., p. 181. When Captain Hamlin returned to his hometown of Greenock, Scotland, after this particular voyage, a pamphlet was published by a local minister, John Simpson, detailing the significant spiritual good that had been accomplished during the journey. The portion of the pamphlet relating to Judson's ministry to members of the *Ramsay* is recorded ibid., pp. 182–5.

33

LOSS OF A WORTHY SUCCESSOR
(1842-1845)

Judson continued to be troubled by a cough but his voice was strong enough for him to preach at one of the church services each Sunday. He also led every other of the smaller nightly worship services. To avoid overtaxing his voice and suffering a relapse of his throat ailment, Judson never spoke above a conversational level, even when preaching publicly. Maulmain's congregation continued to grow steadily, if slowly, having around 160 members by May of 1842.

That same month Judson somewhat reluctantly set to work on a project that his mission board and colleagues had encouraged him to undertake for quite some time – the production of a full-length Burmese-English dictionary. To the Corresponding Secretary of the mission board he would later write:

> ... I [have] commenced a dictionary of the language, a work which I had resolved and re-resolved never to touch. ... The board and my [missionary] brethren repeatedly urged me to prepare a dictionary, the one printed in 1826 being exceedingly imperfect; and as Burma continued shut against our labors, and there were several missionaries in this place, I concluded that I could not do better than to comply.
>
> ... notwithstanding my long-cherished aversion to the work, I have come to think it very important; and that, having seen the accomplishment of two objects on which I set my heart when I first came out to the East, the establishment of a church of converted natives, and the translation of the

Bible into their language, I now beguile my daily toil with the prospect of compassing a third, which may be compared to a causeway, designed to facilitate the transmission of knowledge, religious and scientific, from one people to the other.[1]

Another son was born to the Judsons on July 7. They named him Henry Hall. His first name was in honor of his brother who died at Serampore not quite one year earlier and his middle name was his mother's maiden name. Toward the end of the following month Judson received word that his mother had passed away earlier that year, on January 31. She was eighty-two years old at the time of her death.

A couple of weeks before Judson received that news, he adopted a fresh set of personal spiritual resolutions. These he entitled "Rules of Life":

1. Be more careful to observe the seasons of secret prayer.

2. Never indulge resentful feelings towards any person.

3. Embrace every opportunity of exercising kind feelings, and doing good to others, especially to the household of faith.

4. Sweet in temper, face, and word,
   To please an ever-present Lord.

He "renewed" his commitment to live by these rules on the final day of the year. That same day he added: "Resolved to make the desire to please Christ the grand motive of all my actions."[2]

Joyous news came in April of the following year, 1843, that George Boardman, now nearing fifteen years of age, had professed faith in Christ. Judson wrote his stepson: "My Dear George: You cannot tell how rejoiced we have been, and thankful to God, on hearing that you have professed religion and given yourself to the Savior. Your fond mother has shed many tears of joy over this

1   Wayland, *Memoir*, vol. 2, pp. 191–2.
2   ibid., p. 190.

happy event."[3] Sarah wrote similarly: "My Beloved George: The last letter which I received from America respecting you, rejoiced my heart more than the reception of any letter before in my life. It was from Doct[or] Bolles, and contained the joyful intelligence of your hopeful conversion to God."[4]

Sarah gave birth to yet another son on December 18 and he was named Charles. In addition to caring for her five young children, Sarah led a weekly prayer meeting and a separate weekly Bible study, both for women. Around that time she was leading a group of fifteen women in a study of the Life of Christ, using some of the Bible Questions she had composed several years earlier. Through the years she had composed a score of hymns in Burmese which her husband described as "probably the best in our Chapel Hymn Book". Her recently-published Burmese translation of "Pilgrim's Progress, Part 1st" had earned high praise for its quality and beauty.

Just over one year after Charlie's birth, Sarah, at age forty-one, bore her last child, a son named Edward, on December 27, 1844. She had birthed eleven children in eighteen years, three to Boardman and eight to Judson. Of that number, seven were still living.

The Judsons had recently enjoyed three peaceful, pleasant years. Unfortunately, that changed for them early in 1845 when Sarah had a recurrence of her old affliction, dysentery. At the beginning of February she was invited by the Commissioner of Maulmain and his wife to join them in a trip down the coast to Tavoy so as to regain her health. Nine-year-old Abby and thirteen-month-old Charlie traveled with her while the four other boys stayed home with their father and newborn Edward under the supervision of a Burmese wet nurse. Sarah returned from the six-week excursion weaker and in poorer health than when she left.

The Judsons' doctors and all their friends were in unanimous agreement that Sarah could not live more than a few weeks unless she took a trip beyond the tropics but such a voyage

3   ibid.
4   Emily Judson, *Memoir of Sarah B. Judson*, p. 204.

would almost certainly insure her recovery. Reflecting priorities and a conflicted sense of duty that many missionaries in that era shared, Judson revealed to his mission board: "I have long fought against the necessity of accompanying her; but she is now so desperately weak, and almost helpless, that all say it would be nothing but savage inhumanity to send her off alone."[5]

On two or three occasions in more recent years, the mission board had encouraged Judson to visit the United States for the sake of his own health. He had always resisted that suggestion, believing it would be a dereliction of duty. But now the decision was made to return to America for a time. That decision brought about another excruciating determination involving the break-up of their family circle. They would leave their three youngest children – Henry, Charlie and Edward – with friends in Burma, trusting the Lord to reunite them as a family upon the parents' return. They would take their three older children – Abby, Adoniram and Elnathan – to America and leave them there to pursue their education. They always knew such a day would come but it was no less painful now that it had arrived. Judson divulged:

> These rendings of parental ties are more severe, and wring out bitterer tears from the heart's core, than any can possibly conceive, who have never felt the wrench. But I hope I can say with truth that I love Christ above all; and I am striving, in the strength of my weak faith, to gird up my mind to face and welcome all his appointments. And I am much helped to bear these trials, by the advice and encouragement of all my dear brethren and sisters of the mission.[6]

Judson asked his two Burmese language assistants to accompany him on the voyage so he could continue his work on the dictionary. While in America he wished to quietly continue his linguistic pursuits rather than needing to travel about the country making speeches as a missions representative. He reminded the mission

5   Wayland, *Memoir*, vol. 2, p. 198.
6   ibid.

board of his weak voice that was so easily overtaxed and damaged. He further stated that, having devoted himself exclusively to the Burmese language for over thirty years, his facility in English had been greatly diminished. He considered himself incapable of adequately carrying out public speaking in America.[7]

The Judsons embarked on the *Paragon*, destined for London, on April 26. From England, Judson intended to take passage immediately to America. The first part of the voyage was very rough, causing their party considerable seasickness. Judson was also heavily occupied caring for his wife. During the second month Sarah began to improve and Judson grew optimistic about her recovery. After crossing the equator the ship sprung a leak and the captain decided to put in at Isle of France. Before they reached the island, Sarah was recovering so well that, according to Judson, "it appeared clearly to be my duty to return to Maulmain, and leave her to proceed alone."

Upon arrival at Port Louis on July 5, they found a vessel ready to leave for Maulmain. Judson was unwilling to leave Sarah until he had seen her off on the next leg of her journey. But he was so sure of returning to Maulmain himself, he sent his two Burmese assistants home on the departing vessel and made a deposit for himself on another ship scheduled to depart for Calcutta in two or three weeks. Meanwhile they met Captain John Codman, Jr, who invited Sarah and the children to take passage on his ship, the *Sophia Walker*, which was preparing to sail direct to America. He offered a generous rate on their fare. The *Sophia Walker* would deliver Sarah and the children "to the very doors of her friends, where also she would arrive a month earlier than if she went by the way of England."

Suddenly, however, Sarah suffered "a dreadful relapse, which reduced her lower than ever before. Judson soon realized he could not possibly leave her. Though he now "bitterly regretted" that he had sent his language assistants back to Maulmain, he embarked with his wife and children when their ship sailed on July 25.

---

7   Given the ornate nature of public orations and the high expectations of audiences in that regard in nineteenth century America and Britain, it is not surprising that Judson thought this of himself (though likely in error).

After several days back at sea Sarah again appeared to improve. In the cold weather off the Cape of Good Hope, Judson's hopes for her recovery revived. But gradually it became apparent that, though she experienced brief periods of improvement, overall she was steadily declining. As she sank ever lower, Judson began to fear she might die before they reached land and would need to be buried at sea. She was still living when the ship reached St Helena on August 26 but by that time Judson had lost all hope that she would recover. After docking at Jamestown she lingered on five more days.

As death approached, Sarah remained perfectly tranquil and showed no sign of doubt, fear or anxiety. She was ready, even desirous, of going to be with Christ. But having been away from America for twenty years, she had been eagerly anticipating seeing her son George, her parents as well as other relatives and friends. As it became increasingly apparent that those fond hopes likely would not be realized, she felt conflicted. Honestly and submissively she stated, "I am in a strait betwixt two – let the will of God be done."

A few days before Sarah died, Judson called the children to her bedside and said in their hearing, "I wish, my love, to ask pardon for every unkind word or deed of which I have ever been guilty. I feel that I have, in many instances, failed of treating you with that kindness and affection which you have ever deserved."

"O," she responded, "you will kill me if you talk so. It is I that should ask pardon of you. And I only want to get well that I may have an opportunity of making some return for all your kindness, and of showing you how much I love you."

When at last it was clear she was nearing death, Judson "congratulated her on the prospect of soon beholding the Savior in all his glory". Quoting a line from a familiar hymn, she eagerly replied, "What can I want beside?"

On the evening of August 31 the children kissed her goodnight and laid down to sleep. Judson sat by her bedside, sensing the end was near. At two o'clock in the morning, he roused her attention, and asked, "Do you still love the Savior?"

"O, yes, I ever love the Lord Jesus Christ."

"Do you still love me?"

When she indicated she did by using "a peculiar expression of her own", Judson said, "Then give me one more kiss."

For the last time they exchanged that token of their love.

After another hour passed, she stopped breathing. "For a moment," Judson later revealed, "I traced her upward flight, and thought of the wonders that were opening to her view." Then he closed her "sightless eyes" and dressed her for the last time. After that, being exhausted from many sleepless nights, he threw himself down and slept.

He awoke the next morning to find his children weeping as they stood around their mother's unresponsive body. A coffin was procured from shore. Rev. Bertram, a zealous missionary in Jamestown, came aboard ship and said a prayer with the family and crew. On shore they were met by a Church of England chaplain who led them to the cemetery. Members of Bertram's congregation and "a large concourse" of the town's inhabitants accompanied them to the gravesite. Sarah's grave was in "a beautiful, shady spot" that, fittingly, was right beside the burial place of Mrs. Chater, wife of the first evangelical missionary to Burma, who afterward ministered for many years in Ceylon. Like Sarah, she died and was buried at St Helena during her passage home from the mission field.

"After the funeral," Judson testified, "the dear friends of Mr. Bertram took me to their houses and their hearts; and their conversation and prayers afforded me unexpected relief and consolation."[8] These new Christian friends and Captain Codman covered all the expenses for Sarah's funeral. Judson could not stay with them long, however, because the *Sophia Walker* set sail again that same evening.

The days that immediately followed were difficult ones for Judson and his children but eventually Christian faith brought consolation and hope:

8   Wayland, *Memoir*, vol. 2, p. 209.

For a few days, in the solitude of my cabin, with my poor children crying around me, I could not help abandoning myself to heart-breaking sorrow. But the promises of the gospel came to my aid, and faith stretched her view to the bright world of eternal life, and anticipated a happy meeting with those beloved beings whose bodies are mouldering at Amherst and St Helena.[9]

Judson afterward wrote and had published a rather extensive obituary of Sarah in which he surveyed the highlights of her missionary career and provided an account of her final illness and death. He praised her highly throughout the obituary and made a point to compare her with equal favor to his first wife, Ann, whose ministry had gained much greater acclaim. Of Sarah he wrote:

Her bereaved husband is the more desirous of bearing this testimony to her various attainments, her labors, and her worth, from the fact that her own unobtrusive and retiring disposition always led her to seek the shade, as well as from the fact that she was often brought into comparison with one whose life and character were uncommonly interesting and brilliant. The memoir of his first beloved wife has been long before the public. It is, therefore, most gratifying to his feelings to be able to say, in truth, that the subject of this notice was, in every point of natural and moral excellence, the worthy successor of Ann H. Judson. He constantly thanks God that he has been blessed with two of the best of wives ...[10]

9   ibid., pp. 209–10.
10   ibid., pp. 206–7. The entire obituary is recorded, ibid., pp. 204–10.

34

AMERICA AND EMILY
(1845)

Judson arrived in Boston on Wednesday, October 15, six weeks after the *Sophia Walker* sailed from Mt Helena. Francis Wayland commented on Judson's enthusiastic and esteemed reception in America:

> His sufferings at Ava, and his labors as a missionary for more than thirty years, had made the world conversant with his history. In the United States his name had become a familiar word. ... But of the millions here who had known of his labors, and revered his character, probably not fifty had ever seen him. A new generation occupied the places of those venerated men who were the active supporters of missions at the time of his embarkation. Hence the desire to see him was intense. The largest houses of public worship were thronged long before the usual hour of divine service, if it was known that he was to be present. Men of all professions and of all beliefs were anxious to make his acquaintance. His movements were chronicled in all the papers, both religious and secular. In a word, a spontaneous tribute of homage, love, and veneration awaited him in every village and city that he visited.[1]

Judson recoiled from the public attention and adulation that was heaped upon him:

---

1   Wayland, *Memoir*, vol. 2, pp. 212–13.

He shrank with instinctive delicacy from crowded assemblies where he himself was the theme on which every speaker dilated. He seemed to himself to stand up, [since] he could not speak, merely to be exhibited. In this matter he appeared to me a little nervous, and somewhat to err in judgment. When earnest Christian men sought to make his acquaintance – men who would never have done it but because they honored his services for Christ – his manner of receiving them was some-times chilling, if not repulsive. ... I witnessed myself some instances of this kind, and regretted to perceive that he had, as I thought, mistaken the motives of those who really honored him as a man who had borne hardness for the sake of Christ.[2]

Two days after Judson's arrival, an evening service was held in Boston's Bowdoin Square Church to publicly welcome him. The auditorium was packed long before the announced start time. Dr Daniel Sharp, pastor of the Charles Street Church and president of the Baptist mission board, presented the official welcome, which was effusive in its admiration of Judson. The honored and humbled missionary then briefly greeted the audience, thanking the American churches for their support of the mission work in Burma. As Judson could not raise his voice, William Hague, pastor of the Federal Street Church, broadcast his remarks sentence by sentence so they could be heard by all in attendance.[3]

After Judson had finished, Hague continued on to review some of the highlights of the missionary's celebrated career. As he did so, a man well into middle age made his way from the back of the auditorium to the platform. There he was welcomed by Judson with surprise and delight. Sharp immediately introduced him to the congregation as the Rev. Samuel Nott, the only

2   ibid., pp. 213–14.

3   On several occasions throughout Judson's stay of nearly nine months in America, others assisted him by repeating his remarks aloud so large audiences could hear them. More than once Judson wrote out full addresses that were publicly read aloud for him by others. A number of public and private addresses made by Judson and other speakers during his time in America are scattered throughout Wayland's record of that period: ibid., pp. 216–59.

survivor besides Judson of the five missionaries who first went out from America to India. Failing health had forced Nott to leave India just four years after his arrival there. He now pastored the Congregational Church in Wareham, Massachusetts. This was the first time Judson and Nott had seen each other since they were separated at Calcutta thirty-three years earlier. Now as they embraced "with deep affection and grateful joy" many in the audience wept. Nott was invited to address the gathering, and one observer reported:

> Mr. Nott referred to the small beginning of the American Board, as well as the Baptist, their trust in God, and the present great and glorious work which is exhibited to us in contrast. The missionary movement in this country originated simultaneously in different hearts; the spirit of the Most High, and not human influence, gave it birth. He deemed it a very trifling question whether Adoniram Judson or Samuel J. Mills was the originator of foreign missions. Samuel Nott, Jr, certainly was not. They were all mere boys, but with God's blessing on their puerile efforts, they had begun an influence which is spreading over the world.[4]

Just then it was discovered that another pioneer missionary was in the audience. Hiram Bingham, an 1819 graduate of Andover Theological Seminary, had gone out that same year with his classmate, Asa Thurston, on the first mission to the Sandwich (Hawaiian) Islands.[5] "Another thrill of pleasure went through the congregation" as Bingham was introduced and addressed the gathering.

From Boston Judson traveled by railroad to Salem. That likely was his first ever journey by rail, as only in recent years had railroad tracks begun to branch out from major American cities. In Salem Judson had the joy of being reunited with his beloved sister,

---

4   ibid., p. 220. Through the years some difference of opinion had existed over exactly who should be credited with having originated foreign missions in America. Nott's perspectives as shared on this occasion were doubtless exactly right.

5   Anderson, *To the Golden Shore*, p. 448.

Abigail. His daughter, Abby Ann, was temporarily entrusted to the sister's care. At some unknown date, Sarah Judson's parents, Ralph and Abiah Hall, moved from Salem to Skaneateles, New York. But if they were still living in Salem at this time, Judson doubtless paid them a visit. From Salem Judson continued by stagecoach to Bradford to visit Ann Judson's widowed mother and two sisters, Mary and Abigail Hasseltine. After returning to Boston, Judson, on November 13, took his two sons, Adoniram and Elnathan, by rail to Worcester, Massachusetts. There the boys were left in the care of Dr and Mrs. Newton, with whom Sarah's son, George Boardman, was also living at the time.

Three days later Judson was in Providence, Rhode Island, for a Sunday evening missionary meeting involving evangelical churches of various denominations. The large, historic First Baptist Church in which the meeting was held was filled to overflowing: "Not a pew in any part of the house, not a place in all the aisles, not the remotest corner, above or below, remained unoccupied."[6] Addresses were given by Dr Francis Wayland, president of Brown University, and three other ministers. The next day Judson visited Brown, where he addressed the entire student body. He also spoke at special meetings of the college's Philermenian Society (in which he had been a member while a student at Brown) and the school's Society for Missionary Inquiry.

A special meeting of the Triennial Convention of the Baptist Church was held in New York just two days later, on Wednesday, November 19. There Judson saw firsthand how the issue of slavery was not only dividing the country but also the churches, thus affecting the foreign missionary movement. Several months earlier the mission board had announced that it could no longer appoint as missionaries individuals who owned slaves. Churches in the south promptly severed their ties with the board and formed the Southern Baptist Convention. In September, while Judson was en route to America, a special session of the General Convention was convened in New York and the American Baptist Missionary Union was organized. Now, two months later, Judson

6   Wayland, *Memoir*, vol. 2, p. 223.

listened to a discussion of the current situation, which Anderson summarizes:

> There was already a debt for missions of some forty thousand dollars which weighed heavily. The disaffiliation of the Southern churches meant that this had to be assumed by the Northern group, to which it was obvious most of the missionaries abroad would adhere [eventually all but one did]. As a result, there was talk of contracting missionary activities, and even abandoning the Arakan mission.[7]

At the latter suggestion, Judson rose to his feet and stated for all to hear, "Though forbidden to speak by my medical adviser, I must say a few words. I must protest against the abandonment of the Arakan mission." His voice then sunk to a husky whisper as he stated the reasons the mission should not be given up. Those remarks as well as his closing appeal were repeated aloud to the assembly by Dr Spencer Cone: "If the convention think my services can be dispensed with in finishing my dictionary, I will go immediately to Arakan. Or if God should spare my life to finish my dictionary, I will go there afterward and labor there and die, and be buried there." Two other Burma missionaries, Kincaid and Abbot, were present at the meeting. They supported Judson's appeal with the result that a decision was reached to continue the Arakan mission and to expand rather than contract the overall missionary movement.

Later that same month, Judson received the saddening intelligence that his son Charles had died in Maulmain the previous August 6. He was just nineteen months old when he preceded his mother in death by twenty-six days.

In December Judson was invited to attend a series of missionary meetings in Philadelphia. Dr A. D. Gillette, pastor of the Eleventh Street Baptist Church, Philadelphia, traveled to Boston to accompany Judson on the journey. Along the way they were detained for two or three hours by a minor railroad accident. While waiting, Gillette handed Judson a copy of a recently

7   Anderson, *To the Golden Shore*, pp. 450–1.

published book entitled *Trippings in Author Land*. It was a collection of fictional short stories – descriptive narratives on a variety of subjects – written by a popular young authoress who went by the penname Fanny Forester.

Rather disinterestedly, Judson opened and began reading the little volume. He soon found his attention captured by the writer's graceful style and sprightly narratives. Noting that the stories had a high moral tone, Judson asked if the authoress was a Christian. When Gillette responded in the affirmative, Judson stated, "I should be glad to know her. A lady who writes so well ought to write better. It is a pity that such fine talents should be employed upon such subjects."

> "You will soon be able to make her acquaintance," Gillette informed him, "as she is currently a guest in my house."
>
> "Is she a Baptist?"
>
> "She is."
>
> "Yes, I should like to meet and converse with her. It truly is a pity that talents so brilliant should not be used more worthily."

While in Philadelphia, Judson was hosted in the home of Mr. and Mrs. W. S. Roberts, active supporters of foreign missions. First thing the morning after his arrival, Judson went to Gillette's house where he was introduced to the author of *Trippings*, whose real name was Emily Chubbuck. Judson led her to a sofa where, according to Emily's biographer, "With characteristic impetuosity he immediately inquired how she could reconcile it with her conscience to employ talents so noble in a species of writing so little useful or spiritual as the sketches which he had read."[8]

Rather than taking offense, Emily opened her heart to the esteemed missionary. Her impoverished parents were largely dependent upon her for support. For several years she had taught school full-time and had written on the side, hoping to generate additional income with which she could assist her family

---

8   A. C. Kendrick, *The Life and Letters of Mrs. Emily C. Judson*, p. 143.

members. She had succeeded in publishing a few children's books aimed at promoting high morals but those works had produced little income. That had led her to pursue another type of writing aimed at a broader, more popular audience, which in the past couple of years had brought her an unexpected degree of success. As her current writing endeavors remained secondary to her ongoing teaching responsibilities and as she sought to carefully avoid anything of a dubious nature in her writings, she did not consider her course of action open to serious strictures.

Softened by her explanation, Judson admitted that even his own strict standards could not censure the direction her filial devotion had taken. He then brought up another subject. He desired to find a person to write a memoir of his recently deceased wife. Having been impressed with the quality and attractive style of Emily's writing, he had wished to make her acquaintance to determine if she would be willing to undertake the composition of Sarah's biography. Emily was open to Judson's book-writing proposal and in the days to follow they spent considerable time together discussing the project.

As they did, Judson soon learned more about Emily's background. She was born on August 22, 1817, in a rural cottage near Eaton, in Madison County, New York. Eaton was a village located four miles northwest of Hamilton, home of a Baptist literary and theological institution subsequently named Madison University (eventually Colgate University). Emily was the fifth of seven children born to Charles and Lavinia Chubbuck. She had three brothers and three sisters.

Emily's childhood was a difficult one. Her parents were pious but extremely poor. Two of Emily's older sisters died of illness during her girlhood. Emily herself was "an exceedingly delicate child" and was not expected to live long. At just ten years of age she went to work splicing rolls at a woolen factory to help support the family. She was educated at home and at the district schoolhouse as health and work demands allowed. Beginning at age fifteen, after her family moved to nearby Morrisville, she taught summer school sessions at area schools, though some of her students were older and bigger than she was.

Emily publicly professed faith in Christ and was baptized in the summer of 1834. She was one of twelve or fifteen youths in the Morrisville Baptist Church baptized by William Dean shortly before he went out from that congregation as a missionary to China. Over the course of the following six years, as Emily continued teaching school, she intermittently needed to return home to assist her parents in their financial and health struggles or to recover her own limited health and strength.

In 1838, at age twenty or twenty-one, Emily divulged to a close friend, "I have felt, ever since I read the memoir of Mrs. Ann H. Judson when I was a small child, that I must become a missionary. I fear it is but a childish fancy, and am making every effort to banish it from my mind. Yet the more I seek to divert my thoughts from it, the more unhappy I am." During that period she never listened to a sermon or read her Bible without feeling condemned. She thought her Savior's "requirements", likely in scriptural passages such as Matthew 10:37-39 and Luke 9:59-62, were in direct conflict with her cherished intentions of providing for the comfort of her parents and for the education of her younger siblings. In her heart she constantly struggled with the seeming collision of her perceived heavenly and earthly duties.

Once during that time she wrote a letter to Rev. Nathaniel Kendrick, pastor of the Baptist Church in Eaton and theological professor in the institution at Hamilton, concerning the possibility of devoting her life to missionary service. He advised her to await the openings of providence. Neither of them ever could have imagined how that word of advice would be fulfilled years later.

In the autumn of 1840 Emily was invited to further her education at the esteemed Utica Female Seminary, some thirty miles northeast of Eaton and Hamilton. In less than a year she was appointed as an instructor, then as head of the school's department of English composition. In addition to carrying out her heavy teaching responsibilities, she began writing short children's books for publication, often depriving herself of sleep or social opportunities to do so. From her dual sources of modest income she paid for her younger sister to start attending the seminary in Utica and made a down-payment on a house for her parents in Hamilton.

In the spring of 1844 Emily penned a playful letter to the editors of the *Evening Mirror*, an extremely popular magazine published in New York City. She offered her literary services to the publication and signed the missive under the pseudonym Fanny Forester. The editors at once spotted literary potential and responded favorably to her offer. An enormous amount of public interest instantly developed in the writings of this obviously-talented but unidentified authoress. Emily soon found her writing efforts experiencing heretofore unimagined success and herself, at least under a penname, gaining immense popularity.

The strain from her teaching responsibilities and writing opportunities sometimes proved too much for her physical capacity. Twice she was invited and ventured to Philadelphia as a more temperate locale in which to regain her health. Both times while there she was a guest in the home of Dr Gillette and his family. It was during the second of those visits to the city of brotherly love that Emily met Adoniram Judson. By that time she had been enjoying her Fanny Forester success for eighteen months.

35

A SURPRISING UNION
(1846)

A mutual admiration and appreciation rapidly developed between Judson and Emily. In addition to her considerable literary abilities, Judson appreciated Emily's keen mind, warm heart and enthusiastic spirit. Apparently he was more attracted by those qualities than by her physical beauty. While existing portraits of Emily reveal that she certainly was not homely, by various accounts she did not possess the striking physical attractiveness of Judson's former wives.

Less than a month after initially making her acquaintance, Judson asked Emily to become his wife, to return with him to Burma, to share his life and ministry, and to be a mother to his two young sons still living there. At first Emily was "filled with perplexity and almost alarm" at a proposal that would involve such a sudden and complete reversal of all her plans and prospects in life. What would all her family and friends, indeed the public, say when they heard that the popular young Fanny Forester "was about to turn her back on her newly commenced career, and quench her rising fame in the night of heathenism"? Her own spiritual deficiencies and lack of consecration requisite for missionary service weighed even more heavily upon her. "She had declined from her earlier consecration, and the path which she once sought the privilege of treading, it now, as she afterwards declared, 'seemed like death for her to enter'."[1]

She openly shared these misgivings with Judson but he dismissed them. He perceived that she longed for a higher purpose

1   Kendrick, *The Life and Letters of Mrs. Emily C. Judson*, p. 145.

in life than the pursuit of temporal fame through the writing of popular literature. He had come to know her well enough to be confident that she would respond appropriately when provided with proper spiritual focus and opportunities. He was certain that God had providentially brought them together at this time. On January 20 he presented Emily with a watch and the following formal proposal:

> I hand you, dearest one, a charmed watch. It always comes back to me, and brings its wearer with it. I gave it to Ann when a hemisphere divided us, and it brought her safely and surely to my arms. I gave it to Sarah during her husband's life-time (not then aware of the secret), and the charm, though slow in its operation, was true at last.
>
> Were it not for the sweet sympathies you have kindly extended to me, and the blessed understanding that "love has taught us to guess at", I should not venture to pray you to accept my present with such a note. Should you cease to "guess" and toss back the article, saying, "Your watch has lost its charm; it comes back to you *but brings not its wearer with it*" – O first dash it to pieces, that it may be an emblem of what will remain of the heart of
>
> Your devoted,
A. Judson.[2]

Before Judson left Philadelphia for Washington, D.C., four days later, Emily accepted his proposal. After his departure, she wrote a close friend:

> My good doctor has now gone away, and I have just said to him the irrevocable *yes*, though I must acknowledge that I have acted it slightly before. ... I have not taken this step without a great, *great deal* of thought, and I would not take it but that I believe the blessing of God is in it. I must acknowledge indeed that I have little of the proper missionary spirit. Perhaps it will increase; I hope so. I would

2   ibid., pp. 147–8.

gladly be useful, and this has influenced me very much in my decision.[3]

In a letter that Emily penned to another acquaintance one month later, she revealed other significant perspectives that had played into her accepting Judson's proposal:

> I am a great admirer of greatness – real, genuine greatness; and goodness has an influence which I have not the power to resist. I believe the reason that I have never loved before (for I think that I have a somewhat loving nature) is, that I never saw the two so beautifully combined in one person. My good Doctor's hair is as black as the raven's wing yet; but if it were not, if he were many years older, it would be all the same: I would go with him the world over. ...
>
> ... Did you ever feel as though all the things that you were engaged in were so trivial, so aimless, that you fairly sickened of them, and longed to do something more worthy of your origin and destiny? I can not describe the feeling entirely; but it has haunted me for the last six months, sleeping and waking – in the crowd and in solitude – till, from being the most contented of humans, I have been growing dissatisfied with everything. True, I had the power to amuse, and make some people momentarily happy. I tried to weave some little moral into all I wrote; and while doing so, endeavored to persuade myself that this was sufficient. But, though I seemed to convince myself, I was not convinced or satisfied. Now it is different. I shall really have an opportunity of spending my short life in the way which would make me most happy – in doing real, permanent good. ...[4]

Judson traveled to Richmond, Virginia, for a meeting with churches of the Southern Baptist Convention on February 8. The Rev. Dr J. B. Jeter, President of the Board of the Southern Baptist Convention and pastor of one of Richmond's Baptist congregations, delivered an eloquent address in which he expressed high esteem and warm

3   ibid., p. 148.
4   ibid., pp. 158–9.

regards for Judson and his missionary endeavors. Jeter stated near the end of his address, "Welcome, thrice welcome are you, my brother, to our city, our churches, our bosoms. I speak as the representative of southern Baptists. We love you for the truth's sake, and for your labors in the cause of Christ. We honor you as the father of American missions."[5]

In his response on that occasion, Judson sought to play a pacifying role in connection with the recent division that had taken place among northern and southern Baptist congregations in America:

> I congratulate the Southern and Southwestern churches on the formation of the Southern Baptist Convention for Foreign Missions. ... Such an organization should have been formed several years ago. Besides other circumstances, the extent of the country called for a separate organization. I have read with much pleasure the proceedings of the Convention at Augusta, Georgia, and commend the dignified and courteous tone of the address sent forth by that body. I am only an humble missionary of the heathen, and do not aspire to be a teacher of Christians in this enlightened country; but if I may be indulged a remark, I would say, that if hereafter the more violent spirits of the North should persist in the use of irritating language, I hope they will be met, on the part of the South, with dignified silence.[6]

Emily left Philadelphia on February 17 and three days later arrived at the Utica Female Seminary. Her friends there warmly welcomed her and enthusiastically supported her new plans for marriage and missionary life. They, along with her friends in Philadelphia, assumed the primary responsibility of supplying the funds needed for her outfit. In the first week of March Emily returned to her parents' home in Hamilton. She had nicknamed the modest but comfortable house she had provided for her

5   Wayland, *Memoir*, vol. 2, p. 247.

6   Edward Judson, *The Life of Adoniram Judson*, pp. 475–6. In referring to "the more violent spirits of the North", Judson doubtless intended certain individuals rather than the northern association of Baptist churches as a whole.

parents "the loggery". Judson joined her on March 12 and spent several days getting acquainted with his future in-laws.

By that time word of their future plans was spreading rapidly and beginning to create a significant stir. Many in both religious and secular circles responded with marked incredulity and criticism of their intentions. Christians who, contrary to Judson's wishes, had insisted on lionizing and revering him to an almost superhuman level were now shocked to learn that he intended to marry a popular young authoress who wrote secular fiction under an assumed name. Only twenty-eight years old, she was not quite half his age of fifty-seven. Little was known of her religious upbringing or her present spiritual commitment. She hardly seemed a suitable spousal successor to the saintly Ann Hasseltine Judson and Sarah Boardman Judson.

Those in the secular literary world, publishers and readers alike, were likewise astounded and appalled at the recently-revealed intentions and prospects of the popular Fanny Forester. They could not fathom how she could sacrifice her considerable talents and brilliant career prospects by going to minister to heathens on the other side of the globe. Further, they "could hardly stigmatize severely enough the sorceries by which Dr Judson had wrought upon that youthful heart, and lured it to so wanton a sacrifice."[7]

Toward the end of March Judson and Emily again temporarily parted company. Emily returned to Utica while Judson made his way back to Plymouth for what he thought might be a final visit with his children and sister, at whose house they gathered. After a few days there, Judson sent Adoniram and Elnathan on the train back to the Newtons in Worcester. He took Abby Ann to Bradford where she would remain with the Hasseltines. George Boardman was intending to enter Brown University in the fall.

Emily, with her high-strung and sensitive spirit, became overwrought at the considerable public gossip that continued to swirl concerning her future intentions. As a result, she lost her appetite and had difficulty sleeping, which doubtless worsened

---

7   Kendrick, *The Life and Letters of Mrs. Emily C. Judson*, p. 167.

her anxiety. She gave vent to her vexation in a letter to Judson on April 3:

> I am distressed to death with the thousand things which I am called to endure, and I can not help letting you know it. I wonder if men – Christians or infidels – have any human feelings about them, that they should think their fellows made of stone. ... I don't care whether they praise or censure me ... I wish they would just let me alone. ... I am heart-sick now, and if the feeling be not wicked, would rather die than live. ... It seems that all New York is alive about the affair. It is the common subject of conversation on steamboat and in hotel, in parlor and in grog-shop. H. Anable, who has just returned from New York, says there is no place nor circle where my name is not heard. There is even talk of preventing such an insane proceeding as F.F.'s "throwing herself away". They say such a senseless sacrifice is unparalleled.[8]

Four days later, back in Boston, Judson wrote to encourage her in her trials:

> As to what the newspapers and the public say, can you not receive it with that cool, quiet composure which best becomes you, nor let any one but me know that it disturbs you. In fact, be not disturbed. There is nothing that ought to disturb one of your pure and high purpose. ... The opinion of one such man as President W[ayland] is worth that of ten thousand, and here it is under March 26th: "I know not where you are, but hear you are tripping in author-land under the guidance of a fair Forester. I am pleased to hear of your engagement, as far as I know of it. Miss C. is every where spoken of as a pious, sensible, cultivated, and engaging person. I pray God it may prove a great and mutual blessing. ..."[9]

The next day Judson added:

8   ibid., p. 176.
9   ibid., p. 179.

I have been so cried down at different periods of my life – especially when I became a Baptist and lost all, all but Ann – that I suppose I am a little hardened. But I feel for you, for it is your first [battle]field. Whatever of strength or shield is mine, or I can draw down from heaven, is yours.[10]

In her letter of response on April 10, Emily's spirit was once again calm and composed:

Thanks for your beautiful letter. You do take all the trouble away so sweetly! I don't know why you should be so good and kind to me when I get out of patience. Yes, I do know that you will never repent the step you have taken, though the entire world should disapprove of it, and with full faith in that I will not be disturbed by trifles. I know these are all trifles – things that I shall laugh at when I get away from them; but sometimes they seem terrible now. They shall not any more, though; I will rest in your love, and in a holier. ...[11]

One month later Emily penned a letter to Dr Gillette which revealed that the peace and composure she had gained was lasting:

I thank you for your warm, kind interest; but I am not troubled now by what people say. Indeed, I never in my life before was so perfectly indifferent to any thing relating to myself. I am very happy in my new prospects – though there are terrible sacrifices close at hand – and in my happiness I can afford to hear the wind blowing around me. It is all wind – "only that and nothing more." Do not be troubled for me. "If God be for us, who can be against us?" I feel in my very soul that I have the approbation of God in this step; and really the approval or disapproval of men, who are incapable of understanding or appreciating the matter, is an exceedingly small thing. Let it pass.[12]

10 ibid., p. 180.
11 ibid.
12 ibid., p. 187.

The middle of April Judson traveled to Maine to visit the senior George Boardman's alma mater, Waterville College. There he addressed the school's Boardman Missionary Society. Early in May Judson rejoined Emily in Utica and together they visited her parents in Hamilton. Through a loan from Judson, which Emily insisted she would repay through the sale of her books, she was able to pay off the remaining mortgage on the house she had been purchasing for her parents.

One Sunday Judson and Emily visited the Baptist church in Morrisville where she had professed her Christian faith and been baptized as a teenager. After the pastor finished his sermon, Judson was invited to address the congregation. For about fifteen minutes he spoke with simplicity and pathos of what the precious Savior had done for His people and what they owed to Him. As Judson sat down it was apparent that most of the listeners were disappointed. After the service, several individuals asked Emily why Judson had not shared, instead, a story from his colorful missionary experiences. When she mentioned the matter to him on the way home he responded, "Why, what did they want? I presented the most interesting subject in the world, to the best of my ability."

"But they wanted something different – a story."

"Well, I am sure I gave them a story – the most thrilling one that can be conceived of."

"But they had heard it before. They wanted something new of a man who had just come from the antipodes."

"Then I am glad to have it to say, that a man coming from the antipodes had nothing better to tell than the wondrous story of Jesus' dying love. My business is to preach the Gospel of Christ, and when I can speak at all, I dare not trifle with my commission. When I looked upon those people today and remembered where I should next meet them, how could I stand up and furnish food to vain curiosity – tickle their fancies with amusing stories, however decently strung together on a thread of religion? That is not what Christ meant by preaching the Gospel. And then, how could I hereafter meet the fearful charge, "I gave you one opportunity to tell them of me – you spent it describing your own adventures!"

From Hamilton Emily again returned to Utica and Judson set out for religious meetings in New York City and Philadelphia. Emily desired to make arrangements for the publication of a revised collection of her various stories and sketches, including those she had written since *Trippings in Author-Land* had been published. Judson actively assisted her in that desire by contacting and visiting a number of publishers in New York and Philadelphia. In the end, arrangements were made with a publisher in Boston and the desired new work was brought out in two attractive volumes under the title *Alderbrook*.[13]

Judson and Emily were wed on June 2 in Hamilton. The "strictly private" wedding took place in the home of Emily's parents. Some of Emily's family members and two of her special friends from the Utica Female Seminary, Miss Cynthia Sheldon and Miss Anna Maria Anable, comprised the small audience. The ceremony was officiated by the elderly Rev. Dr Nathaniel Kendrick, who years earlier had advised Emily to await the openings of providence when she shared with him her interest in dedicating her life to missionary service. The aged, ailing Kendrick, pale and feeble, arose from his couch and walked the short distance from his house to the Chubbucks' home in order to conduct the marriage ceremony. That was the last or nearly the last occasion when he left his home before his death.

In the weeks that followed the newlyweds paid final visits to Utica, New York City, Boston, Plymouth and Bradford. A sizeable farewell service was held at the Baldwin Place Church in Boston on Tuesday afternoon, June 30, for the Judsons and five new missionaries who were going with them to Burma – the John Beechers, the Norman Harrises, and Miss Lydia Lillybridge, who had been one of Emily's teaching associates at Utica. When it came time for Judson to address the audience, he made a few brief remarks in a voice loud enough for the large audience to

13   ibid., pp. 192, 197, 200–204, detail Judson's efforts in Emily's behalf in this regard.

hear. William Hague, who had assisted Judson in addressing the congregation at his welcoming service in Boston eight months earlier, then read aloud for all to hear a longer parting statement that the veteran missionary had prepared for the occasion.

Originally the mission party was to sail aboard the ship *Faneuil Hall*, bound for Maulmain, on July 1, but the vessel did not actually embark until the eleventh. Judson took advantage of the delay to visit Adoniram and Elnathan one final time in Worcester on July 4, and Abby Ann in Bradford on the ninth. Two days later, "amidst the tearful adieus of hundreds", the Judsons and their fellow missionaries boarded the *Faneuil Hall* and set sail for Burma. Among the hundreds or even thousands of well-wishers who were there to see them off was Judson's stepson, George Boardman.

36

RETURN TO BURMA AND RANGOON
(1846-1847)

"None ever had a pleasanter passage than we have been favored with, though rather long, from the prevalence of head winds. The *Faneuil Hall* was a good sailer, an excellent sea boat, and furnished with the best accommodations."[1] Thus Judson wrote to an acquaintance in Boston as the mountains of Burma appeared on the horizon on Monday, November 27, 139 days after they sailed from America. The ship's Captain Hallet not only showed "unremitting kindness" toward the missionaries but also shared "congenial sentiments and feelings on the subject of religion" with them. Each Lord's Day the missionaries held a Bible class in the saloon and a worship service on deck with the crew. Those services as well as a time of worship each evening "have given the character of a Bethel [house of God] to our floating home".

Judson caught a bad cold about the time they sailed from Boston. That and "some small attempts at public speaking" on the ship irritated his throat and produced a severe cough the first month of the voyage. During the course of the passage he managed to revise and transcribe the first half of the English to Burmese portion of the dictionary that had been done earlier. Emily suffered from sickness and the cold weather they encountered, while the other members of the missionary party enjoyed good health. She busied her pen in recording elaborate descriptions of the new sights and experiences she was having – gales encountered off the Cape of Good Hope, a supper of dolphin, curious types

1   Wayland, *Memoir*, vol. 2, p. 266.

of fish, a Portuguese man of war, constellations of the southern hemisphere.[2]

In a letter to her sister Katy, Emily also provided a colorful portrayal of the joyous reception they received from the Burmese Christians at Amherst on Tuesday:

> We were scarcely anchored this morning when a boat of six or seven men came bounding toward us, who, by the fluttering of gay silks, and the display of snowy jackets and turbans, were judged to be something above mere boatmen. As they drew sufficiently near to be distinguishable by their features, one of our number [Judson] who had been for some time silently watching them from the side of the vessel, leaned far over for a moment gazing at them intently, and then sent forth a glad wild hail. In a moment the glancing of oars ceased, a half dozen men sprang to their feet to the imminent peril of the odd nut-shell in which they floated, and a wilder, longer, and if possible more joyous cry, showed that the voice of the salutation was recognized. Christian [Emily's nickname for Judson, borrowed from *Pilgrim's Progress*] beckoned me to his side. "They are our Amherst friends," he said; "the dear, faithful fellows!" And these were some of the Christians of Burma! ... In a few moments the men had brought the boat along side, and were scrambling up the sides of the vessel. How the black eyes danced beneath their grave brows, and the rough lips curled with smiles behind the bristling beards! Then came a quick grasping of hands, and half-choked words of salutation, in a strange, deep guttural, which he only to whom they were addressed could understand; while I, like the full-grown baby that I am, retreated to the nearest shadow, actually sobbing; for what, I am sure I do not know, unless I might have fancied myself a sort of flood-gate for the relief of other people's eyes and voices. However, though it had been pretty strongly intimated that "mamma" must not be out of sight, just at present, I do not think her

---

2   Those descriptions are preserved in Kendrick, *The Life and Letters of Mrs. Emily C. Judson*, pp. 218-31.

madamship was missed until she had made herself tolerably presentable, and then she was again beckoned forward. The Burmans gave my hand a cordial American grip, but their dusky palms were so velvety that I do not think even your fingers would have complained under the pressure. Then a venerable old man, who, as I afterward learned, is a deacon in the church, came forward, and bending his turbaned head respectfully, commenced an animated address, waving his hand occasionally to the troop behind him, who bowed as in assent. I have no doubt it was a rare specimen of eloquence, but, of course, I could not understand a word of it, and could only curtsey and simper very foolishly in acknowledgment. You will laugh when I tell you I have seldom been so embarrassed in my life. I soon learned that the men had reserved nicely matted seats for us in the boat, and that several of their wives and daughters were waiting at the jetty, with cart and oxen, to take me up to the village. ... Our visitors had brought us bottles of milk, eggs, fish, shrimps, yams, sweet potatoes, plantains, and oranges for our comfort ...[3]

Judson and Emily reached Maulmain two days later, on November 30. There they settled in Judson's former residence with Henry and Edward, both of whom they found in good health. "Emily makes one of the best wives and kindest mothers to the children that ever man was blessed with," Judson wrote to his sister Abigail. "Emily loves the children as if they were her own," he similarly testified in a subsequent letter.[4] Emily's personal journal entries from the opening days of the new year revealed her joys and challenges in adjusting to her new roles and varied demands as a mother and missionary:

January 1, 1847. Actually in Burma! And is it really myself? Is the past year a reality, or am I still dreaming up there in Dominie Gillette's chamber, where I lay down (seemingly)

3   ibid., pp. 239–40.
4   Wayland, Memoir, vol. 2, pp. 264, 270.

a year ago? If it *be* a dream, I pray God that I may never wake, for I believe that it would break my heart to be other than I am. Thank God, it is a reality – a blessed reality; and I am in the very spot I so longed to plant my foot upon, years and years gone by.

January 2. I have got a teacher, and made a beginning in the language, but the children absorb so much of my time that I can not study much. They are dear little fellows, but *so* full of mischief! Precious gems they are; may they not be spoiled by so inexperienced a polisher as I am.

January 5. It seems to me as though I do nothing but get up, turn round, and then go to bed again! I believe there never was such a novice in housekeeping; and then the children, and the language, and the thousand and one other botherations! I expected to make a rush at the language, take it by storm, then get a parcel of natives about me, and go to work in "true apostolic style". Not that I had the vanity to think myself very apostle-like, but I know, O my Heavenly Father, that Thou canst bless the very meanest of Thy children if they but look up to Thee. And I will continue to look; for though my work is not what I expected, Thou canst bring great results from little causes. It is all of Thy ordering.[5]

Judson was gratified to learn that evident progress had been made in every department of the mission work at Maulmain and its outstations during his absence. But he was interested in returning to ministry in "Burma proper", that part of the country not under British authority. A new monarch, Pagan Min, the son of the previous emperor, had recently come to the throne.[6] Though his administration professed greater friendliness toward foreigners than had the previous rulers, it maintained a rigid intolerance of any religions other than Buddhism among the indigenous

5   Kendrick, *The Life and Letters of Mrs. Emily C. Judson*, pp. 246–7.

6   Anderson, *To the Golden Shore*, p. 475, summarizes: "King Bagyidaw had become insane. In 1837, the 'Tharrawaddy prince' [the king's brother] had deposed him. Tharrawaddy in turn became sadistically insane and died in confinement in 1846. He was succeeded by his eldest son, Pagan Min, a debauched tyrant atop a crumbling central administration riddled with gangster dacoits."

population. As a result, Karen Christians north of Rangoon were currently experiencing persecution and not a single missionary was serving anywhere in Burma proper. Judson thought if he could quietly settle in Rangoon, he might "be instrumental of saving a few souls, who would otherwise be lost". In addition, in Rangoon he would have access to more "learned men and books" to assist him in his production of a Burmese dictionary. There he would also "be in the way of the openings of Providence into the heart of the country" should God suddenly open up those opportunities. "My faith, however, is not very strong, nor my expectations very sanguine," Judson admitted.[7]

The latter half of January 1847, he made a brief exploratory trip to Rangoon to determine the feasibility of settling there with his family. He was received "in the most kind and encouraging manner" by the city governor, a man with whom Judson had enjoyed some friendly acquaintance about twenty years earlier. The governor invited him to settle in Rangoon and promised to provide him a place for an English church. But the governor made it clear by implication that Judson was welcome as a minister to foreigners rather than as a propagator of a foreign religion to the Burmese. The magistrate also warmly approved of Judson's intention to produce a Burmese-English dictionary and stated his willingness to mention the work favorably to the king.

The only housing Judson could locate to rent was the upper story of a large brick home on a street inhabited by Muslims. While the house afforded several large rooms, it had only a few small windows for lighting, so seemed "as gloomy as a prison". The owner demanded one hundred rupees a month but Judson managed to talk him down to fifty. Still, at nearly twenty-five dollars per month, that was an exorbitant amount to pay for rent. Apparently the accommodations left much to be desired, for Judson initially wrote disconsolately about it to Emily from Rangoon: "I shrink at taking you and the children into such a den, and fear you would pine and die in it."

Despite such reservations, the Judsons left Maulmain the middle of the following month to relocate to Rangoon. Emily

7   Wayland, *Memoir*, vol. 2, p. 269.

described their rented living quarters, which she dubbed "Bat Castle", in a letter to her sister Katy:

> I write you from walls as massive as any you read of in old stories and a great deal uglier ... Think of me in an immense brick house with rooms as large as the entire "loggery" (our centre room is twice as large, and has *no* window), and only one small window apiece. When I speak of windows, do not think I make any allusion to glass – of course not. The windows (holes) are closed by means of heavy board or plank shutters, tinned over on the outside, as a preventive of fire. ... Imagine us, then, on the second floor of this immense den, with nine rooms at our command, the smallest of which (bathing-room and a kind of pantry) are, I think, quite as large as your dining-room, and the rest very much larger. Part of the floors are of brick, and part of boards; but old "Green Turban" white-washed them all, with the walls, before we came, because the Doctor told him, when he was over here, that he must "make the house shine for madam". He did make it shine with a vengeance, between white-washing and greasing. They oil furniture in this country, as Americans do mahogany; but all his doors and other wood-work were fairly dripping, and we have not got rid of the smell yet; nor, with all our rubbing, is it quite safe to hold too long on the door. The partitions are all of brick, and very thick, and the door-sills are *built up*, so that I go over them at three or four steps, Henry mounts and falls off, and Edward gets on all-fours, and accomplishes the pass with more safety.[8]

As its nickname suggested, the house was home to a sizeable population of bats, as well as numerous other undesirable creatures:

> The floor overhead is quite low, and the beams, which are frequent, afford shelter to thousands and thousands of bats, that disturb us in the day-time only by a little cricket-like

8   Kendrick, *The Life and Letters of Mrs. Emily C. Judson*, pp. 270–1.

music, but in the night – Oh, if you could only hear them carouse! The mosquito curtains are our only safe-guard; and getting up [during the night] is horrible. ... We have had men at work nearly a week trying to thin them out, and have killed a great many hundreds, but I suppose their little demoniac souls come back, each with an attendant, for I am sure there are twice as many as at first. Every thing, walls, tables, chairs, etc., are stained by them. Besides the bats, we are blessed with our full share of cockroaches, beetles, spiders, lizards, rats, ants, mosquitoes, and bed-bugs. With the last the wood-work is all alive, and the ants troop over the house in great droves, though there are scattering ones beside. Perhaps twenty have crossed my paper since I have been writing. Only one cockroach has paid me a visit, but the neglect of these gentlemen has been fully made up by a company of black bugs about the size of the end of your little finger – nameless adventurers.[9]

When the Judsons departed from Maulmain they left two large trunks of their belongings, valued by Judson at 700–800 rupees (about 350-400 dollars), with the Stevens. Less than a week after they arrived in Rangoon, word came that the Stevens's house had caught fire and burned to the ground. While no lives were lost, all the belongings in the house, including the Judsons' possessions, were completely destroyed. Of this loss and more serious trials the missionaries had faced in past years, Judson expressed remarkable, unwavering trust in God in a letter he wrote to Edward Stevens on March 11:

I have recommenced the work of the dictionary, which has been suspended nearly two years. Why has this grievous interruption been permitted, and all this precious time lost? And why are our houses and property allowed to be burned up? And why are those most dear to us, and most qualified to be useful in the cause, torn from our arms, and dashed into the grave, and all their knowledge and qualification

9   ibid., pp. 271-2.

with them? Because infinite wisdom and love will have it so. Because it is best for us, and best for them, and best for the cause, and best for the interests of eternity, that it should be so. And blessed be God, we know it, and are thankful, and rejoice, and say, Glory be to God.[10]

In addition to his work on the dictionary, Judson resumed evangelistic labors, though the latter was carried out only privately. He was not able to preach or even distribute Christian literature publicly. But he devoted considerable time ministering to several Burmese who secretly visited him as well as to a number of Karens who came to Rangoon from area villages. While most of those individuals were already Christians, Judson was soon able to report four "hopeful inquirers" after salvation. A private weekly Lord's Day worship service was begun. On Sunday, March 7, communion was observed, with ten Burmans, one Karen, Judson and Emily participating. Three weeks later Judson baptized a Burmese convert in the same pond where he had immersed the very first Burman Christian, Maung Nau, twenty-eight years earlier.

Emily was kept fully occupied as well. Besides superintending the running of the household, she took up the writing of Sarah Judson's biography shortly after their settlement in Rangoon. The strain of the sustained writing project, added to her other responsibilities, overtaxed Emily's limited strength. Early in June, she wrote Katy: "For myself, I am utterly prostrated; and, although I have taken care of everything [overseeing household affairs] and written a little, I have not sat up an hour at a time for six weeks. I have my table by my couch and write a few lines, and then lie down."[11] Still, through dogged determination, she completed the memoir over the course of six months while in Rangoon.[12] Though

<hr>

10 Wayland, *Memoir*, vol. 2, p. 281.

11 Kendrick, *The Life and Letters of Mrs. Emily C. Judson*, p. 277.

12 Joan Jacobs Brumberg, *Mission for Life* (New York: Free Press, 1980), p. 138. Kendrick, *The Life and Letters of Mrs. Emily C. Judson*, p. 272, claims that Emily completed the biography in just six weeks. That seems unlikely, especially given her health limitations and other household responsibilities, as she would have needed to write an average of more than forty pages in each of the six weeks in order to complete the work that quickly. Initially published in 1848, *Memoir of Sarah B. Judson* proved a top seller with 20,000 copies being printed in the first two years alone.

it was never mentioned in any of their correspondence, another significant factor may well have played into Emily's physical condition just at that time. She was pregnant with a child to whom she would give birth by year's end.

37

"A Sudden Tornado in a Sunny Day"
(1847)

In spite of their efforts at maintaining secrecy in their missionary activities, suspicions were eventually raised by the number of people who visited the Judson's home. On Friday, May 28, "a private order of government" was issued that their house was to be watched by police officers. The police were to arrest any who were suspected of favoring "Jesus Christ's religion". However, Judson and the Christian disciples were tipped off by "friends at court" that this order had been issued. Judson sent out messengers to warn believers of the danger. As a result, only two Christians from the country (who had been made aware of the situation) went to his home that Sunday.

A ruthless vice-governor had issued the order for Judson's house to be placed under surveillance. The Governor of Rangoon, whom Judson described as "a weak old man", was nearing the end of his term of office. The vice-governor despised his superior and had begun wresting authority from him. In a letter to his mission board, Judson related of this dangerous official and the very real threat he posed:

> The vice-governor of the place, who is, indeed, the acting governor at present, is the most ferocious, bloodthirsty monster I have ever known in Burma. It is said that his house and court yard resound, day and night, with the screams of people under torture. He lately wreaked his rage on some

Armenians and Mussulmans [Muslims], and one of the latter class died in the hands of a subordinate officer. His crime was quite a venial one; but in order to extort money, he was tortured so barbarously that the blood streamed from his mouth, and he was dead in an hour.[1]

That Sunday evening, May 30, a deeply discouraged Judson, his face clouded, paced back and forth in Emily's room. She tried in vain to comfort him by reminding him that the Lord would take care of His own cause. When her efforts failed to have the desired effect, she gave up and sat down in silence. Suddenly another thought flashed into her mind, and turning to him, she asked, "Would you like to know the first couplet that I ever learned to repeat?" Judson turned his head toward her but said nothing. "I learned it," she continued, "before I could read, and I afterwards used to write it every where – sometimes, even, at the top of the page, when I was preparing the story on whose success more depended than its readers ever dreamed."

She had clearly gained his attention and interest. "What was it?" he inquired. Emily recited:

Beware of desperate steps; the darkest day,

(Live till to-morrow), will have passed away.

"I declare," Judson exclaimed as his face brightened, "if I could only believe in transmigration, I should have no doubt that we had spent ages together in some other sphere, we are so alike in every thing. Why, those two lines have been my motto. I used to repeat them over and over in prison, and I have them now, written on a slip of paper, for a bookmark."

Three days later marked their first wedding anniversary. Emily reflected:

It has been far the happiest year of my life; and, what is in my eyes still more important, my husband says it has been among the happiest of his. We have been in circumstances to be almost constantly together; and I never met with any

1   Wayland, *Memoir*, vol. 2, p. 289.

man who could talk so well, day after day, on every subject, religious, literary, scientific, political, and – and nice baby-talk. He has a mind which seems exhaustless, and so, even here in Rangoon, where all the English I hear, from week's end to week's end, is from him, I never think of wanting more society. I have been ill a great deal, but not in a way to hinder him; and he treats me as gently and tenderly as though I were an infant.[2]

No formal worship service was held the following Sunday, June 6, either. But three or four brave Burmans, including "a fine young man" who had recently been approved for baptism and church membership, dared to spend the day with Judson. At nightfall the small band made its way "to the remote side of the old baptizing place" where, "under cover of the bushes", the missionary baptized the new convert.

Judson had already obtained permission from the aging Governor of Rangoon to journey upriver to Ava. There he hoped "to obtain some countenance" from the king, with which he would be able to continue living in Rangoon without constantly being subjected to potential molestation. Just as he was beginning to plan for such a trip, however, he received stunning and dismaying news, of which he wrote on June 13:

> ... I learn from my last letters from Maulmain, that the annual appropriation [from America] for the Burman mission is ten thousand rupees [equaling around five thousand dollars] less than the current expenses require. The brethren have been obliged to retrench in every department, instead of being able to make an appropriation for a new enterprise. My extra expense in Rangoon for assistants and house rent is eighty-six rupees in a month, and they have been able to allow me seventeen and a half only. The mission secretary writes me, that for any thing beyond that sum, I must look, not to their treasury, but to the board. Instead, therefore, of entering on a new and expensive undertaking, I find myself unable to remain in Rangoon.[3]

2   ibid., pp. 275–6.
3   ibid., p. 292.

Other severe trials were beginning to descend on the Judsons at that same time. The season of Burman lent had already begun and that year Buddhist enthusiasm held such strong sway in Rangoon that the general population was forbidden to eat meat throughout that four-month period. Meat from livestock and fowl was nowhere to be found in the marketplace and even fish was not sold until it had started turning rancid. Judson had no recollection of an earlier year when such severe dietary strictures had been placed on the populace during lent.

The Judsons were forced to subsist almost entirely on boiled rice and fruits. Unfortunately, Emily had developed "an unconquerable disgust" for rice. Sometimes "heavy, black, sour" bread was available for purchase. "Our milk is a mixture of buffaloes' milk, water, and something else which we cannot make out," Emily reported. "As for living, I must own that I am within an inch of starvation," she further revealed.[4] Emily's strength became so depleted from lack of proper nutrition that sometimes when merely walking across a room, even though not ill, she slid down on the floor "not from faintness, but sheer physical weakness". Judson described her as becoming "as thin as the shad that went up Niagra".

One day Judson sent a servant to the marketplace with the directive, "You must contrive and get something that mamma can eat. She will starve to death."

"What shall I get?"

"Anything."

"Anything?"

"Anything."

That day the family did have "a capital dinner", eating some type of creature that they could not identify by the bones. Henry guessed it was a certain species of lizard. "Cook said he *didn't know*," Emily afterward related, "but he grinned a horrible grin which made my stomach heave a little, notwithstanding the deliciousness of the meal."

4   Kendrick, *The Life and Letters of Mrs. Emily C. Judson*, p. 276.

After they had finished, Judson asked the servant whom he had sent to the bazaar, "What did we have for dinner to-day?"

"Were they good?"

"Excellent."

The servant erupted in "a tremendous explosion of laughter". From his dish room the cook joined in the laughter "as loud as he dared".

"What were they?" Judson again queried.

"Rats!" came the bemused response.

The rainy season had also commenced, adding to the family's discomfort. Emily wrote at the beginning of June:

> As for the house, it was very comfortable during the hot weather, for there is a brick floor overhead, but we suffer very much since the coming on of the rains. We are obliged to get directly before the window in order to see, and we suffer unaccountably from the damp air. We frequently shut all up, and light candles at noon. The doctor has severe rheumatism in his writing shoulder and constant headaches, but his lungs do not trouble him so much as during the first storms. For myself, I am utterly prostrated ... The wooden ceiling overhead is covered with a kind of green mold, and the doors get the same way in two days if they are not carefully rubbed.[5]

Shortly thereafter a time of widespread, serious sickness descended on Rangoon and on the Judson household. Emily wrote in mid-June: "But it is a very sickly time, almost everybody is ill, and funeral processions pass our house every day. There has been of late a funeral feast in nearly every house in our neighborhood, and the constant tap-tap of nailing up coffins in the night is dreadful."[6] A few days later she added: "The music and mourners have set up their screeching and howling at a house

5   ibid., p. 277.
6   ibid., p. 278.

nearly opposite, and men are busy decorating the funeral car in the streets. We seem to be hemmed in by death."[7]

The third week of June, Judson came down with an agonizing case of dysentery. For a time Emily feared for his life. The ailment proved ongoing and Judson was not able to return to his work on the dictionary for six weeks. Several days after Judson fell ill, Edward, then two and a half years old, began manifesting peculiar, distressing symptoms of some undetermined ailment. On two consecutive days the youngster would suddenly scream, as if in sharp pain, and run to Emily. He was too young to explain what he was feeling. After a moment his distress would pass and he returned to his play. To make matters worse, on the second day of Edward's difficulties, Henry was suddenly seized by a violent fever.

The next day – Sunday, June 27 – Edward's face was covered with purple spots and so swollen that his eyes were nearly closed. The Judsons concluded he was suffering from erysipelas. In the days that followed, alarming abscesses developed on his head and neck. On July 1 Emily recorded:

> There is an abscess in his forehead and the acrid matter has eaten back into the bone, we can not tell how far; there is another immense one on the back of the head in a shocking state, and two lesser ones on his neck. ... He is the loveliest child that I ever saw; there is something which seems to me angelic in his patience and calmness. He could not help crying when his papa lanced his head; but the moment the sharpest pain was over, he nestled down in my bosom, and though quivering all over, he kept lifting his eyes to my face, and trying to smile, oh, so sweetly! He watched his papa while he sharpened the lancet to open another, and when it was ready, turned and laid his little head on his knee of his own accord.[8]

Thankfully, the worst of their physical sufferings had passed. Gradually the Judsons began to recover their health and several

7   ibid., p. 280.
8   ibid., pp. 281–2.

boxes of biscuits were received from their fellow missionaries in Maulmain. Judson exchanged a supply of those biscuits for a favor from a Muslim in their neighborhood who worked for the government. With the restrictions of the lenten season still in force, the minor official secretly supplied the Judsons with fifty fowl for eating at a cost of thirty-six rupees. The arrangement did not work out as well as anticipated, however, as Judson good-naturedly explained to a colleague in Maulmain in a letter dated July 21:

> Three nights after we had cooped them, our friend's jackals, we know, stole twenty of them; and soon after our friend himself borrowed eight more, because he let us have them so cheap, I suppose. The rest we are bolting as fast as possible, for fear he will want to borrow them too. By we, I mean I, for wife has become a sort of Grahamite, living chiefly, or vegetating rather, on Mrs. Stevens's gingerbread, your coffee, and the scrapings of yams which we pick up now and then – the article being now out of season.[9]

Despite all the hardships they had recently encountered, the Judsons could not reconcile themselves to the thought of losing their foothold in Rangoon. As soon as Judson began to recover from his attack of dysentery, he went to visit the Governor of Rangoon again about his intended trip to Ava, presumably to assure he still had the governor's official permission in that undertaking. In the end, however, the Judsons did not journey to Ava. There is no indication that the governor revoked his earlier permission. Instead, Judson and Emily both indicated the venture was not undertaken due to lack of funding from the mission. Perhaps only after Judson's heart led him to seek permission again from the governor did his mind accept the fact that the necessary financial resources for such an undertaking simply were not available.

For a brief time Judson dipped into discouragement and even bitterness over this unexpected development, which Emily

---

9   Wayland, *Memoir*, vol. 2, p. 294. Sylvester Graham (1794–1851) was a Presbyterian minister and an early dietary reformer in America. An advocate of vegetarianism and the temperance movement, he is best known today as the father of Graham crackers.

stated came upon them "like a sudden tornado in a sunny day". But Judson soon acquiesced to the directives of providence. Emily feared that in doing so he was misunderstood by some of his missionary brethren. Of all this she related:

> "I thought they loved me," he would say, mournfully, "and they would scarcely have known it if I had died." "All through our troubles, I was comforted with the thought that my brethren in Maulmain, and in America, were praying for us, and they have never once thought of us." At other times he would draw startling pictures of missionaries abandoning the spirit of their mission, and sacrificing everything to some darling project; and at others he would talk hopelessly of the impulsive nature of the home movements, and then pray, in a voice of agony, that these sins of the children of God might not be visited on the heathen. This was an unnatural state of excitement – for *him* peculiarly unnatural – and he was not long in recovering from it. He very soon began to devise apologies for everybody, and said we must remember that so far as *we* were concerned, or the missionary cause itself, God had done this thing, and done it, as he always does, for good. It was not his will that we should go to Ava then, and we had no right to complain of the means he made use of to prevent it. He insisted, too, that our obedience was not to be yielded grudgingly; that it must be a cheerful acquiescence in all that God had done, and a sincere, careful study of the indications of his providence afterwards, without any suspicion that our ways were hedged by any thing harder or thornier than his love and mercy. By the time he had an opportunity to send letters to Maulmain and Boston, his mind was restored to its usual serenity. ... He wrote more hopefully to Maulmain, but I have sometimes thought that his generosity took the point from his letter, and that his meaning was not understood in saying that it was *for the best*. I think now that they mistook resignation to God for a personal willingness to abandon the enterprise.[10]

10   ibid., pp. 302–3.

The Judsons had actually been forced into the undesired conclusion that it was untenable for them to remain in Rangoon. Reluctantly they sailed from Rangoon on the last day of August to return to Maulmain.

38

WORKING LIKE A GALLEY SLAVE
(1847-1849)

For the first six months that Judson was back in Maulmain, beginning early in September of 1847, he "remained at some distance" from preaching and pastoral duties in the Burmese congregation. He did this in order to focus most of his attention on the production of the Burmese dictionary and to keep himself from becoming "so entangled with the church as to make it difficult to leave" should the hoped-for opportunity arise to venture to Ava. Judson disapproved of the fact that twenty-four of the twenty-nine Baptist missionaries in Burma at that time were clustered together in Maulmain. He longed to minister elsewhere should such an opportunity present itself.

As Judson once again set to work on his dictionary, Emily resumed her study of the Burmese language. She had needed to set aside language study during the six and a half months they had spent in Rangoon due to her writing of Sarah's biography and her health limitations. Emily gave birth to a daughter on December 24. The infant was named Emily Frances. Emily continued to mother Henry and Edward as affectionately and attentively as though they were her own. She beautifully described a touching incident involving Edward that occurred around the time of his third birthday:

> One night Edward, who slept in a little room by himself, called out that he was "afraid", and would not be comforted. I have never taught them a [memorized] prayer to repeat, because I do not like the formality, but I assist them in

discovering what they need, and then have them repeat the words after me. So I prayed with little E., kissed him good night, and left him apparently satisfied. Pretty soon, however, I heard him call out, as though in great distress, "O, Dod!" The poor little fellow had not sufficient acquaintance with language to know what to say next; but this up-lifting of the heart evidently relieved him, for in a few minutes after he again called out, "O, Dod!" but in a tone much softened. I stepped to the door but hesitated about entering. In a few minutes he again repeated "O, Dod!" but in a tone so confiding that I thought I had better go back to my room, and leave him with his Great Protector. I heard no more of him for some time, when I at last went in and found him on his knees fast asleep. He never fails now to remind me of asking "Dod to tate tare of him," if I neglect it, and I have never heard him say a word since of being afraid.[1]

Judson, too, took time for the children. Edward later testified:

And the two little boys who formed a part of the family group at Maulmain, often found in their father an ardent companion in their play. One of them well remembers how his father used to come into his room in the morning and greet him upon his first awakening with a delicious piece of Burmese cake, or with the joyful tidings that a rat had been caught in a trap the night before![2]

As Judson had done earlier when his stepson George Boardman was sent from Burma to the United States, so now, ever since leaving Abby Ann, Adoniram and Elnathan in America, he regularly wrote them. In those letters of paternal affection, concern and advice, Judson frequently urged his children to come to faith in Christ. In May of 1848, Judson was overjoyed to receive letters from Adoniram and Elnathan for the first time since he parted from them nearly two years earlier. He was especially delighted to learn that Elnathan had come to trust in Jesus as Savior. Again

1 Kendrick, *The Life and Letters of Mrs. Emily C. Judson*, p. 292.
2 Edward Judson, *The Life of Adoniram Judson*, pp. 523–4.

Judson earnestly impressed on both boys the foremost importance of obtaining salvation:

> I am so glad to hear of your welfare, and especially that you have both been under religious impressions, and that Elnathan begins to entertain a hope in Christ! O, this is the most blessed news. Go on, my dear boys, and not rest until you have made your calling and election sure [2 Pet. 1:10]. I believe that you both and Abby Ann will become true Christians, and meet me in heaven; for I never pray without praying for your conversion, and I think I pray in faith. Go to school, attend to your studies, be good scholars, try to get a good education; but, O, heaven is all. Life, life, eternal life! Without this, without an interest in the Lord of life, you are lost, lost forever. ...[3]

Sometime in the latter months of 1848, Judson resumed his spiritual care of Maulmain's Burmese congregation. He was assisted in the preaching and other pastoral responsibilities by Edward Stevens. As the year progressed, Emily gained enough proficiency in the Burmese language to begin conducting a Bible class and a separate prayer meeting for women. She also finished the volume of "Scripture Questions" on the book of Acts that Sarah had started before her death. In addition, Emily began preparing an extensive set of endnotes on various aspects of Burmese culture and history to be appended to a new edition of her memoir of Sarah.

Judson completed the English to Burmese portion of his dictionary by the end of the year. Early in 1849 a modest edition of 300 copies was being printed. It consisted of some 600 quarto pages. Judson immediately set to work on the Burmese to English part of the dictionary which he supposed would be a similar length.

For nearly a year following the birth of Emily Frances, mother and daughter both enjoyed relatively good health. But then Baby Emily fell "dangerously ill" with cholera. As the infant began to

3   Wayland, *Memoir*, vol. 2, pp. 307–8.

recover, Mother Emily developed a cough that grew increasingly serious as 1849 dawned. Previously Emily had joined Judson in his brisk early morning walks. But now they purchased a pony for her to ride as an alternative form of exercise. When Emily's health continued to decline, leaving her "a mere skeleton and very weak indeed", the Judsons made arrangements for her to travel down the coast by steamer to visit the Bennetts in Tavoy. There she was treated by a doctor who ventured his opinion that her symptoms – cough, fever, night sweats, pain in the side and difficulty breathing – were indications of consumption that would likely prove fatal. Her missionary hosts in Tavoy became alarmed, lest she should die while away from her husband. After only a week in Tavoy she returned to Maulmain, convinced that she was in a dying state.

The Judsons' physician in Maulmain, a Dr Morton, diagnosed the problem as congestion of the liver rather than a disease of the lungs. He began administering a course of treatment which included digitalis as a primary ingredient. For a time Emily's condition did not improve but eventually she began to recover. The George Houghs sent their carriage for Emily to use in taking a drive each morning. The salutary effects were so encouraging that the Judsons began contemplating the purchase of a horse and buggy of their own. Just then an unexpected cash gift, intended for some personal need they might have, arrived in the mail from an acquaintance in New York. They used it to make the desired purchase. By the latter half of April Emily was considerably improved.

On April 20 Judson penned a letter to Abby Ann in which he expressed fervent concern for her eternal welfare:

> When I think of you and your brothers at Worcester, O, I have such a longing to see you that it seems as if I could not always stay on the other side of the globe, "severed from you by stormy seas and the wide world's expanse". But O, if you are not in Christ, a wider expanse – even the impassable gulf – will soon lie between us, and the wide expanse of eternity itself will show no point of meeting, no spot where

I and your departed mother will be able to take you to our longing arms.[4]

"Mr. J. is looking, I think, much younger than he did in America, and is so well as to be a proverb among Europeans," Emily wrote of her husband to a friend on June 2. Six weeks later she described Judson to her sister Katy:

"The goodman" works like a galley slave; and really it quite distresses me sometimes, but he seems to get fat on it, so I try not to worry. He walks – or rather *runs* – like a boy over the hills, a mile or two every morning; then down to his books, scratch-scratch, puzzle-puzzle, and when he gets deep in the mire, out on the veranda with your humble servant by his side, walking and talking ... till the point is elucidated, and then down again – and so on till ten o'clock in the evening. It is this *walking* which is keeping him out of the grave.[5]

Four days before his sixty-first birthday that August, Judson provided a status report of the missionary enterprise in Maulmain and other parts of Burma:

There are three Baptist churches in this town: a Burmese church, containing about one hundred and fifty members, of which I am pastor; a Karen church, containing about one hundred members ...; and an English church, containing about twenty-five members ... There are two other Burmese churches in these regions, and above a dozen Karen churches. I suppose there are between fifteen hundred and two thousand baptized communicants in all the churches under our supervision in these parts, besides double that number, or more, exclusively Karen, attached to the Arakan mission. ... We find it impossible, at present, to penetrate into Burma proper ... But now and then we baptize an individual from the empire; so that we trust the seed is sowing there, which

4   ibid., p. 322.
5   Kendrick, *The Life and Letters of Mrs. Emily C. Judson*, p. 307.

will finally spring up in large and flourishing churches to the glory of God.[6]

Unfortunately, Emily's health had continued to be rather iffy. She revealed to an intimate friend in a letter dated September 21:

I have a slight cough, sometimes with bloody expectorations, and a continued pain in my right side – the latter, Dr M. says, occasioned by congestion of the liver. My stomach is very weak and so sensitive to the touch that I seldom wear a tight dress, and my throat is shockingly ulcerated. I have a slight difficulty of breathing, and just now can not read aloud at all. The physician says that my lungs are perfectly sound, but admits that there is more danger of their becoming diseased than there would be if my throat was well, and every fresh attack on my throat is worse than the last, although he succeeds tolerably well in subduing the fever. I am not so thin as I was, and some of my worst symptoms, such as night sweats, have totally disappeared. I work little, study little, walk in the veranda for exercise, drive out every day, and keep in excellent spirits. I suppose it would not be a surprising thing if I were to die in a few weeks, nor be considered a miraculous interposition if I were to live to be eighty years old ...[7]

Emily was likely then aware of another reason she had to be concerned about her health. Two months earlier she had become pregnant. Throughout that year Judson's health had been relatively good while Emily's remained precarious. Few would have then imagined that within mere months he rather than she would be the one to step into eternity.

6   Wayland, *Memoir*, vol. 2, p. 325.

7   Kendrick, *The Life and Letters of Mrs. Emily C. Judson*, p. 316. ibid., pp. 317–28, record a number of Emily's worthwhile reflections on life and death from this period when she faced her own mortality.

39

STRONG IN CHRIST TO THE END
(1849-1850)

Judson had always been deeply spiritual throughout the time Emily had known him. But she bore testimony that during the final year of his life she observed a further quickening and development of his spiritual perspectives and character:

> Every subject on which we conversed, every book we read, every incident that occurred, whether trivial or important, had a tendency to suggest some peculiarly spiritual train of thought, till it seemed to me that, more than ever before, "Christ was all his theme". Something of the same nature was also noted in his preaching, to which I then had not the privilege of listening [due to illness]. He was in the habit, however, of studying his subject for the Sabbath, audibly, and in my presence, at which time he was frequently so much affected as to weep, and sometimes so overwhelmed with the vastness of his conceptions as to be obliged to abandon his theme and choose another. My own illness at the commencement of the year had brought eternity very near to us, and rendered death, the grave, and the bright heaven beyond it, familiar subjects of conversation.[1]

Though experiencing highs and lows due to his intense temperamental makeup, Judson exhibited a prevailing spirit of joy and trust, as Emily commented:

1 Wayland, *Memoir*, vol. 2, p. 337.

He was of a singularly happy temperament, although not of that even cast which never rises above a certain level, and is never depressed. Possessing acute sensibilities, suffering with those who suffered, and entering as readily into the joys of the prosperous and happy, he was variable in his moods; but religion formed such an essential element in his character, and his trust in Providence was so implicit and habitual, that He was never gloomy, and seldom more than momentarily disheartened. On the other hand, being accustomed to regard all the events of this life, however minute or painful, as ordered in wisdom, and tending to one great and glorious end, he lived in almost constant obedience to the apostolic injunction, "Rejoice evermore!" [1 Thess. 5:16]. He often told me that although he had endured much personal suffering, and passed through many fearful trials in the course of his eventful life, a kind Providence had also hedged him round with precious, peculiar blessings, so that his joys had far outnumbered his sorrows.[2]

Despite his characteristic joy, Emily could not help but notice that Judson's literary labor was becoming increasingly burdensome to him. He often referred to it using such expressions as "my heavy work", "a tedious work" and "that wearisome dictionary". He longed to be engaged in activities that he considered "more legitimate missionary labor" like Gospel preaching and personal evangelism.

He sometimes anticipated with delight the future time when he would be able to devote himself full time to preaching and prayer. But at other times he supposed he would not complete the dictionary. "People will call it a strange providence," he remarked significantly one day, "if I do not live to finish my dictionary. But to me it will be a strange providence if I do. Men almost always leave some work, that they or their friends consider vastly important, unfinished. It is a way God has of showing us what really worthless creatures we are, and how altogether unnecessary, as active agents, in the working out of his plans."[3]

2   ibid., pp. 339-40.
3   ibid., p. 366.

Judson's physical health also seemed quite good to Emily during that period:

> In person he had grown somewhat stouter than when in America; his complexion had a healthful hue, compared with that of his associates generally; and though by no means a person of uniformly firm health, he seemed to possess such vigor and strength of constitution, that I thought his life as likely to be extended twenty years longer, as that of any member of the mission. He continued his system of morning exercise, commenced when a student at Andover, and was not satisfied with a common walk on level ground, but always chose an up-hill path, and then frequently went bounding on his way with all the exuberant activity of boyhood.[4]

"What deep cause have we for gratitude to God!" Judson exclaimed to Emily one evening near the end of September 1849. "Do you believe there are any other two persons in the wide world so happy as we are?" He proceeded to enumerate several sources of their happiness, including their missionary work and their eternal prospects.

"A heavy cloud" lay upon Emily's spirits that evening. When Judson had finished his "glowing" portrayal, she responded pensively, "We are certainly very happy now, but it cannot be so always. I am thinking of the time when one of us must stand beside the bed, and see the other die."

"Yes," he acknowledged, "that will be a sad moment. I felt it most deeply a little while ago. But now it would not be strange if your life were prolonged beyond mine. Though I would wish, if it were possible, to spare you that pain. It is the one left alone who suffers, not the one who goes to be with Christ. ... But He will order all things well, and we can safely trust our future to His hands."

Later that same night Judson and Emily were awakened by the sudden illness of one of their children. The air was chilly and

4   ibid., p. 339.

damp that evening, and Judson soon began to shiver violently. The next morning he awoke with a severe cold and a slight fever, which at first seemed to pose no special cause for concern. But soon he experienced an attack of dysentery. That was followed by "a burning fever twice a day" for nearly a month. His health gradually declined until, in late November, he was forced to lay aside his work on the dictionary. When his condition continued to worsen, Judson made plans to take a short trip by steamer down the coast to Mergui. Though he suffered intense pain "some hours of every day", his spirits remained buoyant and his disposition uncomplaining. He had so frequently faced similar periods of protracted illness in the past that neither he nor any of his acquaintances were alarmed over his condition.

During the weeks leading up to that trip Judson devoted much time to prayer, especially focusing on progressing in personal sanctification. One day shortly before their departure in January, Judson looked up from his pillow and declared to Emily, "I have gained the victory at last. I love every one of Christ's redeemed, as I believe He would have me love them – in the same manner, though not probably to the same degree as we shall love one another in heaven. And gladly would I prefer the meanest of His creatures, who bears His name, before myself." After further conversation along a similar line, he concluded, "And now here I lie at peace with all the world, and what is better still, at peace with my own conscience. I know that I am a miserable sinner in the sight of God, with no hope but in the blessed Savior's merits. But I cannot think of any particular fault, any peculiarly besetting sin, which it is now my duty to correct. Can you tell me of any?"

In the days that followed he repeatedly spoke of himself as a great sinner who had been overwhelmed with divine benefits. He stated that never before had he enjoyed such precious views of the Savior's "unfathomable love and infinite condescension" as were then opening to his understanding. "O, the love of Christ! The love of Christ!" he would suddenly exclaim as his eyes brightened and tears streamed down his cheeks. "We cannot understand it now. But what a beautiful study for eternity!"

Though Judson seemed slightly improved by their trip to Mergui, he suffered a relapse shortly after their return to Maulmain. His doctor recommended he spend a longer period of time at Amherst, taking advantage of the fresh ocean air as well as sea bathing. The Judsons accordingly went there for nearly a month. Of that time, Emily related:

> This to me was the darkest period of his illness – no medical adviser, no friend at hand, and he daily growing weaker and weaker. He began to totter in walking, clinging to the furniture and walls, when he thought he was unobserved (for he was not willing to acknowledge the extent of his debility), and his wan face was of a ghastly paleness. His sufferings too were sometimes fearfully intense, so that, in spite of his habitual self-control, his groans would fill the house. At other times a kind of lethargy seemed to steal over him, and he would sleep almost incessantly for twenty-four hours, seeming annoyed if he were aroused or disturbed. Yet there were portions of the time when he was comparatively comfortable, and conversed intelligently; but his mind seemed to revert to former scenes, and he tried to amuse me with stories of his boyhood, his college days, his imprisonment in France, and his early missionary life. He had a great deal also to say on his favorite theme, "the love of Christ"; but his strength was too much impaired for any continuous mental effort. Even a short prayer, made audibly, exhausted him to such a degree that he was obliged to discontinue the practice.[5]

Upon their return to Maulmain, Judson's doctor advised him to take a long voyage in hopes of recovering his health. For a time Judson hesitated, especially since Emily would not be able to accompany him. Her baby was due in several weeks, and in light of how she suffered from seasickness, a voyage could prove disastrous for her and the yet unborn child. In addition, just at that time there were no vessels at Maulmain or Amherst intending to sail for a distant

5   ibid., p. 342.

port. In the meanwhile the doctors had pronounced the Judsons' house "unhealthy", so they needed to move to another dwelling. At first that change seemed beneficial but before long Judson again declined. In the end, the couple concluded that though a voyage would involve a painful separation, it was the only hope, under God, of preserving Judson's life, so must be attempted as a matter of duty.

Finally, toward the end of March, Judson's little remaining strength gave out entirely and he lay prostrate on his bed, completely unable to help himself. As he watched the swelling of his feet and "other alarming symptoms" he became extremely anxious to set out to sea. The doctor was of the opinion that Judson had only a fifty-fifty chance of continuing to live, even if he took the voyage. Fellow missionaries seemed even less optimistic.

Judson's bodily sufferings had become so great by then that he spoke but little, and usually only to indicate some need he had. But late one night as Emily was assisting him, he suddenly looked up at her and exclaimed, "This will never do! You are killing yourself for me, and I will not permit it. You must have some one to relieve you. If I had not been made selfish by suffering, I should have insisted upon it long ago."

His considerate remark was so like his old self and his tone sounded so healthy that momentarily Emily "felt almost bewildered with sudden hope". Her exact reply to him was not preserved, but likely it was to the effect that she did not consider caring for him to be a burden. He responded to her statement with "a half-pitying, half-gratified smile". But then, just as suddenly, his facial expression changed before her very eyes and once again clearly manifested "the marks of excessive debility". "It is only a little while, you know," she added.

> "Only a little while," he echoed sorrowfully. "This separation
> is a bitter thing. But it does not distress me now as it did –
> I am too weak."

> "You have no reason to be distressed with such glorious
> prospects before you. You have often told me it is the one left
> alone who suffers, not the one who goes to be with Christ."

He gave her a rapid, questioning glance, then fell into deep thought. At last he fixed his eyes on her and stated in a calm, earnest tone, "I do not believe I am going to die. I think I know why this illness has been sent upon me. I needed it. I feel that it has done me good. And it is my impression that I shall now recover and be a better and more useful man."

"Then it is your wish to recover?"

"If it should be the will of God, yes. I should like to complete the dictionary, on which I have bestowed so much labor, now that it is so nearly done; for though it has not been a work that pleased my taste, or quite satisfied my feelings, I have never underrated its importance. Then after that come all the plans that we have formed. O, I feel as if I were only just beginning to be prepared for usefulness."

"It is the opinion of most of the mission that you will not recover."

"I know it is. And I suppose they think me an old man and imagine it is nothing for one like me to resign a life so full of trials. But I am not old – at least in that sense. You know I am not. O, no man ever left this world with more inviting prospects, with brighter hopes or warmer feelings."

"Warmer feelings," he repeated, then began to weep freely. His face remained "perfectly placid" even as the tears rolled from behind closed eyelids and down his cheeks to the pillow.

After a few moments he continued, "Lying here on my bed, when I could not talk, I have had such views of the loving condescension of Christ, and the glories of heaven, as I believe are seldom granted to mortal man. It is not because I shrink from death that I wish to live. Neither is it because the ties that bind me here, though some of them are very sweet, bear any comparison with the drawings I at times feel towards heaven. But a few years would not be missed from my eternity of bliss, and I can well afford to spare them, both for your sake and for the sake of the poor Burmans. I am not tired of my work, neither am I tired of the world. Yet when Christ calls me home, I shall go with the gladness of a boy bounding away from his school. Perhaps I feel something like the young bride, when she contemplates resigning the pleasant associations of her childhood for a yet dearer home – though only a very little like her, for *there is no doubt resting on my future*."

> "Then death would not take you by surprise if it should come even before you could get on board ship?"

> "Oh, no, death will never take me by surprise. Do not be afraid of that. I feel *so strong in Christ*. He has not led me so tenderly thus far, to forsake me at the very gate of heaven. No, no. I am willing to live a few years longer, if it should be so ordered. And if otherwise, I am willing and glad to die now. I leave myself entirely in the hands of God, to be disposed of according to His holy will."

Judson was able to book passage on a French bark, the *Aristide Marie*, which was destined for the Isle of Bourbon (modern Island of Reunion), one of the Mascarene Islands east of Madagascar. It was decided that Thomas Ranney, superintendent of the mission's printing press in Maulmain, and a Burmese servant named Panapah would accompany Judson on the voyage. On Wednesday, April 3, Judson was carried aboard the vessel on a palanquin. Emily spent the entire day with him before returning home to be with the children at night.

In order to get the ship downriver as quickly as possible, arrangements had been made with Maulmain's civil commissioner for the bark to be towed to Amherst by a steamer. After Judson had already been carried aboard, however, it was learned that the vessel would not be towed by the steamer, which was transporting troops. A military commander claimed that towing the ship might endanger the soldiers' lives and asserted that since the steamer was being used as a troop transport it was not subject to the commissioner's order. As a result, it took the *Aristide Marie* five days rather than twenty-four hours to reach Amherst. Meanwhile, Judson's life continued to slip away.

The ship's creeping progress downriver allowed Emily, three other missionaries and Judson's loyal Burmese assistants,

Ko En and Ko Shway Doke, to visit him repeatedly in the days immediately following his departure from Maulmain. Ko En and Ko Shway Doke begged that Judson would be taken back to Maulmain. They were convinced he was about to die and wished him to be buried in Maulmain where the Christian disciples could look upon his grave. Each day Emily took a smaller boat downriver to visit Judson aboard the bark. When she boarded the vessel about two o'clock Saturday afternoon, she found her husband noticeably weaker and barely able to speak. His mind was so absorbed with his bodily pain that he hardly seemed aware of his surroundings. When Emily said her final sorrowful farewell to Judson at nightfall, his lips moved as if to communicate some response but no sound came from them. She returned to her "desolate home" that night with a heavy, breaking heart, fearing she might never see him again.

The next day Judson was in less pain and able to describe in some detail the nature of his physical afflictions and his responses to them. Ranney afterward related:

> He said that no one could conceive the intensity of his sufferings. Death would have been a glad relief. The idea of death caused no peculiar emotion of either fear or transport. His mind was so afflicted by suffering that he could not think, or even pray. Nay, he could not think of his wife and family. ... Yet he felt he had nothing to complain of. He knew it was the will of God, and therefore right.[6]

The *Aristide Marie* sailed from Amherst on Monday, April 8. At Judson's request, Ranney wrote to Emily that her husband "went out to sea with a strong feeling that he should recover". But later that same day his violent pains returned.

Tuesday morning the Tenasserim coast faded from their view and they enjoyed a fresh, invigorating breeze. Before long, however, they encountered a violent thunderstorm, followed by a calm. That morning Judson suffered from distressing hiccups and by the afternoon began to vomit frequently. A number of

6   ibid., pp. 349-50.

prescriptions were administered without success. The days and nights that followed were oppressively hot and humid as the ship, for the most part, continued to languish in calms.

Wednesday evening, as Ranney sat by Judson's bedside, the latter stated, "I am glad you are here. I do not feel so abandoned. You are my only kindred now – the only one on board who loves Christ, I mean. And it is a great comfort to have one near me who loves Christ."

"I hope," responded Ranney, "you feel that Christ is now near, sustaining you."

"O, yes, *it is all right there*. I believe He gives me just so much pain and suffering as is necessary to fit me to die – to make me submissive to His will."

The next morning Judson's eyes "seemed glassy and death-like" and remained half open while he slept. His stomach continued to reject all nourishment. When suffering from acute nausea, he declared, "O that I could die at once and go immediately into paradise, where there is no pain!" A while later he said, "O, how few there are who suffer such great torment – who die so hard!"

By Friday morning Judson's "countenance was that of a dying man". At three in the afternoon he stated to the servant Panapah, "It is done. I am going." A little later he made a downward sign with his hand that was not understood. Ranney bent over him with his ear near his mouth. "Brother Ranney," Judson said convulsively, "will you bury me? Bury me? Quick! Quick!" Ranney thought this likely was Judson's request as the thought of burial at sea crossed his mind. When Ranney was briefly called from the cabin, Judson again addressed Panapah, this time admonishing him to "take care of poor mistress".

The ship's captain and other officers neglected their dinner, which had been set out as usual in the cuddy, to gather at the doorway of Judson's cabin. Solemnly, respectfully they watched the closing scene of the missionary's earthly life. Mercifully, by that time Judson's suffering had passed. Ranney felt Judson's grip on his hand "growing more and more feeble as life waned". At four fifteen that afternoon – Friday, April 12, 1850 – Judson quietly expired. "His death was like falling asleep," Ranney afterward related. "Not the movement of a muscle was perceptible, and the moment of the going out of life was indicated only by his ceasing to breathe."

"A strong plank coffin" was constructed immediately. Along with Judson's body, several buckets of sand were placed in the coffin to make it sink. At eight o'clock that evening the ship's occupants gathered "in perfect silence". The only voice heard was the captain's as he issued commands for the coffin to be slid through the larboard port as Judson's body was committed to the deep. Strangely, Ranney did not offer so much as a public prayer at the brief burial ceremony. Emily later graciously stated: "They lowered him to his ocean grave without a prayer. His freed spirit had soared above the reach of earthly intercession, and to the foreigners who stood around it would have been a senseless form."[7]

Judson's burial at sea took place in latitude thirteen degrees north, longitude ninety-three degrees east, more than 300 miles southwest of Amherst and not many miles east of the Andaman Islands. The *Aristide Marie* had embarked from Burma only four days earlier but four anxious months would pass before Emily would receive word of her husband's death.

7   ibid., p. 348.

EPILOGUE

Ten days after Judson's death, Emily gave birth to a son. She named him Charles, after her father. Sadly, the infant was stillborn.

It was not until the latter half of August that Emily learned of her husband's passing. She poured out her grief in a letter to a close friend:

> ... I am so, *so* desolate. He lived only four days after they left the river, and suffered so intensely that he longed for the release of death. And here for four long months have I been so anxious about him, when he was wearing his crown in heaven? I ought to rejoice and be glad that he is so happy and glorious: sometime, perhaps, I may get strength for it; but now I can think of nothing, and see nothing, but the black shadows that have fallen upon my own heart and life. Oh, it is a terrible thing to lose a friend and guide like him.[1]

A few days before his departure from Maulmain, Judson had instructed Emily, should he not return, to turn over all his papers and study notes for the Burmese dictionary to Edward Stevens. Judson had completed an extensive portion of the dictionary but it was left to Stevens to finish the work. Eighty-seven years later, Stacy Warburton testified of the abiding value of Judson's dictionary:

> All Christian work in Burma since his day is indebted to him for his dictionary. And his contribution was of great value as well to the Burmans themselves. ... Revisions have been

1   Kendrick, *The Life and Letters of Mrs. Emily C. Judson*, p. 344.

made by the Indian Civil Service and by Dr F. H. Eveleth of the Burma mission. But Judson's work is still the basis of the revised dictionary and it bears his name.[2]

At first Emily had a strong desire to remain in Burma and carry out further mission work until the time came for the three younger Judson children to be taken to America. But when the return of the rainy season again reduced her physical health to a very low state, her doctor informed her in no uncertain terms that to remain in Burma would result in her death. She concluded it was her duty to return to the United States and to care for all the Judson children there. She left Maulmain on January 22, 1851. After brief stays in Calcutta and London along the way, she arrived in America early in October. Five and a quarter years had passed since she set sail with Judson for Burma. Though many had doubted her fitness for missionary service as she departed, none questioned it at her return.

Emily's limited health and financial resources prevented her from fulfilling her desire of caring for all the Judson children. Loyal friends continued to provide loving homes for Abby Ann, Adoniram and Elnathan. In addition to parenting the three younger children, Emily was called upon to provide extensive assistance to Francis Wayland, President of Brown University, the individual selected by the mission board to write Judson's official biography. Emily collected and compiled elaborate original resource materials, contributed numerous reminiscences of her own and assisted in the final production of the massive two-volume work. In addition, she contributed articles to *The Macedonian*, a Baptist missionary periodical, and had three volumes of her own published – a book of her poems, a collection of her missionary essays and a memoir of her two older sisters, both of whom had died in young womanhood.

An unfortunate development relative to the publication of Judson's biography occurred late in 1853. Wayland had announced that all profits from the sale of his official biography would be devoted to helping support Emily and the Judson children. In October, about a month after Wayland's two-volume work was published, a Baptist publisher in New York named E. H. Fletcher announced his intentions

2   Warburton, *Eastward!*, p. 221.

to release a shorter and more affordable single-volume memoir of Judson's life. Fletcher proposed to do so for the benefit of Sabbath schools and for those who were unable or unwilling to purchase Wayland's more voluminous and expensive work.

Emily wrote to Fletcher, urging him not to follow through with the alternative memoir. She pointed out that it would doubtless hamper sales of the officially recognized biography and would effectively rob Judson's own family of much-needed support. But Fletcher would not be dissuaded and not long thereafter published *Burmah's Great Missionary: Records of the Life, Character and Achievements of Adoniram Judson*. It had been written by Robert Middleditch but was originally published anonymously.[3] Reportedly, however, Fletcher's publication "was soon after consigned, by the moral sense of the public, to oblivion".[4] Wayland's biography, on the other hand, sold well, 26,000 copies in the first year alone.[5]

Emily never fully regained her health after returning from Burma. Instead, she continued to experience relapses from what appears to have been tuberculosis or pleurisy. During the final few months of her life, spent with family members at her home in Hamilton, New York, she became a complete invalid, too weak even to write. In her closing days Emily suffered horrifically from intense pain and a recurring suffocating sensation. Finally, on June 1, 1854, "She lingered until ten in the evening in great agony; the pain then subsided, and after a few minutes, sweetly and tranquilly, without a groan or the movement of a muscle, she breathed out her life on the bosom of her sister [Katy]."[6] Emily was thirty-six years old at the time of her death.

Judson's sister, Abigail, continued to live in the old family home in Plymouth until her death at age ninety-three in 1884. After Judson stayed in the home in 1846, shortly before returning to Burma, Abigail reportedly closed up his bedroom and preserved it, untouched just as he had left it, to the end of her life.

3   Anderson, *To the Golden Shore*, p. 512.

4   Kendrick, *The Life and Letters of Mrs. Emily C. Judson*, p. 404.

5   Brumberg, *Mission for Life*, p. 143.

6   Kendrick, *The Life and Letters of Mrs. Emily C. Judson*, p. 408.

After graduating from Brown University in 1855, Judson's stepson, George Boardman (1828–1903), went on to serve as a minister for four decades. The final thirty of those years he pastored the prestigious First Baptist Church of Philadelphia.[7]

Abby Ann Judson (1835–1902) publicly professed her Christian faith at age seventeen. For twenty-five years she taught at schools or served as governess for families in Massachusetts, Rhode Island, New York and Ohio. In 1879 she moved to Minneapolis, Minnesota, where she founded the Judson Female Institute, an interdenominational school for girls, which she led for a decade. For years, however, Abby Ann had lived with doubts about her Christian faith and had entertained beliefs in spiritism. In 1890, at age sixty-five, she publicly proclaimed herself a Spiritualist. In the years immediately following she went on record as opposing many orthodox Christian tenets, including the Trinity, a divinely inspired Bible, human depravity, predestination, Christ's vicarious atonement, conversion, miracles, physical resurrection and the final judgment.

Following his graduation from Brown in 1859, Judson's son, Adoniram (1837–1916), attended Harvard Medical School, Jefferson Medical College in Philadelphia and Columbia University's College of Physicians and Surgeons. He practiced medicine in New York City for forty-eight years and became an outstanding orthopedic specialist.

Elnathan (1838–1897) prepared for the ministry and graduated from Union Theological Seminary in 1862. Tragically, however, after suffering sunstroke and "brain fever", he was pronounced insane in 1864 and was institutionalized in asylums for the next thirty-two years. Abby Ann moved to Worcester, Massachusetts, and assumed complete care of Elnathan the final year of his life in her own rented quarters.

Henry (1842–1918) attended Brown University for a year then transferred to Williams College. In January 1864, during his junior year, he enlisted to fight for the Union Army in the

---

7   Brumberg, *Mission for Life*, pp. 145-216, 274-88, provides much biographical information on the adult years of George Boardman and the surviving Judson children.

Civil War. Battle injuries he sustained left him permanently disabled.

Edward (1844–1913) graduated from Madison University in Hamilton in 1864. After serving a wealthy congregation in New Jersey for several years, he accepted the call to pastor the struggling Berean Baptist Church in New York City in 1875. There he built up a ministry aimed at reaching and assisting the city's burgeoning immigrant poor population. Generous financial contributions from various sources enabled Edward to expand the ministry. A fine new edifice was completed in 1891 and called the Judson Memorial Church. In addition, in 1883, with Wayland's comprehensive biography out of print, Edward compiled his own thorough account of his father's life and ministry, drawing largely from previous publications.

At age twenty-three, Emily Frances (1847–1911) married Thomas Hanna, a Baptist minister. For decades they served in pastorates, home missions work and other denominational capacities in Connecticut and Pennsylvania. Emily Francis bore eight children.

Besides the initial biographies written about Judson and his three wives, dozens of other books were written about them in the century following their deaths. Likely no other family stirred up greater interest in foreign missions in America during the nineteenth and first half of the twentieth century than did Judson's. Accounts of Judson's life were translated into French, German, Spanish, Swedish and Hindi, thus spreading an awareness of his ministry around the world. In addition to Judson Memorial Church in New York City, a Baptist publishing company and two colleges were named in his honor.[8]

In the front lawn of the house where Judson was born in Malden, Massachusetts, a bronze plate was affixed to an inconspicuous stone, inscribed with this fitting tribute:

---

8 Those were Judson Press of Valley Forge, Pennsylvania, the American Baptist Mission's Judson College in Rangoon (part of modern Yangon University), and Judson University in Elgin, Illinois. Judson College in Marion, Alabama, originally named Judson Female Institute, was founded in memory of Ann H. Judson.

REV. ADONIRAM JUDSON

America's First Foreign Missionary

1788 – 1850

Malden, His Birthplace

The Ocean, His Sepulchre

Converted Burmans and the

Burman Bible, His Monument

His Record Is On High[9]

9   Warburton, *Eastward!*, p. 231.

FOR FURTHER READING

Anderson, Courtney. *To the Golden Shore, The Life of Adoniram Judson*. Grand Rapids: Zondervan, 1972.

Brumberg, Joan Jacobs. *Mission for Life: The story of the family of Adoniram Judson, the dramatic events of the first American foreign mission, and the course of evangelical religion in the nineteenth century*. New York: Free Press, 1980.

Carey, S. Pearce. *William Carey, 'The Father of Modern Missions'*. London: Wakeman Trust, 2008.

Judson, Ann H. *An Account of the American Baptist Mission to the Burman Empire, In a Series of Letters Addressed to a Gentleman in London*. London: Joseph Butterworth, 1827.

Judson, Edward. *The Life of Adoniram Judson*. Philadelphia: Judson Press, 1938.

Judson, Emily C. *Memoir of Sarah B. Judson, Member of the American Mission to Burmah*. New York: Lewis Colby, 1849.

Kendrick, A. C. *The Life and Letters of Mrs. Emily C. Judson*. New York: Sheldon, 1860.

Knowles, James D. *Memoir of Mrs. Ann H. Judson, Late Missionary to Burmah*. Boston: Lincoln & Edmands, 1829.

Warburton, Stacy R. *Eastward! The Story of Adoniram Judson*. New York: Round Table Press, 1937.

Wayland, Francis. *Memoir of the Life and Labors of the Rev. Adoniram Judson, D.D.*, vols. 1 & 2. Boston: Phillips, Sampson and Co., 1853.

DAVID BRAINERD

A FLAME FOR GOD
Vance Christie

ISBN 978-1-84550-478-6

David Brainerd

A Flame for God

Vance Christie

'...I hardly ever so longed to live to God and to be altogether devoted to Him; I wanted to wear out my life in His service and for His glory ...'

David Brainerd

'The poor man was sick, and his devotion to Christ and his self-sacrificial labours among indigenous Americans stand as a testimony to what God can do through weak and damaged people. And the story is not by any means all bleak; Brainerd certainly knew times of real closeness to God, and saw touches of revival in his ministry.'

Evangelicals Now

Introduction by John Macarthur. David Brainerd was devoted to live for his Lord. He lived a short life but in his four years as a missionary he was blessed with a period of revival amongst the Indians to whom he had been ministering. As you consider the life of Brainerd, this book will be of tremendous spiritual benefit to you as you read of a young man plagued with depression and yet made so effective under God.

History Maker biographies bring you the best classic biographies of important people and movements in church history together with important new biographical works of the same. They have gained a reputation as an important new resource for the church.

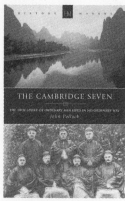

The Cambridge Seven
The True Story of Ordinary Men Used in no Ordinary Way

John Pollock – *award-winning biographer, acclaimed as one of Britain's leading historical writers with a flair for telling a dramatic story.*

Harold Schofield, brilliant Oxford doctor and a missionary in China for many years, was on his knees praying, *"Lord, give me missionaries from British Universities to help in China'*. The day he died, Schofield's prayer was answered as seven Cambridge students volunteered to leave behind cosy lives of wealth and privilege to serve God in whatever way they were led. In turn these seven inspired thousands of others to think seriously about missionary service.

ISBN 978-1-84550-177-8
128 Pages

George Müller
Delighted in God

Roger Steer – *writer, broadcaster, online tutor, author of twelve books and a leader in his local church in Devon, England.*

Still considered to be the best biography of George Müller's life and a powerful answer to modern scepticism. Müller's name has become a by-word for faith throughout the world. Disturbed by the faithlessness of the Church in general, he longed to have something to point to as *"visible proof that our God and Father is*

ISBN 978-1-84550-120-4
256 Pages

the same faithful creator as he ever was'. Praying in every penny of the costs, he supervised the building of orphanages to house thousands of children. He was insistent that under no circumstances would any individual ever be asked for money or materials. He was more successful than anyone could have believed possible and is as much an example to our generation, as he was to his.

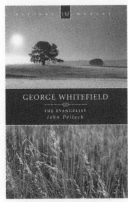

ISBN 978-1-84550-454-0
272 Pages

George Whitefield
The Evangelist
John Pollock – *award-winning biographer*
John Pollock vividly portrays George Whitefield and his times. The story is told of how God worked in a remarkable way through Whitefield in Britain and the then Colonies of America. As he travelled many miles by horseback, crossing the Atlantic on countless occasions, sometimes experiencing illness and fatigue, countless people were drawn to Christ through this man. Come and catch the drama and also the passion and commitment George Whitefield had for the gospel. *'May the rising generation catch a spark of that flame which shone with such distinguished lustre in the Spirit and practice of this faithful servant of the most high God.'* **John Wesley speaking about George Whitefield after his death**

John G Paton
Missionary to the New Hebrides
James Paton – *This is the abridged version of the material collected by John G. Paton and was compiled by his brother Rev. James Paton an author and Presbyterian Minister in Scotland.*
The story of the Scottish missionary pioneer John Gibson Paton (1824-1907). Born in Dumfries-shire, trained at Medical school and spent ten years as city missionary in Glasgow and felt compelled by God to be a missionary in the South Sea Islands. This is the

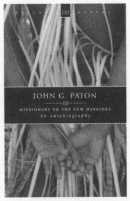

ISBN 978-1-84550-453-3
368 Pages

inspirational account of Scottish Missionary John G. Paton's pioneering mission work among cannibals in the New Hebrides (now Vanuatu). Living among constant dangers and death threats, battling against illness and enduring great personal loss and sacrifice, Paton labored on and showed great love for the island peoples. He had the joy eventually of seeing people come to Christ and living a totally transformed lifestyle.

Other titles in the *History Maker* Series:

Charles Simeon
The Pastor of a Generation
Handley Moule
ISBN 978-1-85792-310-0

D.L. Moody
Moody without Sankey
John Pollock
ISBN 978-1-85792-167-0

F.B. Meyer
If I had a hundred lives…
Bob Holman
ISBN 978-1-84550-243-0

A Fistful of Heroes
Christians at the Forefront of Change
John Pollock
ISBN 978-1-84550-346-8

Gordon of Khartoum
An Extraordinary Soldier
John Pollock
ISBN 978-1-84550-063-4

Hudson Taylor and Maria
A Match Made in Heaven
John Pollock
ISBN 978-1-85792-223-3

J. C. Ryle
That Man of Granite – with the Heart of a Child
Eric Russell
ISBN 978-1-84550-387-1

John Calvin
Revolutionary, Theologian, Pastor
Williston Walker
ISBN 978-1-84550-104-4

John Owen
Prince of Puritans
Andrew Thomson
ISBN 978-1-85792-267-7

Martin Luther

The Man who Started the
Reformation

Thomas Lindsay

ISBN 978-1-85792-261-5

Pastor Hsi

A Struggle for Chinese
Christianity

Geraldine Taylor

ISBN 978-1-85792-159-5

Richard Baxter

The Pastor's pastor

Andrew Thomson

ISBN 978-1-85792-380-3

**Robert Murray
McCheyne**

A Burning Light

Alexander Smellie

ISBN 978-1-85792-184-7

Thomas Boston

His Life and Times

Andrew Thomson

ISBN 978-1-85792-379-7

The Way to Glory

Major General Sir Henry
Havelock

John Pollock

ISBN 978-1-85792-245-5

Christian Focus Publications

Our mission statement –

STAYING FAITHFUL
In dependence upon God we seek to impact the world through literature faithful to His infallible Word, the Bible. Our aim is to ensure that the Lord Jesus Christ is presented as the only hope to obtain forgiveness of sin, live a useful life and look forward to heaven with Him.

Our Books are published in four imprints:

CHRISTIAN FOCUS

popular works including biographies, commentaries, basic doctrine and Christian living.

CHRISTIAN HERITAGE

books representing some of the best material from the rich heritage of the church.

MENTOR

books written at a level suitable for Bible College and seminary students, pastors, and other serious readers. The imprint includes commentaries, doctrinal studies, examination of current issues and church history.

CF4•K

children's books for quality Bible teaching and for all age groups: Sunday school curriculum, puzzle and activity books; personal and family devotional titles, biographies and inspirational stories – Because you are never too young to know Jesus!

Christian Focus Publications Ltd,
Geanies House, Fearn, Ross-shire,
IV20 1TW, Scotland, United Kingdom.
www.christianfocus.com